PERFORMANCE PRACTICE

PERFORMANCE PRACTICE

ETHNOMUSICOLOGICAL PERSPECTIVES

Edited by
Gerard Béhague

Contributions in Intercultural and Comparative Studies, Number 12

GREENWOOD PRESS
Westport, Connecticut • London, England

Library of Congress Cataloging in Publication Data
Main entry under title:

Performance practice.

(Contributions in intercultural and comparative
studies, ISSN 0147-1031 ; no. 12)
Bibliography: p.
Includes index.
1. Ethnomusicology—Addresses, essays, lectures.
2. Music—Performance—Addresses, essays, lectures.
I. Béhague, Gerard.   II. Series.
ML3799.P47   1984   781.7   83-10842
ISBN 0-313-24160-0 (lib. bdg.)

Library of Congress Catalog Card Number: 83-10842
ISBN: 0-313-24160-0
ISSN: 0147-1031

First published in 1984

Greenwood Press
A division of Congressional Information Service, Inc.
88 Post Road West, Westport, Connecticut 06881

Printed in the United States of America

10 9 8 7 6 5 4 3 2 1

Contents

Acknowledgments ⸻⸻⸻⸻⸻⸻⸻⸻

I wish to express my gratitude to a number of individuals who helped me in different ways in the long process of this project. First and foremost, I am grateful to my colleagues and friends, Linda C. Burman-Hall, Bonnie C. Wade, Rod Knight and Philip Schuyler, for their excellent contributions and their patience in the completion of the project. I thank Elaine Brody, New York University, for suggesting the idea of the project in the first place. My thanks also go to the late Alan P. Merriam who shared with me his first reactions to my formulation of performance practice from an ethnomusicological perspective. I gratefully acknowledge my friends and colleagues, Norma McLeod and Marcia Herndon, for providing challenging dialogues about music in and as performance ever since 1974. Finally, I express my thanks to Ann M. Pescatello, Director of the Council on Intercultural and Comparative Studies, University of California, Berkeley, for her support and interest in seeing this volume in print.

—Gerard Béhague

PERFORMANCE PRACTICE

Introduction _____

Gerard Béhague

Traditionally the concept of performance practice elaborated by musicologists has been limited to attempting to reconstruct the original sound of early European music of various periods through the study of a variety of literary and historical (including iconographic) sources. In focusing their attention on the sound structure phenomena, musicologists have generally isolated some performance traits for a given period or "style," which they came to consider essential to a historically "correct" performance of early music. Moreover, the quest for the historical authenticity of sound reproduction has led scholars to assume that contextual differences in the performance of a piece of music matter little since different contexts of performance could not account logically for a substantial modification of the essential elements of that piece. This assumption, which only recently has begun to be questioned, relegated the consideration of performance factors in the overall style analysis of a given corpus of music to the lowest level in the hierarchy of stylistic elements. Comparative musicologists and later ethnomusicologists inherited the numerous shortcomings of such an approach in the study of *Aufführungspraxis*. Consequently, as applied to non-Western and folk musics, this study has been generally limited to detailed aspects of performance dealing with the idiosyncratic qualities of vocal and instrumental sound production in a given culture, generally applying Western concepts of sound.

Heretofore few ethnomusicologists have paid close attention to the study of music performance as an event. But because ethnomusicologists concern themselves, in most cases, with musics of non-literate societies, they have come to realize, if only empirically, that performance is actually their primary source of study and have tended, therefore, to develop an all-inclusive approach to the study of performance. Recent work in folklore and ethnomusicology allows us to elaborate new perspectives on the study of performance practice, by attempting to integrate context and sound, i.e., performance and practice.

Under the tremendous impact of folklore studies in the "ethnography of speaking," and verbal art as performance (cf. Abrahams 1970, 1972; Bauman and Sherzer 1974; Bauman 1975; Paredes and Bauman 1972) since the early 1970s, the conceptualization of performance as an organizing principle and a process has taken shape. This conceptualization has greatly influenced the orientation taken by ethnomusicologists concerned with musical performance both as an event and a process.[1]

Any discussion of performance practice must of necessity elucidate first the nature of performance in as much of a cross-cultural capacity as possible. Because folklorists and ethnomusicologists have dealt with many different cultures, the nature of performance must also be understood in terms applicable to both general and specific studies. Actually several concepts of performance are available, of which the most useful for our purposes are perhaps those advanced by Milton Singer, Roger Abrahams, Richard Bauman, and Norma McLeod.

Milton Singer, an anthropologist specializing in South Asian studies, includes in what he calls "cultural performances" not only "what we in the West call by that name—for example, plays, music concerts and lectures," but also "prayers, ritual readings and recitations, rites and ceremonies, festivals and all those things which we usually classify under religion and ritual rather than with the 'cultural' or artistic" (Singer 1955: 23). He further defines the actual patterning of a cultural performance as consisting of "a definitely limited time span or, at least, a beginning and an end, an organized program of activity, a set of performers, an audience and a place and occasion of performance" (Ibid.). Moreover, Singer conceives cultural performances as separable portions of activity thought by the members of a social group to be encapsulations of their culture "which they could exhibit to visitors and to themselves" (Ibid.). Singer's extension of the concept of performance to include rituals (sacred and secular), festivals and play, has long been recognized as valid because of its implication that "highly formalized human behavior is a cultural focusing, and that it probably is symbolic and meaningful" (in Herndon and Brunyate 1975: 12; see also Herndon 1971: 339). The question of meaning is paramount and will be examined below.

Both folklorists Roger Abrahams and Richard Bauman, in their conceptualization of verbal art as performance, emphasize and advocate the study of the actual behavior and social interaction of the participants in the performance, and of the rules or codes and contexts of the performance, so that they can ultimately develop the notion of performance as a mode of expression and communication. For Abrahams the "audience" plays an extremely important part of the performance occasion, but this obvious fact has not been recognized because "we come at performance from our highly Western sophisticated artistic conceptions, which have focused for so long on the virtuosic dimension of performance: the means by which the performer himself stuns everybody within the performance environment into silence" (Abrahams 1975: 19). Abrahams coined the term "Pure Performance" to underline the term on not so "specially licensed and set aside occasions" as when we use the term "a performance," to make it into "a term of art," or performance with a capital 'P' (Idem: 20). As he articulates it, Pure Performance is an "intensified (or stylized) behavioral system," including "an occasion, a time, places, codes, and patterns of expectation" (Idem: 25).

Bauman, on the other hand, suggests very pertinently the kind of "interpretive frame performance establishes or represents" (cf. Bauman 1975: 293) and provides useful answers to the question of "how is communication that constitutes performance to be interpreted?" For this purpose, he discusses the patterning of performance in genres, roles, acts and events and, most importantly, develops, with Abrahams, the concept of "the emergent quality of performance" and that of performance as a "display of communicative competence." In addition, in conceiving of performance as "a mode of language use, a way of speaking," Bauman is able to draw a fundamental conclusion regarding the implication of such a concept for a theory of verbal art, namely,

it is no longer necessary to begin with artful texts, identified on independent formal grounds and then reinjected into situations of use, in order to conceptualize verbal art in communicative terms. Rather, in terms of the approach being developed here, performance becomes *constitutive* of the domain of verbal art as spoken communication (Bauman 1975: 293).

Bauman and Abrahams also emphasize that performance is "unique unto itself within every culture" (Abrahams 1975: 25), and that "just as speaking itself, as a cultural system (or as a part of cultural systems defined in other terms) will vary from speech community to speech community, so too will the nature and extent of the realm of performance and verbal art" (Bauman 1975: 294). This view advocates the nature of performance as culture- and community-specific and the role of the folklorist and ethnomusicologist in the study of performance as consisting of elucidating ethnographically the extent of the domain of performance in a given community. But, while supporting strongly the necessity of determining the *emic* conceptions of performance, Bauman, in his discussion of how performance is keyed, provides "an etic list of communicative means . . . as serving to key performance," including at least eight categories:

(1) special codes, reserved for and diagnostic of performance; (2) special formulae that signal performance; (3) figurative language such as metaphor; (4) formal stylistic devices; (5) special prosodic patterns of tempo, stress, pitch; (6) special paralinguistic patterns of voice quality and vocalization; (7) appeal to tradition; and (8) disclaimer of performance (Bauman 1975: 295).

Such a list, however, is felt to be of limited utility in the ethnography of performance because the essential task of performance is seen as the determination of community-specific "constellations of communicative means that serve to key performance in particular communities" (Bauman 1975: 296). Furthermore, Bauman recognizes the need to determine these means empirically and, despite variations from one community to another, admits the probable existence of universal tendencies of conventionalized means.

Finally, the concepts of competence and of the emergent quality of all performance discussed by both folklorists are crucial for the study of performance, "as a means toward comprehending the uniqueness of particular performances within the context of performance as a generalized cultural system in a community" (Bauman 1975: 302). For Abrahams, the role of an individual performer is paramount because of the fact that he brings patterns of performance into play, exhibits technical control over registers and codes of the performance, "has the ability to recognize where these occasions arise," and "can capitalize upon them and invest them with his own sense of energy" (Abrahams 1975: 25). In Bauman's terms, "the emergent quality of performance resides in the interplay between communicative resources, individual competence, and the goals of the participants, within the context of a particular situation" (Bauman 1975: 302). Furthermore, he sees performance as offering "to the participants a special enhancement of experience, bringing with it a heightened intensity of communicative interaction which binds the audience to the performer in a way that is specific to performance as a mode of communication" (Idem: 305), and that is part of the essence of performance.

Norma McLeod's concept of musical occasion carries essential implications for the study of performance as an event. She coined the term "musical occasion" in her doctoral thesis (1966) and used it in a contextual sense, i.e., as a cultural performance of music. From her study of musical occasions in Tikopia, she concluded that "there is a very clear relationship between what we would call content, that is the performance item, and context, the occasion. As the general social texture of an occasion becomes thicker, with more forms of social structural principles present, music becomes more ordered" (McLeod 1975: 15). She also perceived a continuum of "ordering and complexity" and "a shift toward more complexity in the performance item, as complexity in the larger order of events increases," and "as anxiety [a funeral, for example] on the part of the participants increases, the music, at least, increases in level of redundancy" (Idem: 16). In her study of the Cherokee Ball Game, Marcia Herndon isolated the musical occasion as one particular aspect of the social context of music. For her, "the occasion may be regarded as an encapsulated expression of the shared cognitive forms and values of a society, which includes not only the music itself, but also the totality of associated behavior and underlying concepts. It is usually a named event with a beginning and an end, varying degrees of organization of activity, audience, performances, and location" (Herndon 1971: 340). This definition suggests that, from the point of view of individual composition, one aspect of its social context derives from the fact that it is part of a larger cognitive and social entity, a musical occasion in which many pieces of music are performed.

From such concepts, the ethnomusicologist should be able to consider some theoretical and methodological implications for the study of musical performance and performance practices. The ethnography of musical performance should bring to light the ways non-musical elements in a performance occasion or event influence the musical outcome of a performance. Practices of performance result from the relationship of content and context. To isolate the sound contents of a performance and call such an operation "Performance Practice" is no longer justifiable. In McLeod's words, "music provides sufficient density of marking to enable scholars to separate it from its context. That is, when music is being performed, it is usually quite clear that this is the case. With the development of notation systems, and, later, of recording devices, it is all too easy to separate musical sound from its cultural context. This is both a curse and a blessing. While the separability of music from its performance context allows us to compare this part of human behavior with other areas, it also tempts us to regard music as separate from culture, simply because it is separable from culture" (McLeod 1975: 17). The curse, however, far outweighs the blessing. Although it is easy to contend that the sound phenomena remain our primary source of study and that practice can only be ascertained through the minute examination and measurement of sound, the study of Performance Practice involves numerous levels of analysis so as to consider the multi-dimensionality of music. Moreover, no one will deny that performance practice (in its traditional sense) exists only in oral tradition. The distinctions between written and oral traditions of music have been overstressed. Behind all notational systems rests a dynamic oral tradition of performance, subject to change in time and space. This is true of all (written or oral) musical traditions, including that of Western art music. This oral tradition of performance represents one of the most essential sources for the study of cultural values, communication, and meaning.

THE STUDY OF MUSIC AS PERFORMANCE

Ideally, then, the study of music performance as an event and a process and of the resulting performance practices or products should concentrate on the actual musical and extra-musical behavior of participants (performers and audience), the consequent social interaction, the meaning of that interaction for the participants, and the rules or codes of performance defined by the community for a specific context or occasion. Such a study would rely on "symbolic interactionism" (cf. Blumer 1969) and semiotics, to be able to assess the process of interaction in emic terms and the meanings constructed from the subjective interpretation of the various signs and symbols of the performance by the participants. The ethnomusicologist will have to focus his attention on that interpretation and in doing so will also engage in social interaction, either as observer or participant. The meaning of the latter's social interaction will generally differ considerably from the interpretation by the participants mentioned above. To a great extent, however, one can state that the ethnomusicologist's analytical evaluation of the folk evaluation is in itself a folk evaluation, since it is from his inference of the interpretative process of the performer that the analyst constructs his own understanding of the musical occasion and assigns specific meaning to it. Musical meaning, however, cannot be derived from a single source. Just as there exist "constellations of communicative means" in performance there are also many different perceptions of the performance situation. The ethnography of musical performance must be based, therefore, on numerous ethnic views and evaluations of any musical situation, specific events, musical systems, and practices, so that the researcher will, in most cases, base his perception on the commonalities of the evaluations. Such a procedure is clearly tied up to the question of musical meaning. "Creative, critical listening is a sign of musical competence no less than is musical performance" (Blacking 1971: 30). In addition, the result of that critical listening and the consequent behavior affects the outcome of the performance. The audience's behavior (musical, verbal or kinesic) is then an integral part of the performance situation.

In focusing our study of performance on the musical occasion (taken as a unit of study), it becomes imperative to document the total and often multiple contextual dimensions of that occasion. The musical organization of the occasion will almost always be determined by these dimensions. The course and structure of the music performance will also depend more or less clearly on the same contextual coordinates. But while recognizing the contention of numerous scholars in ethnomusicology that the social context of a composition or piece is not external to its music sound-structure, we must confess that our analytical tools for establishing that relationship unequivocally lack in sophistication. The theoretical foundation proposed by the method of Cantometrics, for example, assumes too much of that relationship to prove satisfactory. Rather minute musical elements among the 37 parameters of the Cantometrics' coding sheet are supposed to symbolize major cultural patterns, and the comparative, cross-cultural results of song trait measurements related to culture appear too unspecific to be of real usefulness. Furthermore, John Blacking's insistence that "no musical style has 'its own terms': its terms are the terms of its society and culture, and of the bodies of the human beings who listen to it, and create and perform it" (Blacking 1973b: 25), is convincing enough, but his application of structural linguistic concepts of deep and surface structures to traditional musical realms needs considerably more empirical evidence to prove feasible cross-culturally.

Once more, a possible hierarchy of levels of meaning and of structure cannot be elucidated through observation alone but through various degrees of participation. Among the various field techniques available to ethnomusicologists in the study of the musical occasion, those involving several forms of participation and observation have proved the most useful. Total participation, as advocated by Blacking, appears, in most cases, unrealistic because it is generally unattainable. Total observation, on the other hand, while possible, neglects social interaction. Participant observation offers, therefore, the highest probabilities of eliciting accurate information and interpretation of the musical occasion and should be complemented by other traditional techniques of research, such as interviews (rejecting once and for all the idea that musicians are generally unable to verbalize about their own music-making process), field experiment (as used by Blacking, for example, see Blacking 1973a: 215), the staging of musical performance, and the "staged interaction" as proposed by Spradley (1972). Although somewhat artificial, a "staged interaction," which consists of bringing together the participants of a specific performance for discussing whatever aspect of it they may wish to discuss, can reveal substantial insights about the meanings and expectations of that occasion for the participants. The basic advantage of such an "interaction" over the simple interviews is clear: the eliciting of information is not directed by the outsider/researcher but results from "natural" exchanges between the participants. The effects of staging music performances are quite varied according to a given culture and a community. Numerous musical occasions are actually staged in their original context, so that the staging becomes an integral part of the context. As a field technique, however, the staging of a performance is useful for bringing forth and clarifying certain aspects of musical performance practices, generally not as readily obtainable in the natural context, and the corresponding musical texts that such a staging might generate.

The present volume is conceived as an illustration of the study of music performance as an event and the corresponding performance practices. Each chapter represents a case study of performance, culture-, process- and community-specific. Within the variety of performance contexts offered in this volume, the conceptualization of Performance Practice as the integrated study of sound and context is quite homogeneous among the five case studies. Given the different nature of empirical data gathered and interpreted by each of the five authors, the individual treatment of performance events and the relative importance given to aspects of those events are naturally quite different, thereby demonstrating the culture-, community-specific nature of the problem at hand. In addition, it is clear that the nature of individual data dictates to a great extent the orientation of the theoretical framework of each study presented here. Yet all studies resulted from participant observation in natural contexts of performance, and while the holistic perspective in the study of Performance Practice as advocated here is recognized by all authors, some chose to stress the musical aspects or the social contexts of performance in their study.

In her detailed essay, Bonnie Wade addresses herself first to the identity of the performers of North and South Indian Classical music, both vocalists and instrumentalists in their soloistic and accompanimental functions. After considering the main types of performance contexts, she illustrates with specific examples the musical process of performance par excellence, i.e., improvisation, and the roles and responsibilities of the soloist in this creative art. She stresses also the Indian esthetic criteria associated with "style" of performance and, most importantly, provides a thorough comparative discussion of the nature of improvisation and performance in the Hindustani and Karnatak traditions. Her consideration of audience-performers relationships, of individual competence, constraints and discipline, and their influences on the performer's creative behavior (i.e., the keying of performance) sheds a rich light on the nature of performance in Classical music outside the Western European tradition.

In a very engaging manner, Roderic Knight sets the stage for his socio-historical account of the musician's status and role in the Old Mali Empire. Specifically, he opposes and contrasts the duality of Manding music, represented on one hand by the *jali*, a professional balladeer-historian, and on the other by the drummer, a popular entertainer. His all-inclusive approach to the study of performance brings forth the determinants of style in both the *jali*'s music (*jaliya*) and drum music, including the consideration of instruments, tonal material, rhythmic organization, song style, the teaching and learning process, and the various musical occasions. Attention is also paid here to the Manding categories of excellence in performance and to the levels of social interaction operating in the various musical events described.

Professional musicians, this time from North Africa, are the focus of the study by Philip D. Schuyler. The Berber musicians known as *rwais* wander through Southwestern Morocco providing music in various contexts. In studying four different contexts of performance, namely the marketplace, private parties, commercial establishments and recording studios, Schuyler is able to establish the text-context relationships specifically by analyzing and revealing the influences of the contextual factors on the performance contents. In so doing he also provides a vivid picture of the sociology of these musicians and their adaptive mechanisms, in musical terms, operative in the performance contexts under study.

Linda Burman-Hall's essay penetrates the dynamic tradition of Anglo-American folk fiddling. This tradition is clearly traced to Western European dance violin practices presumably imported to the American colonies, as shown in specific Baroque violin techniques preserved in the Southeastern states of the United States, as in the Blue Ridge and Southern Appalachian fiddling styles. The author reveals through analyses some of the traditional performance techniques, such as bowing patterns and idiomatic melodic realization, preserved in more recent commercial styles arising from folk fiddling such as the String Band, Western Swing, and Bluegrass. Here again special attention is given to the various social contexts of performance, to the significance of the conventions and mannerisms of performance, and the importance of the fiddle tune as the essential cognitive structure of the fiddle repertory.

My own essay, dealing with a specific religious ritual context, illustrates the organic functionality that music performance possesses inherently in several musical events, and the ways it contributes to the expression of sociocultural meanings of ritual. Since the ritual structure dictates, to a great extent, the corresponding musical structure of song repertories, it is considered in detail. In my exemplification of performance contexts, close attention is also paid to the relationship of liturgical dogmas and practices, musical behavior of participants, and specific music repertories. That relationship is, in fact, so pervasive that music performance appears truly constitutive of the liturgy itself.

NOTE

1. This concern was internationally recognized at the Twelfth Congress of the International Musicological Society in Berkeley in 1977 with the inclusion of a panel and study sessions on "The Ethnography of Musical Performance" (Heartz and Wade 1981). Earlier, a symposium on "Form in Performance, Hard-Core Ethnography" was held at the University of Texas at Austin in 1975, with the participation of several scholars in ethnomusicology and related disciplines. See also N. McLeod and M. Herndon (1980).

REFERENCES CITED

Abrahams, Roger D.
    1970   A Performance-Centered Approach to Gossip. *Man* 5: 290-301.
    1972   Folklore and Literature as Performance. *Journal of the Folklore Institute* 9: 75-94.
    1975   The Theoretical Boundaries of Performance. In Marcia Herndon and Roger Brunyate, eds., *Form in Performance, Hard-Core Ethnography*. 18-27.
Bauman, Richard
    1975   Verbal Art as Performance. *American Anthropologist* 77: 290-311.
Bauman, Richard and Sherzer, Joel, eds.
    1974   *Explorations in the Ethnography of Speaking*. New York: Cambridge University Press.

Blacking, John
  1971   Towards a Theory of Musical Competence. In E. J. DeJager, ed., *Man:
            Anthropological Essays Presented to O. F. Raum*. Capetown: Struik.
            19-34.
  1973a   Field Work in African Music. In Dominique René DeLerma, ed.,
            Reflections on Afro-American Music. Kent, Ohio: Kent State Univer-
            sity Press. 207-221.
  1973b   *How Musical is Man?* Seattle and London: University of Washington
            Press.
Blumer, Herbert
  1969   *Symbolic Interactionism: Perspective and Method*. Englewood Cliffs,
            New Jersey: Prentice-Hall, Inc.
Heartz, Daniel and Wade, Bonnie, eds.
  1981   *Report of the Twelfth Congress* (International Musicological Society),
            Berkeley, 1977. Kassel-Basel-London: Bärenreiter.
Herndon, Marcia
  1971   The Cherokee Ballgame Cycle: An Ethnomusicologist's View. *Ethno-
            musicology* 15: 339-352.
Herndon, Marcia and Brunyate, Roger, eds.
  1975   *Form in Performance, Hard-Core Ethnography*. Austin, Texas: Office
            of the College of Fine Arts.
McLeod, Norma
  1966   *Some Techniques for the Analysis of Non-Western Music*. Doctoral
            dissertation. Northwestern University.
  1975   Keynote address. *Form in Performance, Hard-Core Ethnography*.
            Austin, Texas: Office of the College of Fine Arts. 1-17.
McLeod, Norma and Herndon, Marcia
  1980   *The Ethnography of Musical Performance*. Norwood, Pennsylvania:
            Norwood Editions.
Paredes, Américo and Bauman, Richard, eds.
  1972   *Towards New Perspectives in Folklore*. Austin: University of Texas
            Press.
Singer, Milton
  1955   The Cultural Pattern of India. *The Far Eastern Quarterly* 15: 23-26.
Spradley, James P.
  1972   Adaptive Strategies of Urban Nomads. In *Culture and Cognition*. San
            Francisco: Chandler. 235-262.

1

Performance Practice in Indian Classical Music

Bonnie C. Wade

An article on performance practice in Indian art music could take any one of a number of forms. "Indian art music" encompasses an enormous amount of music, just as the rubric "Western art music" does. Formulation of an article which would encompass much music, or one which considers some music in any detail, is made possible only by the relative degree of cohesion in "the tradition."

Given the difficulty of the assignment, this article takes only a first step in an effort to establish a framework for the consideration of the subject. This has been conceived with two purposes in mind. One is to explore for scholars of Western music—for whom the rubric "performance practice" has relatively concrete connotations—what that rubric could connote for Indian art music. The second purpose is to put forth for ethnomusicologists and others who wish to study Indian music a set of factors to consider (i.e., a research methodology) for any topic which falls under the rubric "performance practice." To speak to both those audiences in the same essay is indeed a formidable task, and thus the result is more a "thinkpiece" than a research report.[1]

Since so little has been written under the rubric "performance practice" for any music other than Western art music, the format had to be formulated on an ad hoc basis. Folklore studies on performance practice contexts and performers have been most useful, particularly those by Roger Abrahams, Dan Ben-Amos, and Michael Owens Jones. It might be argued by musicologists that ideas of "folk" derivation are not applicable to a tradition of art music. Indian musicians and musicologists might argue further that they are inappropriate especially for their musical traditions. And indeed, the methods, models, and concepts dealing with performance which have been generated in folklore scholarship have a varying range of applicability to genres other than those for which they were developed. I have found them more useful in the shaping of some sections of this essay than for others. In general, however, the approach in this essay is derived from the music itself.

Defining what constitutes "performance practice" in the art musics of North and South India is complex and multifaceted.[2] Many of the topics discussed for Western art music by scholars involved with performance practice are of equal importance in Indic musical traditions: ensembles, the instrumentarium and relationships among the members, specific instruments, performances genres, musical structural principles (cadenza, improvisation, basso continuo, and the like), technique (bowing, fingering), types of musicians (trouvere, castrato), ornamentation, dynamics, expression, rhythm and tempo, texture, particular composers, and time period.[3] This essay encompasses many of these topics in Western music scholarship which are also appropriate to the consideration of performance practice in India.[4]

There is one major characteristic of Indian art music, however, that requires a somewhat different basic approach to the topic of performance practice: what is "practiced" (that is, done) in a performance of Indian art music is improvised to a large extent. What is done in a performance of Indian music is a matter of what must be done, and also what might possibly be done. Therefore, it is important to consider here not only the musical decisions that are made (what the practices in Indian performances are), but also the factors involved in making decisions in the improvisation process. With all of these facets of the topic in mind, this essay is subdivided by three perspectives: audience-performer relationships, performance ensembles, and the nature of performances themselves.

A performance is defined here as a situation in which there are present both music-makers (performers) and listeners who are not part of the music-making ensemble. For the purposes of this essay a performer is an individual who acts with the self-belief, and probably with some group's approval, that (s)he has acquired a respectable amount of knowledge and skill in a particular musical tradition and that (s)he should be able to present those materials for listeners in a coherent, acceptable fashion. Further, (s)he takes that responsibility upon him(her)self and performs for others. The term listener is used here to describe a person who is focusing primary attention on the music-making, as distinguished from a person who is hearing music while focusing primary attention on something other than the music.[5] The listeners are referred to hereafter as the audience.

The performance being addressed here is therefore further specified as a situation in which music-making is the primary focus of attention. Furthermore, the music which is being made is the central concern of the event.[6]

Contexts for such performances have been diverse and have been determined by the nature of the patronage system for music; that is, who the patrons have been, what settings the patrons have provided, and what types of occasions have been held in those settings.

Patrons of the type of musical performance under consideration here traditionally have been both institutions and individuals. "Institutions" refers here primarily to royal courts (which existed until 1947 in India), and cultural organizations of various types. "Individuals" refer to persons who operated within the "institutions" of the royal courts and to other wealthy citizens. Such patrons of art music in India have been predominantly members of an elite group—elite socially, politically, economically, or a combination thereof. This has been due to two ideas of Indic culture—the association of patronage with status, and the association of elitism with a knowledge of music. A third set of individual patrons has been made up of musicians themselves, members of the cultural elite (if not the social elite, as well).

The settings and occasions which have been provided by the patrons for the type of musical performance under consideration have been diverse. In a court, for example, formal *darbār* sessions have been contrasted with occasions for performance in less formal circumstances such as the ladies' quarters; there were also formal or informal occasions when important guests were honored with the presentation of a concert. Another occasion might be a musical contest arranged by the patrons for highly stimulating listening. The types of music which would have been heard in these diverse settings and occasions differed according to accepted sociocultural ideas of appropriateness. For example, *ālāp-dhrupad* or *khyāl*, sung for formal situations, required a different set of musical emphases than the more romantic, "lighter" types of music that would be appropriate for less formal occasions.

The musicians who performed in each context were likely to be different groups. In keeping with the character of Indic society the high degree of musical specialization was reflective of the high degree of other types of specialization within a stratified, ritually-sanctioned social structure—one in which only certain people supposedly were able to perform certain tasks in certain contexts. Female musicians performed inside female quarters; male musicians performed in court sessions, or for a female audience as long as they remained outside female quarters. But, there could be further division in the larger societal situations, even within those categories of specializations. Some male vocalists specialized in one performance genre while others specialized in another. Members of the famed Dagar family (Muslim), for instance, engaged at the court of Indore (Rajasthan state, western India), sang during the morning devotions of their Hindu rulers because their music (*ālāp-dhrupad* in Dagar style) was considered particularly devotional. Yet, during evening house entertainment when there was drinking, musicians other than the Dagars performed (Owens 1969: 31). Courts and other wealthy households employed either a large number of performers with different specializations, or supported a small number of performers, thereby leaving themselves free to invite musicians to give concerts on an ad hoc basis.

In modern Indian life private concerts in homes, and public concerts under *shāmiyānā* (tents) or in performance halls, are the predominant settings, whether the occasion is the celebration of an auspicious moment, a regular performance event, a music festival, or some other type of occasion. While the variety in the types of music performed still abounds, and while the specialization persists among musicians as to the type of music they perform, the variety in setting and types of occasion for performance have been considerably reduced.

There has been no break, however, in the continuity of performances in which music-making is the primary focus, and where the music being made is the central concern of the event. In the following section of this paper, I will try to show why and how the audience-performer relationship at such a performance has a direct bearing on the music being made, that is, a direct bearing on performance practice in Indian art music.

AUDIENCE-PERFORMER RELATIONSHIPS

Perhaps the most critical factor of audience-performer relationships in the type of musical performance under consideration here is the cultural value which is placed on the very idea that there should be an audience-performer relationship and, more specifically, that the audience should be an active agent in the performance. The carrying out of that idea (in any given performance) and the continuity of the idea (for all such performances) seem to be dependent on several factors of that relationship—the constituency of the audience, the musical knowledge of the members of an audience and the attitudes they bring to different types of occasions, and the attitudes and responses of performers.

In the court contexts for musical performance, the audience consisted almost exclusively of co-members of the patron's social group. The likelihood was strong that most members of the audience were at least somewhat knowledgeable about music. The performers to whom they would be listening were highly trained specialists who constituted an important segment of the cultural elite (but not necessarily a social elite, particularly with Muslim musicians). The relationships between the social elite and cultural elite were played out in the form of musical performance.[7]

One performance context created by royal patrons, in which the audience-performer relationship was displayed in an especially vivid manner, was the musical contest: patrons were often responsible for creating purposefully competitive situations in the form of contests between musicians of the same specialization. Such factors as the great degree of specialization among musicians themselves, the abundant number of musicians, and the pleasure taken by the audience in being sufficiently knowledgeable to judge the performance must have contributed to the creation of an air of competition. (The Hindi term for a listener knowledgeable enough to judge a performance is *samajdarlok* [literally, a person who knows]).

A well-known story of a patron-induced contest involved two of North India's most famous musicians, Tansen and his teacher Swami Haridas. Haridas was a Hindu saint and singer who lived most of his life in Brindaban, birthplace of the Hindu Lord Krishna. Haridas was never attached to any court, but was known as one of the finest musicians in the first half of the sixteenth century. Tansen, a musician at the court of the great Mughal emperor and patron of the arts Akbar, was a student and devotee of Swami Haridas. A story suggests that Akbar sent Tansen to compete in a singing contest with his teacher. Haridas "won" the contest as a result of the great emotional feeling he expressed through his music. When asked why his teacher had won, Tansen responded to Akbar that Haridas could sing with such feeling because he performed out of a sense of devotion to God and he was free to sing when and how he pleased. He, Tansen, had to be at the disposal of his king; such were the roles of the patron and his musician.

The "air of competition" encompassed an attitude of respect for someone who could meet a challenge. Skill, knowledge, and creativity were respected; offering proof of them was a desideratum. While those who were insecure in their musical achievement might have feared such situations, it would appear that those who were secure often were eager to prove themselves. The spirit of challenge was built into certain aspects of performance practice, as will be discussed in the section of this essay on relationships among members of a performing ensemble.

The rewards in musical contests arranged by patrons accrued to both patron and performer. For the patron who was supporting the best musicians, there was increased or maintained status. For the performer there was material as well as status gain. The rewards to both patron and performer were immediate and handsome. In addition, they were personal and highly individualized. The "individualness" in the sphere of music-making in India has been extremely important. It is characteristic particularly of private performance, from the patron's and audience's frame of reference. Individuality is a vital element; indeed, it is at the heart of performance practice in Indian music. It is both a reason for, and reflected in, the improvisatory nature of much musical performance, where the entire performance is produced by the individuals involved at the moment. It puts enormous responsibility on the individual performer, whether in private or public presentations. This is also prominent in non-improvisatory music, although to a lesser degree.

Competition was not only patron-created, but also could come from the listening audience in an otherwise non-competitive concert situation. In the instance to be cited, a fellow musician in the audience was particularly aggressive, but the example serves to reinforce the point that the role of audience in a performance situation is an immediate one. Radhikaprasad Gosvami (b. 1858) of Bengal, famous singer of *dhrupad* and *khyāl*, was admired for his great stress on purity of *rāga* (mode/melody). He attended a performance at which the famous Rampur musician Mushtaq Hussain Khan was the main performer.

Radhikaprasad, who had recently swallowed the hint that Mushtaq Hussain was capable of creating far greater sparkling variety in the rāga Malkosh than he, spent most of the evening interrupting the performance to point out deviations from the correct form of the rāga. Each time Mushtaq Hussain, as well as the audience, agreed that Radhikaprasad was right, but the soloist eventually became so exasperated with the interruptions that he stopped singing. Radhikaprasad then sang his own interpretation of Malkosh, to the audience's great approval, and said to Mushtaq Hussain, "Khan Saheb, we are restricted by our true adherence to the strict forms. We know techniques of *bistar* [improvisation] a little; but because we know the true forms of the rāgas we cannot mix them up. We cannot spoil the form of a rāga in order to get the applause of the listeners" (Owens 1969: 64,n.3).

One of the most rarified performance situations, and one in which the audience-performer relationship is especially intense, is the musical gathering at the home of a musician. Such an occasion would be held for one of several reasons: it might serve to introduce a rising young musician to his fellow musicians, to reconfirm the accomplishment and skill of a musician returned from a prolonged stint abroad, to introduce a musician known in one part of the country to the musical community in a different location, or the concert may be organized in celebration of a wedding or some other similar event. In such a setting the audience will be comprised of a number of musicians, all knowledgeable and the most demanding critics in the musical sphere. Not surprisingly, a spirit of challenge and competition is a vital element in the audience-performer relationship. Here is a description of this in a North Indian context:

In private concerts, open challenge is usually in the form of a 'farmaish' [a verbalized specific musical challenge] . . . in which a musician in the audience asks the tablā soloist to play a particular kind of composition or perform a rhythmic feat. Whether or not there is open challenge, musicians do feel competitive towards each other to the extent of trying to outdo each other. On a tape of a solo performance by the late Kanthe Maharaj which was arranged at the home of Ravi Shankar in 1955, Kanthe Maharaj tells his audience that he is about to play a gat that everyone plays but never as beautifully as he is about to play it: "just listen." He then recites the composition to prepare the audience so that when he plays it they will know what to listen for.

Challenges often come as disparaging remarks made by one musician about another's musicianship behind his back. The remark eventually finds its way to the injured party who seeks an opportune moment to prove himself to be the better of the two musicians.

Thus the listener to whom a tablā solo is played will greatly affect the content of that solo and hence the extent to which it is a true representation of the solo tradition of the artist. Also the element of 'challenge' is a facet of the tablā solo [as it is with North Indian classical music]. The winning over of an audience; the proving of oneself musically; the beating of a fellow musician; are all aspects of a musical performance in which a listener plays a part (Shepherd 1976: 117-118).

In twentieth-century India, there has been a gradual shift in musical performance away from the cloistered contexts fostered almost solely by the social, political, and economic elite. The phenomena of public concerts and a "mass audience" are therefore relatively recent. In these more recent contexts, the mass audience is an impersonal body "out there," the performer is an impersonal figure "up there." While the members of such an audience may accrue some status for going to hear an elitist music, their status is increased no more than that of the many other members of the public audience. The status of the performer may be enhanced in the eyes of the unknowledgeable, but the basis of that status is not the solidly musical basis that matters to elitist-oriented musicians. When there is a reciprocal one-to-one relationship between patron and client, as in the traditional relationship, and each enhances the other in some way (livelihood for status or ritual achievement as well as pleasure), the patronage is a personal one. When groups consisting of unrelated individuals (such as the mass audience) become the sponsor, the patronage is less personal, less individually reciprocal, and the reasons for the attainment of any status are likely to be somewhat different. It becomes patronage of art for the culture's sake rather than of the artist for the culture and elite's sake. That is a more abstract cultural ideal, one which puts the art in a dependent, impersonal position.

Almost every writer on Indian music has at some time addressed the ramifications of this situation. Commentaries speak of decreased knowledge of the subject on the part of the audience, and the traditional assumption that audience approval or disapproval actually and immediately affects a performer's music. The rationale seems to be as follows. If an audience is intimate with a performer's style and skill, they will listen expectantly to his performance. If, for example, an audience knows a *rāga* (the melodic mode in which a piece is performed) well enough to call him on mistakes or to notice a subtle rendition of familiar material then the artist will be careful and will try harder to create that subtle "something different," within his own style and through his own skill. Thus, it is now assumed that if the "new" audience does not know, then the performer need not be so careful as in the past, nor challenge himself musically. Furthermore, it also seems to be assumed that a performer would not continue to challenge himself musically, thereby uphold the highest standards, for reasons of his or her own. If these assumptions are correct, then performance practice will obviously be affected.

An artist knows whether or not his audience is knowledgeable musically by how attentive it is or whether it responds with a nod of the head or a verbal interjection at the right places. He can tell quickly what types of musical detail his auditors will respond to and he may have to tailor his performance to them in order to hold their attention. On the other hand, some artists have felt it their responsibility to educate their audiences.

If the audience simply does not react as it should even to moments the artist feels deserve a reaction, then the members of the performance ensemble—of whom there always will be at least two—will have to adjust in some way, perhaps to interact more with each other. Or the custom will flourish of an artist's insistence that a coterie of friends or students will be there to react. Or the expectation of audience-performer interplay will disappear and the performance practice will change accordingly. It is possible that the more asymmetrical and ritualized the performer-audience relationship becomes, the more ritualized (therefore less individualized) the performance will become.[8]

One further possible result of the shift to public performance with less knowledgeable audiences could be a bifurcation among performers into two groups: those who desire to maintain the tradition of elitism and refuse to react musically by conforming to the tastes of a less elite audience, and musicians who, for whatever reasons, choose to respond to demands of the "newer" consumers of musical performances. Precedents for such a bifurcation can be found in tradition. In South India, the nineteenth-century saint-singer Tyagaraja refused to accept court patronage, preferring instead to sing for Lord Rama; the ramifications for the change in musical styles in the Karnatak tradition were enormous.

Responses to change rarely take such clear-cut form as the formation of two distinct groups of musicians, however, and there are factors in the situation which mediate between the forces for continuity and for change with respect to the audience-performer relationship, and in the music which results from it. Those factors mediate between old and new performance contexts, between elite and general audiences, between musically knowledgeable and non-knowledgeable audiences.

One such factor is a particular segment of the audience which attends a performance. This segment of the audience is the coterie of students and connoisseurs whom one is likely to find at every musical performance, whether private or public. The presence of the coterie is no accident; the artist or the artist's manager is likely to be certain that they will be at the performance because the manager knows how important it is for an Indian musical performance to have audience reaction, particularly a musically knowledgeable one.

Another mediator is the institutional activity of music "training" in schools and universities where large numbers of the citizenry study music. The students in these schools and universities are still largely of the elite due to the structure and recruitment procedures of the Indian educational system and the general demands of the Indian economy, but they are of a less socially restricted elite than in the past. This type of general school and university training results not in producing performers but in producing an audience educated to be musically more knowledgeable.

A third major factor in the mediation process is found in the attitudes of the musicians themselves. This is reflected in the continuing custom of private musician-sponsored concerts where the highest standards are upheld. The spirit of challenge and competition is also upheld, playing not a small part in keeping those standards high. In addition, the continuation of such concerts provides the context where the traditional audience-performer relationship is re-enacted.

To this point in time the cultural value placed on the very idea that there should be an audience-performer relationship seems to remain viable. However, the contexts of performance do not so consistently create the proper "atmosphere" for the carrying out of the idea as they once did. Nor is the proportion of the audience which is musically knowledgeable as large as it once was. Thus, two of the three critical factors of the audience-performance relationship are in the process of radical change. That may eventually erode the cultural value itself. All the while, performance practice is being affected.

PERFORMANCE ENSEMBLES

In Indian art music performance practice is affected greatly by relationships among members of a performance ensemble. Ensembles are not large by Western orchestral standards; they are, rather, chamber ensemble size. Indian ensembles consist of two essential members, described here in terms of performing role: soloist(s) and those who perform with the soloist(s).[9] Soloists are individuals who take primary responsibility for the shaping of the performance; in all except percussion solo performances they are the individuals who produce the primary melody.

The categorizing terms "soloist" and "accompanist" are used differently and carry subtly different connotations, depending on where they are used, and by whom. For example, the terms "soloist" and "accompanist" are used consistently in Indian writing in English about music.[10] However, in Indian languages it is more frequently the custom to refer to an individual performer, not by performance role, but by the instrument (s)he plays; for example, not "I am an accompanist," but "I am a sārangiyā"; not "I am a soloist," but "I am a singer." Particularly in the case of sārangiyās and tablā players this is more precise than saying "I am an accompanist," because in other performance situations (perhaps only privately, in some cases) the same player could be a soloist. Singers might also be known by the genres in which they specialize: "I am a khyāliyā."

At least one of those who performs with the soloist(s) will play a percussion instrument. There is also some person(s) who play(s) a drone-producing instrument. In some ensembles, a second melody-producing instrumentalist or vocalist is also a constituent member, but the melody (s)he produces is related to that of the soloist and does not constitute a second independent melody.

In performance the interrelationships within an ensemble become clear through the musical events. The music-making of a *tablā* player in one *khyāl* performance, for example, may be very different from the music-making of that same *tablā* player with a different *khyāl* singer, who holds different ideas about the performing roles of the members of his/her ensemble. The soloists are expected to take primary responsibility for shaping performances, and control of the relationships in musical ways is a facet of that.

The musical relationships among members of an ensemble are determined to some extent by the particular genre of music which is being performed; thus, where pertinent, the material in each section of this portion of this essay is subdivided by genre. Other considerations are relative levels of skill, degrees of familiarity with each other's capabilities and styles, and considerations of a more personal or social nature. Section A below considers ensembles in which there is one melody-producing medium (voice or instrument) which is, of course, the solo instrument. It also includes ensembles in which two performers in the same medium (voice or instrument[s]) share the solo role. Section B considers ensembles in which there are two or more melody-producing musicians, only one of whom is a soloist. Section C considers percussion solos, and Section D highlights a Karnatak dance accompaniment ensemble in order to show a wider range of possibilities. Within each section, a selection of ensembles of both the Hindustani (H.) and Karnatak (K.) traditions are considered. Chart 1 delineates the organization of this portion of the essay. The reader is cautioned that, as in the entire essay, space prohibits the discussion from being all-encompassing.

As seen in Chart 1, it is particularly in Hindustānī (H) music that the constituency of ensembles is determined to a large extent by the genre of music being performed. In order of presentation below they are: *ālāp-dhrupad/dhamār* (vocal). *ālāp-jod-jhālā-gat*(s) (instrumental); *gāyakī* style (vocal style) instrumental performance; *khyāl*; *ṭhumrī*. Because the constituency of Karnatak ensembles is not determined to the same extent by genre of music being performed, there is greater flexibility in composition of Karnatak performance ensembles; accordingly, they are listed herein by solo instrument. Each Karnatak performance ensemble (except for dance ensembles) is likely to perform two genres: *ālāpana-kriti* and *rāgam-tānam-pallavi* (including *tānī āvartam* listed under C. Percussion Solo). As each genre or solo medium is first introduced in the discussion below, the instrumentarium of its ensemble will be specified. Brackets indicate optional instruments or optional number of an instrument; there could be a greater number of an instrument if the number is bracketed. What is important here are the musical relationships played out among all members of each ensemble, both soloist(s) and the other member(s).

Chart 1

Performance Ensemble Examples

A. Melody-producing Medium

   1. One soloist

      a. H. Ālāp-dhrupad/dhamār (vocal)

      b. H. Ālāp-jod-jhālā-gat(s) (instrumental)

      c. H. Gāyakī-style instrumental performance

   2. Two soloists (sharing the single solo role)

      a. H. Ālāp-dhrupad/dhamār

      b. H. instrumental performance

B. Two or more Melody-producing Media

   1. One soloist and accompanist(s)

      a. H. Khyāl

      b. H. Ṭhumrī (soloist may self-accompany)

      c. K. Vocal

      d. K. Flute

      e. K. Vīṇā

   2. Two soloists (sharing the single solo role) and
      accompanist(s)

      a. H. Khyāl

      b. H. Ṭhumrī

      c. K. Vocal

C. Percussion Solo

   1. H. Tablā

   2. K. Tāni āvartam

D. K. Dance Accompaniment Ensemble (Bharata Natyam)

   1. Bharata Natyam tāna varṇam

A. One Melody-Producing Medium

1. One Soloist

1a. In a Hindustānī *ālāp-dhrupad* or *ālāp-dhamār* performance, a vocalist is the primary melody-producing agent. In structural terms, the vocalist(s) hold a shifting relationship with the percussionist.[11] During the *ālāp* movement the percussionist is

```
Ālāp-Dhrupad/Dhamār

1 or 2 voices (male)

1 pakhāvaj (male)

[1] tamburā (male or

                  female)
```

a silent partner; he is present onstage, but, since there is no meter in that portion of the performance, he does not play. He is expected to be attentive and to react to the music being created by the singer.[12] The percussionist offers encouragement and, by being attentive and appreciative is both a bridge between the soloist and the audience, and also part of the audience himself. This role is reinforced by his sitting position, for traditionally he sits to the vocalist's right side, turned somewhat to face him, so that he is not directly facing the audience. When the *dhrupad* and therefore the metered portion of the performance begins, the percussionist becomes solely a member of the performing ensemble.

A bridge between audience and performers remains, as far as functional roles are concerned, however, in the person of the individual playing drone on the *tamburā*. (S)he usually sits facing the audience behind the soloist, therefore visible to the audience but not to the singer. (S)he is expected to listen attentively and to react visibly and vocally to the music as a member of the audience would. Because the soloist cannot easily see the *tamburā* player, one logically assumes that the reactions of the *tamburā* player are partly for the benefit of the audience. While this role is crucial musically in the performance ensemble, the *tamburā* player usually is not named in program notes or concert billing; (s)he is as anonymous as are members of the audience.[13]

During *dhrupad* or *dhamār* the role of the *pakhāvaj* player is to reinforce the rhythmic element. This is done by keeping pace with the vocalist, attempting to anticipate—not imitate—the rhythm that the vocalist will sing and thus to play it with him. This musical relationship and the playing on the *pakhāvaj* that is involved with it are known as *paral*; it is conceptualized as musically challenging but not competitive. The challenge is to improvise almost simultaneously, to keep track of the meter throughout, and occasionally to attempt to confuse at the ends of segments when vocalist and accompanist should arrive at the crucial metric/rhythmic point (*sam*) together.[14] The challenge is specifically between the musicians involved, but the audience, who expects to be able to understand the intricacies that are being created, also finds it a challenge to follow. This is necessary if the release of tension at the proper point is to be felt and appreciated.

1b. In the predominant Hindustānī instrumental performance genre—the sequence *ālāp-jod-jhālā-gat*(s)—a single melody-producing instrument is always joined by a percussion instrument. In the ensemble with the stringed instruments,

```
Ālāp-jod-jhālā-Gat(s)

Sitār, Sarod, Violin,        Shahnāī

Flute, Sārangī

1 tablā                      (1) naārā  (or tablā)

1 tamburā                    Drone shahnāī (surpeti)
```

sitār and *sarod*, the drone may be omitted. The drone may be produced on specific strings on the *sitār* or *sarod* rather than on *tamburā*, thereby reducing the ensemble by one person and changing the drone itself from a constant to a "sometime" element, and that "sometime" involved with rhythm production that is not a factor in constant drone.

In Hindustani *sitār* and *sarod* performances the structural relationship between the soloist and percussionist is a shifting one. During the unmetered *ālāp-jod-jhālā* portions of the performance sequence, the *tablā* player's role as participant audience is the same as the *pakhāvaj* player's role in the *ālāp* of an *ālāp-dhrupad* performance. The relationship of the drummer to the melody-instrumentalist in the *gat* (the metered portion of the sequence) depends on the individual soloist. The ideal relationship in at least part of the *gat* would be one of equal solo opportunities (called *pārī-pārā*) (Sahai, November 26, 1975). In such a case the meter-keeping role that must be filled in some fashion is traded off between sitārist/sarodist and the *tablā* player: while the former improvises, the latter plays a basic drum composition that delineates the meter (*tāla*); and while the latter plays solo, the former keeps time by repeating the *gat* melody. The element of competition is present only in the effort to make all equally effective. Most instrumentalists are unwilling to share the solo spot equally in the *gat*, however, so the element of competition is present but for reasons of time and attention allotment, thus resulting in the clear definition of soloist and accompanist roles.

It is traditional to speak of the *tablā* role in such a performance as an accompanying one (*sangat*), in any case. Ravi Shankar discusses this in his autobiography, although in doing so he also highlights one of the most important changes in recent Hindustānī performance practice, the "rise to importance" of the *tablā* player as soloist:

The accompaniment of the *tabla* now has an extremely important role in Indian music, and instrumental music in particular. Even so, the status of the *tabla* accompanist until about thirty years ago was not especially high. . . . Rarely did the *tabla* player have a chance to do more than a few very short pieces of solo improvisation during an entire performance. Even now, there are still some musicians who prefer the more passive accompaniment of the *tabla* player. It was primarily because my *guru* Allauddin Khan liked and encouraged the more active participation of the *tabla* accompanist, and because Aki Akbar and I later promoted this, that the status of the *tabla* player as well as the proportion of *tabla* accompaniment in any piece have come to have so large a part in our music today (R. Shankar 1968: 30-31).

Also, Western audiences generally have been positively responsive to drum work and have encouraged *tablā* artistry. It is possible that the increased attention given to *tablā* players who perform in Western concert contexts has accelerated the process of change in status of the *tablā* player, both in the West and in India.

Larānt, or challenging each other by improvising simultaneously, trying to play exactly the same stress and rhythms, can also be a feature in instrumental performances. Ravi Shankar distinguishes between degrees of this type of relationship:

Another *tabla* accompaniment is the *sath* [together] *sangat*, wherein the *tabla* tries to follow very closely the rhythmic patterns of the main instrument, playing almost simultaneously the same phrases, and the two must end a phrase together on the *sam*. This is a very exhilarating and exciting moment for the listeners as well as the players, provided they have an excellent mutual understanding. When there is even more tension in the *sitar-tabla* or *sarod-tabla* dialogues, the *sangat* is known as *larant* ("fighting") (R. Shankar 1968: 31; see n.14 above).

In *larānt* and also in the dialogue called *sawāl-jawāb* (question-answer) where the rhythm played on the melody instrument is repeated on the *tablā*, the element of competition and challenge is a shaping force in the performance. Part of the challenge in *sawāl-jawāb* is that neither instrumentalist keeps the meter; one plays while the other listens or strums on a drone string. They must keep the *tāla* within their heads and come together again on *sam* (a count 1) in the end.

1c. A second Hindustānī instrumental performance genre is based on a vocal genre called *khyāl*; it is thus called *gāyakī*-style instrumental music. The ensemble

```
Gāyakī Style (Vocal Style) Instrumental Performance

    Flute, Violin, Sitār, Sārangī

    1 tablā

    1 tamburā
```

composition is given here because it is similar to the ensembles given above, but since the relationship between the soloist and percussionist is closer to that relationship in *khyāl*, the reader is referred to that discussion in Section B.

2. Two Soloists (Sharing the Single Solo Role)

2a. Ālāp-dhrupad/dhamār.

Hindustānī performances in which two individuals share equally in the role of soloist are called *jugalbandi* (duets);[15] this term refers to two solo-melody-producing instrumentalists. Such duets have been a tradition in the Dagar family of *dhrupad* singers: Zakiruddin and Allahbande Khan (d. 1926) performed together;[16] two generations later Allahbande Khan's grandsons Mohinuddin and Aminuddin followed suit; their younger brothers Faiyazuddin and Zahiruddin now perform *dhrupad* together. According to Owens, the musical relationship between the two soloists in the Dagar family, at least between the two soloists Mohinuddin and Aminuddin, was one of deference of the younger (Aminuddin) to the elder: "Before a concert, Mohinuddin would ask Aminuddin what rāga he wished to sing but Aminuddin would hold back his suggestion in deference to his brother's authority" (Owens 1968: 27).[17]

The attitude of deference may be present in other elements in the performance, as well, such as who takes the pitch higher in *ālāp*, who initiates or ends a segment of the performance, who sings first when improvisation begins, and time allotments in the alternation of solos. When asked about their *jugalbandi* relationship with respect to all the possibilities just mentioned, the younger Dagar brothers acknowledged no such attitude of deference in their own performance practice. Rather, they insisted that an attitude of flexibility prevails, allowing for such changeable factors as one of them being "in voice" more than the other on a given occasion, or mood—if one felt definitely like singing one *rāga* or another, while the other felt amenable to any suggestion, or one felt particularly inspired on a given occasion (Interview May 1978).

2b. Instrumental *jugalbandi* performances are frequent and it appears that any two instruments can be featured together—flute and violin,[18] flute and *shahnāī*, violin and *shahnāī*, sitār and *sarod*, sitār and *surbahār*, and the like. In instrumental *jugalbandi* the dialogue that would have been likely to develop between melody soloist and percussionist (in the usual instrumental performance) is given over to dialogue between the two featured instrumentalists. That "dialogue" is likely to be at least somewhat competitive, but very subtly so. Each soloist must appear at least as good as the other, but to appear better is best. The aim overall is to give a balanced, creative performance with the same concentrated intensity that a single soloist would evince.

B. Two or More Melody-Producing Media

1. One Soloist and Accompanist(s)

The next set of relationships to be discussed are those in which the soloist is joined by a secondary melody-producing instrument. The genres presented are Hindustānī *khyāl* and Karnatak *rāgālāpana-kriti* and *pallavi*, in which the secondary melody-producing instrument is played by a performer other than the soloist, and Hindustānī *thumrī*, in which one secondary melody-producing instrument is likely to be played by the soloist.

1a. In the vocal genry *khyāl*, since the nineteenth century the most widely-performed Hindustānī vocal form, the relationships among the members of the

```
    Karnatak Ensemble

1 or 2 solo voices

[1 Supporting singer]

1 violin

1 mrdangam

[1] tamburā

[1 śruti box]

[1 kanjira]

[1 ghaṭam]

Flute

Violin

Mrdangam

[other percussion]

Vīṇā

[Violin]

Mrdangam

[other percussion]
```

ensemble are different in some respects from those in *ālāp-dhrupad/dhamār*. The relationship between the singer and percussionist (*tablā* player in *khyāl*) seems both to have changed through time and to have differed according to the particular soloist. It is said that *khyāl* used to involve a great deal of musical challenge.[19] Some musicians of the present century who (have) maintained that custom in *khyāl* have been Omkarnath Thakur, Faiyaz Khan, Dilip Chandra Vedi, Sharafat Hussain Khan, Nisar Hussain Khan, Vinayak Rao Patwardhan, and Yunus Hussain Khan.

Most singers of *khyāl*, however, prefer to restrict the drummer to meter-keeping through constant repetition of the *theka* (a drumming composition one cycle of the *tāla* long) by which the singer always can tell where (s)he is in the *tāla*. The role is thereby one of support without competition. In fast speed *khyāl* (*choṭā khyāl*) the drum sounds much more prominent due to the speed at which the *theka* is played and the drummer sometimes has an opportunity to play a brief solo when the singer rests for a cycle or two of the *tāla*. The musical relationship between singer and drummer is not significantly different in the two types of *khyāl*, however.

The singer is accompanied on a second melody-producing instrument, the *sāraṅgī*, which takes over the simultaneous improvisation role which was fulfilled by the drum in *dhrupad/dhamār*.[20] The *sārangī* player must, of course, deal with melody as well as rhythm in playing out this relationship.

The ensemble relationships in *khyāl* are extremely hierarchical, however, with the singer garnering almost all the attention to him or herself. With the exception of a few singers of *khyāl* who treat the *sārangīyā* more as a partner in the ensemble, these vocalists find musical means in the course of a performance to assert their position of soloist. Neuman describes such means, from the perspective of the *sārangī* player.

The sarangiyas also have little snatches of solo playing, but the vocalist can, and often does, interrupt the sarangiya. This apparently irritates the sarangiyas since it is the only opportunity that they have for their own expression. The sarangiya is not supposed to play a note that has not yet been elaborated by the vocalist, and is also not supposed to introduce a new melodic idea, except perhaps when the vocalist is a novice (Neuman 1974: 165).

The means found by the soloist are of two types: allotment of time in the performance for a member of the ensemble to be the center of attention; and control of the musical content of the performance. Both of these are basic to performance practice in an improvisatory tradition.

Level of musical accomplishment is also a factor in performance practice. In *khyāl*, this is most crucial if there is an imbalance in the musical acumen of the two melody producers, that is, when an accomplished accompanist and "novice" soloist perform together.

If the vocalist is inexperienced, the sarangiya might suggest a musical idea to him. Most vocalists, however, do not accept this "musical" advice, and it is not uncommon to hear a vocalist complain that the sarangiya attempted to anticipate him, and thus to mislead his own melodic development (Neuman 1974: 170).

1b. In Hindustānī *thumrī*, another vocal genre in which the solo vocalist is joined by a secondary melody-producing instrument, the relationships among the members of the ensemble are somewhat different. The most prominent differences in this

```
Khyāl

1 or 2 voices (male or female)

1 tablā

1 sārangī (or harmonium or violin)

[1] tamburā

[svaramandal]
```

respect from *khyāl*—which developed at the same time as *thumrī*—are two: 1) The secondary melody-producing instrument, the harmonium, is frequently played by the singer her(him)self and the idea of simultaneous iteration on the accompanying instrument is fulfilled more completely than when someone else takes that musical role.[21] When the traditional *sārangī* is present, the role continues to be as described above. Also, the amount of embellishment on the accompanying melody is usually increased. 2) The *tablā* player is given at least one solo section (called *laggī*) in the course of a selection, a time when he can and does show his skill in playing very fast. Otherwise, the drummer's role is to keep the *theka* as in *khyāl*. Since the speed is not as slow as in very slow *khyāl*, however, the *tablā* appears to be much more prominent throughout. As in *khyāl*, musical competition does not appear to be conceptualized as a determinant of performance practice within the *thumrī* performance ensemble. It is striking that *khyāl* and *thumrī* developed at about the same time with the same ensemble of singer(s), *tablā, sārangī,* and *tamburā,* and that both are essentially non-competitive in musical conception.

The Kathak style of North Indian dance, which also developed into its current form in that context and time frame, is closely associated with *thumrī* and with the same performance ensemble, as well. When *tablā* players perform with Kathak dancers, the principle of *paral* comes into play (Sahai, November 26, 1975). That is, the *tablā* players achieve as close rhythmic coordination as possible with the dancers. The term *paral* is not used, however, because that refers specifically to *pakhāvaj* drum strokes and patterns, not to *tablā*.

1c, d, e. In some genres of South Indian art music, as well, soloists are joined in ensemble by a secondary melody-producing instrument—the violin. The relationship between the soloist and violinist is both one of cooperation and competition. The following commentary by a violinist in the Karnatak tradition, speaks to the role of the accompanist.[22]

```
                          Thumrī

            1 or 2 voices (female or male)

            1 tablā

            (1) sārangī

            (1) harmonium
```

It is one of constant learning and of quiet and creative awareness. . . . exposed to others' styles. . . . he is expected to merge with them. . . . His obligation to repeat and to lend support representation of an original. . . . This view of imitation . . . must be dispelled if the role of yet involve himself as a musician (L. Shankar 1974: 4).

Shankar is sensitive to the likely Western interpretation of such a performance role and endeavors to explain the Indian regard for "imitation" in music-making, including what has been referred to as "oral memory."

In South Indian music there is a premium placed on the ability to recreate immediately the music that one has heard . . . to imitate. Imitation is normally given the bad connotation of "copy" or "counterfeit." It is not considered a creative process for it is seen as a parasitical representation of an original. . . . This view of imitation . . . must be dispelled if the role of the violinist as an accompanist is to be fully understood and appreciated. The accompanist actively reconstructs the soloist's music; he is not a passive repeater (L. Shankar 1974: 32).

In repeating a soloist's phrase or playing an approximation of it, the accompanist crystallizes the idea of the phrase, and provides a bridge to the next solo phrase, making it mean all the more "by recalling the very stuff from which it was born" (Shankar 1974: 45).

The relationship between accompanying violinist and solo vocalist in Karnatak music is spoken of by Shankar in terms of tension, as well as support and cooperation on the part of the violinist. Tension arises due to three primary reasons: 1) unfamiliarity with the musician one is accompanying; 2) the expectations concerning the musical relationship in a particular segment of a performance; 3) imbalance in the skill of the two performers.

Occasionally a violinist may be called upon to accompany a musician he does not know. This places him in a disadvantageous position, for if he has accompanied an artist several times he knows him musically—his repertoire, his favorite *rāgas*, and how he deals with music. With an unfamiliar artist it is difficult to predict what will come next.

The second source of tensions, the nature of the musical relationship in a particular segment of a performance, comes into play in *pallavi*. The *pallavi* mentioned in the quote is part of the *pièce de résistance* among improvisatory performance genres in the Karnatak tradition: *rāgam-tānam-pallavi*. The *pallavi* is the portion of that sequence in which meter begins. The term *pallavi* refers to two things: 1) a metered melody that is either traditional or newly composed, and 2) the entire segment of the sequence which begins with the rendering of that composition by the soloist and includes improvisation in which the *pallavi* is a structural element. The accompanist is expected to repeat the *pallavi* (composition) exactly, immediately after the soloist first states it. The moment of repetition is an extremely tense one for the accompanist:

The soloist prepares an intricate *pallavi*, and most often surprises the accompanist at the platform. This area is the soloist's territory, and it is sometimes dangerous territory for an accompanist; the platform could become a battlefield. . . . every accompanist should have a vast knowledge of the form, so that he can face any situation. Otherwise, a *pallavi* can be used as a weapon against his reputation and dignity (L. Shankar 1974: 115).

Svara kalpana is another type of improvisation in Karnatak music that is built around the competitive spirit between soloist and accompanist. *Svara kalpana* is the improvisation within a *rāga* using the solmization system as text,[23] developing rhythmic intricacies and mathematically proportioned rhythmic patterns fitting within the *tāla* structure. It is a type of improvisation that can occur in two Karnatak performance genres—*kriti* and *rāgam-tānam-pallavi*. In *svara kalpana* the violinist has his choice: whether to duplicate note for note what the soloist has played, or to play his own variations (L. Shankar 1974: 105). In the latter case, the soloist, then the violinist, alternate in continuous improvisation. The violinist conforms to the soloist's line only in respect to the length of the improvisation and melodic range. When an excellent soloist and an excellent accompanist challenge each other in this exchange of musical ideas, the result can be delightful musical dialogues.[24]

The percussion accompaniment to *svara kalpana* also contributes to the excitement. Frequently, each melody instrument will have its own accompanying percussion instrument: voice and *mṛdaṅgam*, violin and *kanjira* or *ghaṭam*.[25] Each percussionist attempts to match the rhythmic improvisation of his "soloist," so that the same type of "simultaneous improvisation" seen in Hindustānī *larānt* is played out here.[26] Thus, the spirit of competition is multiplied and intensified, and performance practice is determined by it.

The third reason for tension between soloist and accompanist is imbalance of skill between the two performers, that is, an accompanist who is more accomplished than the soloist. While this is not a common situation, it must be coped with when it occurs. Shankar speaks to this from the point of view of the accompanist, for whom it is an awkward position and one which forces him to exercise "good judgment." The "good judgment" is the quandary. It is especially difficult if the soloist is a weaker musician. If a soloist makes a mistake in rendering the *rāga*, for example, or in rendering a mathematical rhythmic pattern, or even plays out of tune or loses the *tāla*, should the violinist repeat the mistake or correct it? Shankar suggests with wit: "Perhaps the truly clever accompanist will pretend to be tuning his instrument (1974: 30).

In order to avoid an "improper" imbalance musically, or even to put themselves in the best light possible, some Karnatak (as well as Hindustānī) soloists eschew accompanists known for their strong musicianship. Other Karnatak soloists prefer an accomplished accompanist. These differing preferences can undoubtedly be heard in the resulting musical performances.

For those Karnatak musicians who are secure in their capabilities, the spirit of challenge is a positive element in performance. It creates a relationship of interdependence (which seems to be particularly important in the eyes of the accompanist) and keeps the elements of the performance in balance, and keeps everyone "on their creative toes." It becomes a natural part of the performance, manifested in very subtle as well as very obvious ways which may or may not be apparent to the audience. "The stages of action and counteraction are so quickly . . . responded to that the tension . . . between the players in effect appears as harmonious balance" (L. Shankar 1974: 23).

In accompanying a *vīṇā* rather than a vocal soloist, the violinist might take a somewhat different relationship. In the *rāga ālāpana* portion of a performance the violinist's role is more subordinate than it is in a vocal solo: "The violinist is expected not to play as much. . . . And he takes his turn only when the soloist has finished."[27] In the metered portion of even a *vīṇā* performance, however, the relationship is as described above.

Thus, the relationship between soloist and melody-producing accompanist in the Karnatak performances is a shifting one, dependent upon the structure of the performance genre and the particular solo instrument involved. Both of those are crucial factors for Karnatak performance practice.

The trend at present in *mṛdaṅgam* accompaniment has been close support of the melodic phrases; this is a trend attributed largely to the innovative drummer Palghat Mani Iyer. Formerly the drummer "played in a more independent style of cross-rhythmical counterpoint with the soloist. . . . The older style is more often used today with the vina. . . ."[28] Nowadays the drummer is more likely to reinforce and embellish the rhythm of the vocal melody in close rapport. In vocal performance, the accompaniment is hand-in-glove with the solo part, while in *vīṇā* performance the violinist supports the solo instrumental part while the *mṛdaṅgam* player might remain rather independent rhythmically. Since most first-rate drummers know the song repertoire quite well, these relationships carry little competition.

2. Two Soloists (Sharing the Single Solo Role) and Accompanists

2a, b, c. In Karnatak vocal performances and Hindustānī *khyāl* and *ṭhumrī* (vocal) performances—all of which feature a soloist with secondary melody-producing medium—the solo role may be shared between two individuals. It is far more frequent in the Hindustānī tradition, however. In the Karnatak tradition when a second vocalist is added to the ensemble, that person's role is conceived of neither as equal nor as accompanying; it is most frequently spoken of as "supporting." (Earlier in this century this happened frequently in Hindustānī *khyāl*, as well as that the solo vocalist had the support of both the *sāraṅgīyā* and a singer.) In both Karnatak and Hindustānī music the supporting vocalist will be a disciple of the soloist; this is a very effective means of teaching/learning performance practice. In addition, the musical contribution of that person to the performance is another factor in determining performance practice in these improvisatory traditions.

C. Percussion Solo

1. Hindustānī tablā

In a *tablā* solo the percussionist takes the limelight. He plays only with a *tāla*-keeper who sits beside him, also facing the audience. The *tāla*-keeper's role is fulfilled by playing a one-cycle-of-the-*tāla* long melody (*laharā*) over and over again steadily, and with little or no ornamentation; the *laharā* is played preferably on *sāraṅgī* or harmonium, instruments that produce sustained pitches and the desired feeling of an unending cyclic flow.[29] The *laharā* player is not in competition with the *tablā* player; rather he is supportive. He must have a perfect sense of timing and be absolutely certain at all times where he is in the *tāla* cycle. Only if the *tablā* player can be certain of this, can he use the *tāla* as a framework which he can defy in intricate ways.

2. Karnatak Tānī āvartam

The percussion instrumentalists have greater opportunity for sharing the solo spot in Karnatak musical performance than they do in Hindustānī music. After the main item of a concert—whether it be *rāgam-tānam-pallavi* or a long *kriti* (usually in Aditāla)—the percussionists have opportunity afforded by a section in the *pallavi* portion called *tānī āvartam*; if the *mṛdangam* is the only percussion instrument in the ensemble, the player is a soloist and he can go on for a prolonged time, developing rhythmic ideas within the framework of the *tāla*. All melody stops at this point (something that is foreign to Hindustānī performance practice except for brief moments in instrumental performance), and the singer or instrumental soloist keeps *tāla* with obvious hand motions for the drummer and audience.

If there are more percussions in the performance ensemble, the *tānī āvartam* becomes a *tāla vādya kacceri* (gathering of *tāla* instruments). It is usually a "kind of contest in rhythmic dexterity, with each of the several performers on the different instruments trying to outdo the others in imaginative play." (Brown 1974: vol. 1, 50).

Perhaps because of this performance tradition, the playing techniques for *kanjira,* *ghaṭam,* and other percussive instruments are very highly developed.

D. Karnatak Dance Accompaniment Ensemble (Bharata Natyam)

This last example of performance roles and relationships was chosen because of the unusual independence among multiple melody-producing instruments. The ensemble providing the music for a Bharata Natyam dance performance resembles the ensembles already discussed, in that it must include both melodic and percussion instruments.

A Bharata Natyam performance includes a succession of genres. One of those genres, the *tāna varṇam,* is danced with an ensemble consisting of singer(s) either male or female, flutist, *vīṇā* player (or clarinetist in the case of the ensemble cited below), *tamburā* and maybe a *śruti* box, and *mṛdaṅgam.* The *varṇam* is a learned composition; singers render it without improvisation, responsible for communicating the text clearly. The unusual aspect of the performance practice here is the "freedom" of the flute and—in this case—clarinet.

Flute and clarinet enjoy far greater freedom than the singers to improvise melodic and rhythmic variations upon the set musical theme. And the drummer, working always within the four-avarta (cycles of the tāla) setting of the theme, supports the entire ensemble with an underlying rapid-fire succession of rhythmic accents; he also occasionally exploits pitches available to him on the drum (principally the tonic and major second) to highlight the melody (Higgins 1973: 179-180).

The same type of relationship occurs in the *ālāpana* which precedes the *varṇam* and also in the short *ālāpana* which precedes an earlier portion of the Bharata Natyam sequence (*jātisvaram*). The singer assumes informal melodic leadership. Both flute and clarinet for the most part elaborate on what the singer has just done; they improvise their own variations within the range and style of the singer. Sometimes, however, "Both clarinet and flute move in semi-independent fashion, creating what seems like a dissonantly contrapuntal 'free-for-all'" (Higgins 1973: 100). A graph notation of a portion of the pre-*varṇam* *ālāpana* is shown in Example 1 (Higgins 1973: 104-106).

Another factor in a Bharata Natyam performance is relationship between the dancer and her accompanying music ensemble. Part of that relationship is the

unpredictability of a good dancer. While the dance sequence is fixed by tradition, some details within segments of the sequence are determined by the dancer. She may omit or repeat or otherwise lengthen or shorten. These are the options of a dancer who refuses to tie herself to an inflexible plan, knowing that her greatest moments as an artist spring from the freedom to make spontaneous choices. The effect all this has on her musicians, no matter how many times they have performed with her, is a kind of creative insecurity (Higgins 1973: 181).

In summary, performance ensembles are an important determinant of performance practices in Indian art music. The factors that have been considered as part of "the relationships among members of a performance

Notated *Varṇam* Raga Bhairavi *Ālāpana* Performed by Voice, Flute, Clarinet. *An Introduction to Bhairavi Varṇam* (Higgins 1973: 104-106).

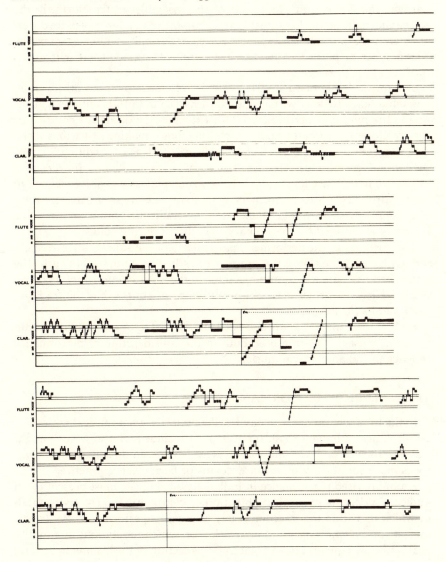

Graph taken from The Music of Bharata Natyam, Jon Higgins, Ann Arbor: University Microfilms, 1973, pp. 104-196. Used with permission.

ensemble" are 1) the association of each particular ensemble in the Hindustānī tradition with a particular performance genre; 2) the instruments in each ensemble (including the voice as an instrument); 3) the musical role of each instrument; 4) the attitudes of the performers in these roles; and 5) the flexibility in some of the above factors.

The composition of each ensemble for a particular genre is stable in Hindustānī practice. *Ṭhumrī*, with the optional *sāraṅgī* in addition to harmonium, is the least predictable of the ensembles in the North. In the Karnatak tradition the instruments and composition of ensembles are different than those of the North and there is greater flexibility within an ensemble. The number of particular percussion instruments included, other than the *mṛdaṅgam*, is flexible.

The musical role of each instrument in relationship to the others in an ensemble tends to shift within one performance in both traditions. This is due to the nature of performance—for example, the desire for contrast or the creation of tension through competitive music-making of various sorts. The element of challenge—whether labelled "challenge," "fighting," "competition," "tension," or "creative insecurity"—is regarded by players who are secure in their abilities and who enjoy such play as a positive element in the performance. Other performers, even some who are secure in their abilities, simply wish to avoid challenge. The challenge within an ensemble normally is initiated by the primary melody-producing soloist.

The attitudes of the performers, particularly of the soloist, are extremely influential in determining the musical roles in the ensemble. In turn, the prescribed roles are a determining factor in the musical content of a performance. Each performer acts within tradition, of course, but the tradition itself admits flexibility.

Each of these major factors and particularly the factor of flexibility within tradition must be taken into account in the consideration of performance practice in Indian classical music.

THE NATURE OF PERFORMANCES

In the final section of this essay I will emphasize what musical material a performance of Indian classical music must include and also what it might possibly include and, to some extent, why.[30] Thus, in this discussion, I will focus more specifically on musical details of performance practice.

An improvised performance in Indian classical music must present to an audience a delicate musical combination of continuity and creativity, both of which lie within the tradition. Only then will a performer make the immediate and memorable good impression on which reputations in a totally oral tradition depend. I have organized this section of the chapter according to criteria of continuity and creativity, as they are manifested in the performance practice of this improvisatory tradition.

Continuity

Pertinent to a discussion of continuity, folklorist Roger Abrahams (1971) posits the following theoretical proposition which I find tenable here: The performer must perpetuate a cohesive body of traditional expression; that body of traditional expression has been and must be approved again by the community. The cohesive body of traditional expression is comprised largely of elements of significant form.[31] *Rāga, tāla,* and performance structures of the various musical genres are those elements of significant form that together constitute the cohesive body of traditional expression in Indian art music.

The opportunity to reapprove the cohesive body of traditional expression is pleasureable to an Indian audience on several levels.[32] Hearing a clear, balanced presentation of those elements executed with artistic sensitivity and a high degree of technical skill will produce aesthetic pleasure on the part of an audience. There is the additional factor of intellectual pleasure when the audience recognizes those elements and knows that the tradition is being perpetuated. This results in approval of the artist and once again of the elements themselves.

A performance must include all three elements; that is the most basic expectation for content of a performance. When a music performance does not include *rāga* (as in *ṭhumrī* sometimes, *ghazal, dhun,* and the like) the music will be dubbed "light" music.

A strong force is at work in the process of maintaining continuity in Indic cultures: high value is given to having traditions; in this instance the value is given to having a cohesive body of traditional musical expression. Furthermore, tradition says that the audience/community is expected to recognize in an intellectual as well as aesthetic way, what the elements of significant form are in their cohesive body of traditional musical expression. These are talked about, written about, and it is expected that they will be reiterated in performance. The importance of audience recognition of the very importance of the elements of significant form, and also of the elements themselves cannot be overstated; it is crucial to the process of maintaining continuity in a tradition.

It appears that *rāga* is the most respected of all the elements of significant form. It also enjoys a reputation as the most complex of the elements in that it encompasses so much musical detail. (That is possibly why it is the most respected.) Not only is the information level high in one *rāga*, but the number of *rāgas* is manifold. If tradition expects the artist to know many *rāgas*, and the audience to recognize details of *rāgas*, the expectation is a demanding one.

How many *rāgas* would an artist "keep" in his or her repertory? It seems that while all artists are familiar with a large number of *rāgas*, many artists choose to concentrate on a relatively small number. In fact, exceptions to this cause comment. One example was Ustad Vilayat Hussain Khan, a *khyāl* singer of the Agra *gharānā* (musical "house" or tradition) who gloried in being able to recount from whom he had learned each of a very large number of *rāgas*. In her discussion of the Vishnapur *gharānā*, Owens cited another example, that of Radhikaprasad Gosvami (b. 1858), a singer of that *gharānā* who was widely admired for his ability to control an unusually wide range of *rāgas* (Owens 1969: 63-64).

One can speculate on reasons for an artist concentrating on a few *rāgas*, The reasons could lie simply with individual preference. An artist might have a selection of his own favorite compositions and cultivate those *rāgas* accordingly. (S)He might prefer complex *rāgas* over less complex ones (or vice versa) or might choose *rāgas* that would suit her/his own temperament. The reasons could also be a matter of circumstances. In a court situation in which many musicians were available for varied functions, each musician naturally would cultivate those *rāgas* appropriate to his specialization, *rāgas* that would, for example, lend themselves to weighty or playful improvisation. If a musician's duties fell at one particular time of day, it would be logical for him to especially cultivate *rāgas* for that time of day. Or as a disciple, an artist might have inherited songs from his *guru* or *usād* on which he placed particular value and therefore cultivated the *rāgas* in which the songs were composed. The possible reasons are many.

How many *rāgas* would an audience hear? In a performance of the instrumental performance genre *ālāp-jod-jhālā-gat*, the soloist will either play all of it in one *rāga*, or change to a second *rāga* at the *gat* section. An artist will probably play that sequence twice in an evening performance and end the concert with one or two lighter selections. Thus, an audience could hear as many as six *rāgas* in a "standard" performance of that type. In vocal performances, one could expect to hear approximately that many, but in any case at least three *rāgas*.

The number of *rāgas* that an audience might hear in a total court context, however, would be considerable, if there were many musicians performing diverse types of music. It is unlikely that the same *rāgas* were cultivated by all or even most artists, and *rāgas* are not all associated with the same genres. In present-day concerts when one artist presents several types of music, the selection of *rāgas* is still diverse, and a number of different concerts would feature a number of different *rāgas*. Thus, it would be quite demanding on a regular concert-goer to recognize the details of the considerable number of *rāgas* (s)he would hear.

While the musically educated audience undoubtedly recognizes many (if not most), it is likely that retention of the details of *rāgas* has rested heavily on the memory of the performers and on their desire to retain them exactly. The quote I cited earlier concerning Rāga Malkosh serves as an example of varying degrees of such a desire. Even a glance through the compendium of information on *rāgas* by Walter Kaufman (1968) reveals the variety in rendition of many *rāgas*. Enough of the detail must be there in cohesive form, however, for that *rāga* to remain that *rāga*.

It is a well documented fact that *rāgas* change through time.[33] I suggest here that one reason why *rāga*, an element of significant form in the cohesive body of traditional expression in Indian art music, is likely to change is that it is such a complex element with so much detail that audiences through time have left the retention of at least some of that detail to the performers themselves, and the performers have held different attitudes toward the detail. In this respect the complexity of the system and the respect for individuality fostered toward and among performers have joined to assure some degree of flexibility.

How, then, can *rāga* be an element of continuity? Because *rāga* is so significant an element of significant form, the community will demand that it be part of the cohesive body of traditional expression; the very artists who take liberties must render enough of the cohesive body of detail intact that their performance will be approved by the community (qua audience) which still includes at least a small group of connoisseurs. Furthermore, the artists themselves usually respect tradition to the extent that the pace of change will be slow. Change is more likely to show up in the community response (if their knowledge is decreased) or in the attitude of the artists (because of their personalities, of the breakdown of cohesive traditions, or from lack of control from the community) than it is to show in the idea that *rāga* (in the abstract) is significant.

The second element of significant form is *tāla* (meter). At present, at least, and especially in Hindustānī music, the listening audience is expected to know more about *rāga* than about either *tāla* or the highly developed art of drumming. *Tālas* themselves do not seem, on the surface, to present the degree of complexity, therefore difficulty (challenge), that *rāgas* hold for audiences. That is, there is relatively little complexity in mastering a feeling for the metric framework that *tālas* are. Count $5 + 2 + 3 + 4$ and you get a cycle of 14 counts that is (Hindustānī) *dhamār tāla*; count $4 + 2 + 2$ and you get the 8 counts that is (Karnatak) *ādī tāla*. Recognizing a cycle and feeling how melodies fit into it is the basic demand on the members of an audience. Furthermore, relatively few *tālas* are in everyday use.

The listener begins to ascertain the complexity of *tālas*, when a cycle of 16 counts subdivided $4 + 4 + 4 + 4$ turns out not to be *tīntāla* but *tilwādā tāla*, distinguished by the drumming pattern. The listener then realizes that recognizing a metric structure calls for one kind of knowledge, but attention to the drumming which is present calls for a more comprehensive degree of awareness. The complexity deepens when one feels called upon to understand the rhythmic and metrical manipulations within the *tāla* and know intellectually how they are working with the *tāla* or against the *tāla*.

The *tāni āvartam* and *tāla vadya kacceri* in South India give Karnatak audiences opportunity to develop awareness and understanding of drumming and rhythmic complexities (whether the audiences use the opportunity is another matter). Such opportunities are less frequent in the Hindustānī tradition. Brief *tablā* solos occur in vocal *ṭhumrī* and somewhat longer ones in instrumental performances, but brief solo moments are hardly to be compared with *tablā* solo performances.[34] The best audience (and practically the only knowledgeable one) for drum solo in North and South India is a group of other drummers.

It would appear that there has been less change in Indian art music with respect to *tāla* than there has been with *rāga*—at least at the basic level of *tāla* structures. I suggest here that continuity at that basic level has been maintained because it is the level of understanding of an enormous number of listeners who hold the performers responsible for maintaining it. Artists must render *tāla* correctly at that level of structure, at least, in order to be approved by the community.

A third element of significant form to be discussed here are the structuring processes through which the *rāga* and *tāla* are manifested. One such process, and an extremely pervasive one, can be described as a presentation of events with sense of proportion and sense of progression. That general structuring process is manifested on various levels. It appears in both Hindustānī and Karnatak music at the level of the total performance. In Hindustānī music there is a progression from "heavy" to "light" that is manifested in a succession of events that carry with them "heavy" to "light" performance genres, choices of *rāgas*, and text content. Proper proportion among these events is determined by the valuation of each; for example, "heavy" forms will be given longer time than "light" forms. In Karnatak musical performance the same basic structuring process is played out, but with different materials.

The same structuring process, or succession of events with a sense of proportion and sense of progression, also is attained at the level of the single performance genre. The "events" in the "succession of events" differ from genre to genre. In fact, the particular types of events utilized are part of the definition of genre. In Hindustānī *khyāl*, for example, it is expected that a major portion of improvisational time in the fast portions will be spent on *tāns* of various sorts; *tāns* are not generally thought of as an element of *dhrupad* or *ṭhumrī* improvisation, however (although one hears them in *ṭhumrī*).

Within a performance genre, the succession of events is clearly observable to the listener due to the use of traditional means of demarcation between them. In Hindustānī *ālāp* the demarcation is created by use of a melodic "cadential formula" called a *mohrā*; it says, "I have just finished one musical segment and now I am going on to another." In the Hindustānī metered forms *khyāl* and *gat*, a particular phrase of melody from the traditional composition (or the whole melody repeated) placed in the crucial point in the *tāla* cycle (approaching and including count 1 of a cycle, from the previous cycle) creates the demarcation. The point in the cycle where the cadence begins is flexible, but the point on which the cadence is considered culminated (count 1) is fixed.

The amount of time devoted to one "event," that is the amount of time between demarcation points, depends on various factors. It could be any length from quite short to quite long. In metered music it could be one cycle of the *tāla* to several cycles of the *tāla*.

The order in which these events occur may differ from performer to performer; the acceptable range of variability also may depend on the genre. In addition, the particular "school" of singing or playing to which a performer belongs may be a factor in determining which types of "events" an artist may include in his performance of a particular genre. There could be several sequential "events" of one type, as in *khyāl* for example, a succession of *boltān* + cadence + *boltān* + cadence + (*akār*) *tān* + cadence.

The succession of clearly demarcated events is prevented from being a series of starts and stops by another of the elements in this primary structure —the sense of progression. There seem to be several "senses of progression." In Hindustānī *ālāp-dhrupad* and instrumental performances a multifaceted progression takes place. As the progression is described below, vertical alignment indicates simultaneity.

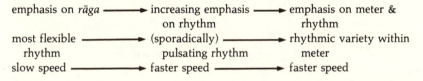

Khyāl also shows this structure, but is metered from the beginning. Those genres of Hindustānī art music which do not manifest this progression— primarily *thumrī* and *ghazal*—are considered "light classical."[35] In Karnatak music this structure—but without the element of progressive acceleration of *tāla* counts—is found in the *rāgam-tānam-pallavi* sequence, in *ālāpana-kriti*.

The "senses of proportion" within the primary structures are manifested at different levels and with different musical materials. As in Western music of medieval and Renaissance eras, proportion in Indian music is most prominently a matter of time. In macro-unit terms, the portions within a largely improvisatory Hindustānī genre can differ, for example, in the amount of time spent emphasizing *rāga* (as in *ālāp*) relative to the time spent improvising with meter and emphasizing rhythmic development. In micro-unit terms, the proportions within *ālāp* can differ, again, by units of time—time spent in low pitch register (*mandra saptak*) relative to middle (*madhya saptak*) and upper (*tār saptak*) register; or smaller units yet, time spent on each new pitch or pitch area within a pitch register.

The sense of proportion, then, is intimately bound to the sense of progression. It therefore differs from genre to genre. With those genres that consist even partially of improvisation, the manipulation of proportion is left to the individual performer. Conscious attention to the macro-unit proportions in melodic music-making is drawn frequently in concert reviews of Hindustānī music,[36] but measurements taken in the few studies that have been done suggest that even at the micro-unit level the sense of proper proportioning (balance) marks the performances of those Hindustānī artists who are considered "the best."[37]

Another type of proportion, one also involved with time, is *tāla*. *Tāla* itself is a delineation of proportion, and drumming in the Indian tradition is calculated to develop an acute sense of proportion. Drum compositions and variation processes exploit proportion as an autonomous element of structure. "Time" becomes linked with "speed." The proportions that are mastered first and manipulated thereafter are mathematical: twice as slow, twice as fast, four times as fast, or three times as fast.

In Hindustānī music the mathematical proportions are named, in a clearly defined system of cross rhythm called *layakārī*. There are four *layakārī* in *tāla* theory: 1) *barābar* (even proportions, i.e., duples); *ādī* (3:2; 3:1, 1½:1; ¾:1); *kuāḍī* (5:1; 2½:1, 1¼:1); *biāḍī* (7:1; 3½:1; 1; ¾:1). Each of the particular proportions within each *layakārī* is named *gun*: for example 1:1, *ekgun*; 1½:1, *dehragun*; 2:1, *dugun*; 3:1 *tigun*, etc.[38]

Not all rhythmic development utilizes these proportions, of course, but they are part of the basic musical vocabulary and are widely used in both drumming and melody-making. Frequently, they come and go quickly in Hindustānī melodic music, however, and are buried among such rhythmic diversity that attention is not constantly drawn to them.

In Karnatak music conscious exploitation of proportions is a primary element of structure. Within a selection in performance there is little (theoretically, no) acceleration of the speed of the *tāla* counts such as there is in Hindustānī music. Rather, speed is increased or decreased through rhythmic density in mathematical proportions. If a performer wishes to accelerate the speed then (s)he must double, triple, half, or otherwise mathematically manipulate the rhythmic density. Cross rhythms are also created by the same process; particularly interesting cross-rhythmic effects are achieved from the doubling and quadrupling of 3, 5, 7, and even 9-count phrases, for example.

Shape (*yati*) is another type of proportion that is developed in Karnatak music. Instances include taking a short melodic motif and gradually expanding it (the *srotovaha* shape), or taking a long line of text and gradually rendering less and less of it (the *gopuccha* shape), or the progressive diminution followed by expansion of a musical unit (the *damaru* shape).

The general performance structure of a succession of events with a sense of proportion and a sense of progression is manifested, then, in different performance genres and on different levels. The broad outlines of that structure are clearly and easily recognizable to an audience and therein probably lies an important reason why they are a strong element of continuity. That is not to say that the particular performance structures (genres) have not changed; most of them have either undergone change or are a result of change through time. In some cases change is documentable, as for example the addition of *saṅgatis* (variations) to Karnatak *kriti* by Tyagaraja. The pace of change, however, has been slow and is, for the most part, undocumented.

While the broad outline of the general performance structure seems to have remained stable, the elements within it—the succession of events, sense of proportion, and sense of progression—are elements of potential flexibility, i.e., creativity. Whether they are in fact flexible and how that flexibility is manifested are peculiar to each genre and/or performer.

Continuity, then, is maintained in performances of Indian classical music when performers perpetuate a cohesive body of traditional expression. That cohesive body of traditional expression consists largely of these elements of significant form: *rāga*, *tāla*, and performance structure. Performers will perpetuate that cohesive body of traditional expression for two intertwined reasons: they respect the tradition; and the performances (and therefore they themselves) are approved by the community (their audiences)—partially because they perpetuate it. A degree of change does occur in the elements of significant form through time, but those same two factors should ensure that the degree of continuity will be far greater than the degree of change.

Those factors also could affect the nature of change. Anthropologist Milton Singer's hypothesis concerning the relation of Little and Great Traditions in Indic civilization could apply to musical tradition: in a primary civilization like India, cultural continuity with the past is so great that even the acceptance of "modernizing" and "progress" ideologies does not result in linear forms of social and cultural change but may result in the "traditionalizing" of apparently "modern" innovations (Singer 1972: 68).

Creativity

At the outset of the discussion of continuity it was stated that the overriding factor in determining a successful performance of Indian art music is that the performer must make a good impression that is both immediate and memorable for an audience. The question was posed: What constitutes a memorable performance for an audience? The answer suggested was: a delicate combination of continuity and creativity, both of which lie within the tradition. This discussion now turns to creativity.

While the "ideals" of the *rāga* and of the performance structure held by the particular soloist who is performing are "models" for that performance, the manner in which (s)he carries out those "models" lies in the realm of creativity. While the "ideal" of the *tāla* is less individualistic because the same "model" is shared by all the performers in an ensemble, rhythmic improvisation within (or without) the *tāla* lies in the realm of creativity. Among other options from which an artist can choose which lie in the realm of creativity are dynamic play, speed, *layakārī*, intonation, and ornamentation.

The use of dynamics (in the Western sense of the word) is one element which a performer can utilize, but it is not an element that one can assume will be utilized to a great extent. In the Dagar style of *dhrupad* singing relatively little use is made of dynamics. In addition, what we hear as dynamic contrast is not necessarily conceptualized as such by Indic tradition. In the Benares school of *tablā* playing, for example, timbral contrast is an underlying principle in structuring stroking patterns. While Indian timbral contrast encompasses what Westerners distinguish as dynamic contrast, Westerners must retrain their minds and ears to hear it as timbral contrast in Indian drumming.

In singing, what we would term dynamics is spoken of in terms of sound production, i.e., singing with power, with chest tones or head tones: ". . . (his fine, flexible voice) lends itself easily to a surprising variety of musical effects—from subtle, sensitive notes to phrases of tremendous force and animation" (*Times of India*, Bombay: October 13, 1969). B. J., a leading *khyāliyā*, is noted for the use of his voice with an effect that we would term partially dynamic: "Lately . . . he plays to the gallery using physical gestures and 'voice-throwing,' and rendering high notes with closed mouth" (*Times of India*, New Delhi: 1969). In singing, such use of the voice is associated with the style of an individual performer, as seen in this review of an artist in a different *gharānā*: "We were glad that (L.) eschewed his preoccupation with the mannerisms of (B. J.), though these did creep in a few times when he rendered the higher notes restfully but with a closed mouth. Crisp and tiny embellishments thrown in between the soft and tranquil strains heightened their effect" (*Times of India*, New Delhi: October 30, 1968).

In *sitār* and *sarod* performances dynamic contrast is cultivated as a major element of performance practice. The extremely soft tones produced on the ebbing vibrations of a struck string contrast markedly with the tremendously powerful percussive striking in the rhythm-oriented portions of improvisation, particularly in the building of climaxes.

Timbral contrast is another option for a performer. "Sweet-sounding phrases," for example, contrasted with "stiff guttural tone." *Tāns* (fast melodic flourishes) are a means of creativity. They are frequently spoken of in terms of shape; this seems to be partially a matter of individual style, sometimes a matter of *gharānā* style in *khyāl* singing. Likewise, ornamentation is a means of creativity, where the type, frequency, and even the very use of them is most often an individual's choice.

Articulation is another means of creativity. One example of this is in the portion of performances where successively plucked/struck/vocally articulated pitches are juxtaposed with multiple pitches produced on one pluck/strike/sung legato unit: in Karnatak *tānam*, Hindustānī *nom-tom* *ālāp* (of *ālāp-dhrupad*) and *joḍ* and *jhālā* (instrumental performances). This articulation is coupled melodically with successively repeated pitches (often a drone pitch) juxtaposed with non-repeated pitches (melody pitches). A style of articulation within this can be developed distinctively by one performer. Ustād Ali Akbar Khan, for example, occasionally performs *jhālā* "backwards," repeating the melody pitches rather than the drone pitches.[39]

Speed is an element of creativity in performance practice. The overall degree of slowness (as in very slow *khyāl*), the degree of fastness (as in *tablā*-playing skill), and use of degrees of speed for contrast are pervasive elements employed from the beginning to the end of every performance. This is an element no matter whether the basic speed of the *tāla* counts changes or not (as discussed in Proportion).

Rhythmic play (*layakārī*) (discussed with Proportion above) is another element that is utilized creatively. Placement of it within a performance, artful use of the text to create it, variety in rhythmic play within a performance, skillful use of it to show off the *rāga*—any number of uses of *layakārī* are available to the creating artist.

Within rendition of a *rāga*, creativity includes "ever-freshness" i.e., not repeating movements and note combinations in the same way to the extent that the performance becomes repetitious. More positively, it was stated in one review: "Then his rich imagination always discovers new avenues of delineating the melody" (*Times of India*, New Delhi: December 10, 1968).

One important means of creativity within a *rāga* can be employed by only the most well-established artists: stepping momentarily out of the *rāga* to draw on non-*rāga* material. Usually this means including a foreign pitch. It will be slipped in very subtly, passing quickly and noticeable only to the most observant; to the listeners it creates a feeling akin to a risqué thrill.

Another means of creativity within *rāga* is intonation. Particularly in vocal music and on instruments without fixed pitches this is an avenue open to each performer. The custom of non-standardized pitch leaves the option open for artists to pitch notes "a little high," "a little low," "very high," "very low." This option is often expressed as "use of microtones" or "use of quartertones" (much too precise an expression). Once established, intentional intonation such as this will be fairly consistent throughout a performance.

Larger units of creativity than options within a performance are the events upon which an entire performance would be built. One such type of creativity is the "composing" of a new *rāga*. Names of some "new" *rāgas* which have now become part of traditional repertoire bear the name of the "composer," for example Miyāṅ kī Todī named for Miyāṅ Tānsen. Today new *rāgas* seem to abound, many introduced by prominent instrumentalists.[40] Only time will determine if they will remain in currency for any long period of time, but the process by which they would become part of the tradition is important to watch for an understanding of this very juxtaposition of continuity and creativity.

One method by which fresh but not entirely new material can be introduced is to combine the characteristics of two traditional *rāgas* into one, as in the case of Ahīr Bhairav and many others. Another route of introducing fresh material is presenting very old musical items (compositions or *rāga* or other) which are so rarely presented that they are ever-fresh. In Hindustānī performance an artist will sometimes introduce a composition by saying that it is his grandfather's, or his great uncle's, or otherwise part of his family tradition which is the way of stating that the composition which will then be heard is old, and known (probably) only to him. "Something old but unknown is new, and as such is an important source of musical innovation" (Neuman 1974: 45).

Furthermore, it is so important that fresh material be considered part of the tradition (old) that composers will attribute their own new composition to a respected predecessor. This occurred with *khyāl cīz* in the eighteenth century when many songs were attributed to Sadārang (including his signature *mudrā* in the text) that do not appear to have been his compositions. The custom apparently continues in Hindustānī music to the present day (Sahai 1975: P. C.). "For India we might write that in order for things to change, they have to appear the same" (Neuman 1974: 291). Stated another way, creativity is often couched in terms of continuity.

The greatest individual creativity within a performance lies, of course, in improvisation, in both the Hindustānī and Karnatak traditions. When improvisation must include a large degree of continuity along with creativity, it stands to reason that moments of creativity stand out all the more as "precious gems." A performer must protect his/her own particular means for attaining freshness and individuality and be able to keep it as sacrosanct as possible. The choices of means to do this range from not performing it at all to performing in such a way that fresh ideas go by too quickly to be learned by the listener.

The circumstances of performance is one means that artists have of ensuring that they can keep the most creative part of their art to themselves. Resistance to recording is one of those means, thereby maintaining the tradition of the one-time event. The content of performance is another means. Taking care not to include an idea or *rāga* or composition too frequently keeps it a potential item of freshness. Likewise does refusing to repeat something exactly within a performance. One *tablā* player relates how in a private solo performance among a gathering of drummers, the artist played a composition that was new to the audience. When asked to repeat the composition, the *tablā* player agreed to do so, and proceeded to play something quite different (Sahai 1975: P. C.). The transmission process is also involved in the preservation of items of freshness. The same *tablā* player, in order to have his "secret" items remain in individual "ownership," taught one group of compositions to one disciple and another group to another disciple; those two are now reluctant to share them even with each other.

In summary, creativity in the performance practice of Indian art music must be viewed in the light of a complex of factors now familiar. It involves not only performance contexts but the role of the individual performer, how he sees his own creativity in relationship to his musical tradition, to his fellow performers, and to his audience. In turn, his creativity is influenced in degree and in kind by the other participants in his musical tradition and his performing ensemble and by his audience—restraining, encouraging, accepting, rejecting, withholding, giving. All of these factors, whether subtle or obvious, must be taken into account in consideration of what happens in a performance, that is in consideration of performance practice.

NOTES

1. I wish to thank several colleagues in Indian music for their suggestions and criticisms. But, in particular, I am indebted to two Indian music specialists who are both musicologists and performers of Indian music: Peter Row of the New England Conservatory, a specialist in the Hindustānī tradition, and Jon Higgins, Wesleyan University, a specialist in the Karnatak tradition, gave the penultimate draft of this chapter a thorough reading and concomitant advice which only performers can give. I wish also to thank my *tablā* teacher of several years, Pandit Sharda Sahai, of the Benares *baj*.

2. These are the two main traditions operative within the sphere of Indian classical music. While the North Indian (Hindustānī) and South Indian (Karnatak) traditions are different in many ways, they do share a common basis in ancient Indic music theory and are two separate and vital traditions within one musical system. The more widespread tradition is the Hindustānī, used throughout central, northern, western, and eastern India, Pakistan, and Bangladesh. The Karnatak tradition is based primarily in Dravidian language areas and the southerly portion of the subcontinent, with its major center Madras city.

3. This list of topics includes a large percentage of the categories by which the index of Vinquist and Zaslow (1971) is organized.

4. This essay does not include explanations of Indian music. For such information see Wade (1979) and other pertinent items listed in the bibliography of this essay. Particularly pertinent is the entry "India, subcontinent of: II, 3 Performing Practice" by Harold S. Powers, in *The New Grove Dictionary of Music and Musicians* (vol. 9, 105-115). In that entry Powers discusses ornamentation, improvisation in terms of major principles and *rāga* exposition, and ensembles.

5. This distinction between listener and hearer is pertinent here because there are contexts where music is present, but as background entertainment. A specific example of this from historic times was the periodic occasion on which a ruler was formally greeted by his or her courtiers (one by one) who would assemble for the ritualized custom of renewing ties and paying respect. Modern-day receptions with background entertainment are a common occurrence.

6. This is distinguished, for example, from a musical event in which religious worship is the central concern.

7. As Roger Abrahams has noted, an expressive product can be and is, in fact, rhetorical of the relationship at play in other spheres of the culture (Abrahams 1968: 143-158).

8. The ritual involved with performance would become based on public decorum rather than on musical response. This is the reverse of a process described by Roger Abrahams: ". . . it is usually the case that the more stylized the performance, the more asymmetrical and ritualized the performer-audience relationship becomes. . . ." (Abrahams 1972: 76).

9. In radio performance announcements, for example, the ensemble is introduced as follows "N H K will sing Rāg Bihag—with him (कं के साथ) on tabla (तबला पर) Shri H.A.K." *Tamburā* players and *śruti* keepers are known neither by the instrument nor by their role.

10. See, for example, Neuman (1980).

11. *Dhrupad* and *dhamār* are two similar types of compositions. They differ mostly in the *tāla*s used and in subject matter of their texts. Each is preceded by an *ālāp: ālāp-dhrupad; ālāp-dhamār*. For further detail about these performance genres see Wade (1979): Chapter 7, and other related sources cited therein.

A *pakhāvaj* is a double-headed membranophone handstruck; it is always played by a male. For further information on the instrument see Krishnaswamy (1967); Wade (1979); Chapters 5 and 6; and Brown (1974).

A *tamburā* is a plucked chordophone used to produce the drone pitches throughout a performance. For further information on the instrument see Krishnaswamy, Wade and Brown cited.

12. If there are two vocalists, they sing together only when they are singing the traditional composition in *dhrupad* or the *mohrā* in *ālāp*; otherwise, they alternate so that in improvisation there is one singer, one percussionist.

13. An interesting example of differences between cultures in this matter is that in western concert situations, the name of the *tamburā* player or *śruti* keeper is almost invariably given.

In South Indian (Karnatak) ensembles, the drone frequently is produced on a small organ-like *śruti* box. According to a Karnatak violinist the person pumping the bellows on the *śruti* box to keep the drone constant is not considered an integral part of the music-making: "I had my first instrumental experience playing a śruti box [a drone instrument] for my brothers and sisters. The task was tiresome and left me discouraged as I was the only member not performing" (L. Shankar 1974: 8).

14. Frequently this is translated as "fight" by Indian musicians; I prefer to render it as "challenge" because the word "fight" tends to conjure up a negative relationship in the American or western European value system, whereas "challenge" does not necessarily do so. This musical challenge usually is not considered a negative one in the Indian value sphere.

15. The western term "duet" is not as precise as the Hindustānī term *"jugalbandi."*

16. Owens: 38. They studied *ālāp* with a descendant of the great Tansen and became famous for spending much more time on *ālāp* performance than their contemporaries did.

17. The structures of musical relationships and familial/social relationships mirror themselves here. As Owens has pointed out the deference and restraint required of younger brothers toward their elder brothers as well as father, also was characteristic of upper-caste Hindu family relationships in the State of Mewar. She suggests that this family, which is thought to have been Brahmin Hindu before they converted to Islam, has retained many of their high-caste Hindu behavior patterns. The family

was employed for several generations at the Hindu court of the Rāja of Mewar at Udaipur in present-day Rajasthan (Owens 1968: 27).

18. The violin is a solo instrument in North India, an accompanying instrument (primarily) in South India.

19. Sharda Sahai (October 29, 1975) suggests that it was appropriate because *khyāls* were sung in medium speed at that time, as *dhrupads* were. *Tablā* are a pair of membranophones, each drum struck by one hand. Formally, it is performed publicly by a male, although a few girls study drumming. For further information see Krishnaswamy (1967) and Wade (1979).

20. This is not known as *paral* or *larānt*; those are terms which refer to rhythmic play only, and with respect to *pakhāvaj* and *tablā*, respectively. *Sārangī* is a bowed chordophone whose sound can be very similar to that of a voice, particularly a female voice. It is always played by a male in public although a few women now are learning to play. For further information see sources cited above. *Sārangī* is sometimes replaced in *khyāl* ensembles by violin.

21. An harmonium is an organ-like aerophone with a keyboard. It is played frequently by the vocalist(s) approximately in close heterophony. For further details see Wade (1979) and Krishnaswamy (1967).

22. L. Shankar is an unusual and valuable source, and I am indebted to him here. Shankar is one of few Indian performing artists who have brought their practical experience to bear in a PhD dissertation. It seems only appropriate to have him be the spokesman in this instance, as well.

23. Sa Ri Ga Ma Pa Dha Ni Sa, corresponding to the western Do Re Mi Fa Sol La Ti Do.

24. Shankar also states that "certain complex forms of *svara* . . . are more premeditated. The soloist can prepare them and surprise the accompanist" (1974: 93). Apparently, he still would not include these in the category of *citta svara*, which means composed passages of *svaras*.

25. *Mṛdaṅgam* is the most prominent Karnatak drum; it is very similar to the Hindustānī *pakhāvaj*. *Kanjira* is a tambourine and *ghaṭam* is a clay pot played against the bare belly of the percussionist. For more detailed information about each of these instruments, see Wade (1979); Krishnaswamy (1967); and Brown (1974).

26. This can be heard performed on the Nonesuch Record, H-72040 *Ramnad Krishnan: Kaccheri* (A Concert of South Indian Classical Music).

27. Shankar 1974: 51. In accompanying *rāga ālāpana*, the violinist can improvise alone for the same length of time that the soloist took and he can either improvise in the soloist's style or in his own style.

28. Brown 1974: vol. 1, 284. Brown is not clear as to which performance genres this pertains, but most likely it is *kriti*.

29. Shepherd 1976: 119. The *laharā* should be flowing rather than "the beating out of every *mātrā*" (count).

30. I refer to both Hindustānī and Karnatak musics throughout this discussion, unless I specify one or the other.

31. What I call "elements of significant form" is equivalent (I think) to Bruno Nettl's "rather precisely defined style characteristics," or "models" on which an improvised performance is based (Nettl 1972). While these "models" also apply in Indian art music compositions, I speak here of improvised performances.

32. Here I am substituting "audience" for Abraham's "community."

33. A fine thesis on why *rāgas* have been changed by performers through time is in Jairazbhoy (1971).

34. For a detailed discussion of *tablā* solo in the Benares *gharānā*, see Shepherd (1976).

35. The reader is reminded that these are gross generalizations and exceptions can always be pointed to.

36. Performers are criticized when they spend little time in slow speed. Performing well in slow speed is most difficult to do successfully and therefore is "the true test" of musicianship.

37. One such study was done by Shirish Korde (Brown University, 1974-75) who concentrated primarily on performances recorded by Ustad Ali Akbar Khan.

38. For a fuller discussion of these properties see Shepherd (1976): 100-103. The reader may find somewhat different definitions of the rhythmic ratios such as *Kuādī* and *biāḍi*.

39. Pointed out to me by Nazir Jairazbhoy during a class at Brown University, Fall 1975.

40. Since it is difficult to document the pace at which new *rāgas* have been introduced in the past, it is impossible to know if this is a recent phenomenon.

REFERENCES CITED

Abrahams, Roger D.
> 1968   Introductory Remarks to a Rhetorical Theory of Folklore. *Journal of American Folklore* 81: 143-158.
> 1971   Personal Power and Social Restraint. *Journal of American Folklore* 84: 16-30.
> 1972   Folklore and Literature as Performance. *Journal of the Folklore Institute* 9: 75-94.

Ben-Amos, Dan
> 1974   Toward a Definition of Folklore in Context. *Journal of American Folklore* 84: 2-15.

Brown, Robert
> 1974   *The Mrdanga: A Study of Drumming in South India.* Ann Arbor, Mich.: University Microfilms. 2 vols.

Goldstein, Dan and Kenneth, eds.
> 1975   *Folklore Performance and Communication.* The Hague: Mouton.

Higgins, Jon
> 1973   *The Music of Bharata Natyam.* Ann Arbor, Mich.: University Microfilms.
> 1976   Personal Correspondence and Personal Communications (verbal). P. C.

Jairazbhoy, Nazir
> 1971   *The Rāgs of North Indian Music.* Middletown, Conn.: Wesleyan University Press.
> 1975   Personal Communications.

Jairazbhoy, Nazir A., Harold S. Powers, Regula Qureshi, Robert Simon, Kapila Vatsyayan, Bonnie C. Wade
> 1980   India, Subcontinent of. In *The New Grove Dictionary of Music and Musicians.* London: Macmillan Publishers Limited. Vol. 9: 69-166.

Kaufmann, Walter
    1968   *The Rāgas of North India*. Bloomington: Indiana University Press.
Krishnaswamy, S.
    n.d.   *Musical Instruments of India*. Delhi: Publications Division, Government of India.
Nettl, Bruno with Bela Foltin, Jr.
    1972   *Daramad of Chahargah: A Study in the Performance Practice of Persian Music*. Detroit, Mich.: Information Coordination.
Neuman, Daniel M.
    1974   *The Cultural Structure and Social Organization of Musicians in India*. Ann Arbor, Mich.: University Microfilms.
    1980   *The Life of Music in North India: The Organization of an Artistic Tradition*. Detroit, Mich.: Wayne State University Press.
Owens, Naomi
    1969   "Two North Indian Musical Gharānas." Chicago: University of Chicago.
Ranade, G. H.
    1961   Some Thoughts about the Laya-Aspect of Modern Music. In *Commemoration Volume in Honour of Dr. S. N. Ratanjakar*. Bombay: K. G. Ginde. 112-121.
Row, Peter
    1976,   Personal Correspondence and Personal Communications.
    1977
Sahai, Pandit Sharda
    1975   Personal Communications.
Shankar, L.
    1974   *The Art of Violin Accompaniment in South Indian Classical Music*. Ann Arbor: University Microfilms.
Shankar, Ravi
    1968   *My Music, My Life*. New York: Simon and Schuster, Inc.
Shepherd, Frances
    1976   *Tablā and the Benares Gharānā*. Ann Arbor: University Microfilms.
Singer, Milton
    1972   Search for a Great Tradition in Cultural Performances. In *When a Great Tradition Modernizes: An Anthropological Approach to Indian Civilization*. New York: Praeger Publishers. 67-80.
Sorrell, Neil and Ram Narayan
    1980   *Indian Music in Performance: A Practical Introduction*. Manchester, England: Manchester University Press. With cassette.
Sunday Statesman
    1969   New Delhi.
Times of India
    1969   Bombay.
Times of India
    1968,   New Delhi.
    1969
Vinquist, Mary and Neal Zaslow
    1971   *Performance Practice: A Bibliography*. New York: Norton, Inc.

Wade, Bonnie
    1979   *Music in India: The Classical Traditions*. Englewood Cliffs, New
            Jersey: Prentice-Hall, Inc.
Wade, Bonnie and Ann Pescatello
    1977   Music "Patronage" in Indic Culture: the *Jajmani* Model. In *Essay for
            a Humanist. An Offering for Klaus Wachsmann*. New York: Town
            House Press, Inc. 277-336.

2

Music in Africa: The Manding Contexts

Roderic Knight

The musicologist studying a medieval manuscript or a nineteenth-century score usually finds it necessary to search for additional information in literary and historical works and often the visual arts to help him understand the way the music on the printed page was actually performed. In like manner the ethnomusicologist listening to a recording of unfamiliar music relies heavily on written sources to help place the music in its proper context. In either case, going beyond the simple fascination with the recorded document—whether on paper or magnetic tape—requires a knowledge of the practices surrounding the performance.

The focus of this book is on those performance practices and the role they play in five different cultural settings. In this chapter the focus will be on Africa, or more specifically, on the Manding people of West Africa.

Music in Manding culture has many facets, from the strictly amateur to some of the most impressive and professional virtuosity to be heard anywhere in Africa. In the present day the music most often heard is either the latter type, performed by the *jali*, a professional musician (or in a wider sense, a verbal artist), or music of the drummer, who is strictly speaking not a jali, but is nonetheless usually referred to as a *tantang jali* (tantang is a type of drum).

Since we are not looking at scores or listening to recordings here, we must be content with describing a series of scenes featuring first the jali, then the drummer. With these scenes as a backdrop, we will then take a closer look at the different elements that make up what we are calling the performance practice: the social setting in which the performance takes place, the role of the musicians in that setting, aesthetic judgments about the music and its performance, the application of those judgments in the teaching of music, and the content of the song texts, especially as this sheds light on the relationship between the performer and the audience.

The following scenes are presented much as a visitor to the Manding area
—that is, southern Senegal, Gambia, Guinea-Bissau, Guinea, southern
Mali, and western Ivory Coast—might see them today.

SCENES WITH THE JALI, OR SCENES OF "JALIYA"

Scene 1.

Outside a large well-kept house in the city a group of *jalolu*[1] is performing. The owner of the house has just taken a new wife and is preparing for
her arrival. Three of the men are sitting side by side on the ground, each
playing the *balo*, a xylophone. Others are singing, and the women add a
festive clanging sound with tubular iron bells as they sing. One of the men is
the lead singer. At the end of his long phrases the others respond in chorus.
After some time the owner of the house appears and calls the lead singer to
him. The music stops and the man speaks softly to the singer, who repeats
what the man has said in a loud, announcing voice. The announcement continues in this way as the man expresses his appreciation for the performance
and makes public his gift of 100 *dalasi* for the musicians' services. After
discussing how best to divide up the money, the musicians disperse, to
return later in the evening to entertain both the man and his wife.

Scene 2.

It is mid-morning, and invited guests are gathering in the compound to
celebrate the *kulio* (lit., head shaving) or naming ceremony for a week-old
child. A jali sits on the veranda, his 21-string *kora* before him as he plays,
and a second jali sits beside him, tapping on the back of the instrument. The
jali women (*jali musolu*) sit nearby, ringing their iron bells and singing.
Soon the child is brought out. The music stops and the jali musolu gather
around as the Imam, prayer leader at the mosque, shaves a patch of hair
from the baby's forehead, announces the baby's name, and leads the assembled guests in prayers for its health. The jali musolu escort the baby and its
mother back inside and the music starts up again. Food and drink are
offered around, and as the guests disperse, the baby's father pays the jalolu
who have come to perform.

Scene 3.

The leading *kontingo*[2] jali and his wife, a fine singer, have been invited to
sumungo, or visiting, at the home of a wealthy but generous merchant.
They were eager to accept, not only because *Duniya mu kacha le ti*
(Conversation is the essence of life), but because it is part of their
profession, and an occasion for music as well. They take a cab to the man's
house since it is far from where they live. Several of the man's friends are
there as well, and the conversation ranges from current politics to the best

choice of a wife for the merchant's son. As the jali plays his slender, skin-covered lute, his wife, singing in a powerful but relaxed and majestic style, tailors her performance to the people there, selecting songs about the merchant's own ancestors and other great men, and extemporizing lines of her own for him as well. The kontingo jali interjects words of encouragement and agreement as he plays, and occasionally narrates some of the stories behind the songs being sung. As with the other events, the expectation of a fitting fee is a major incentive to the couple performing.

Scene 4.

It is the annual Independence Day celebration, and in the capital many events are planned. The national ensemble will perform in the central square, and speeches will be made. Unlike the ensembles of the past, this one includes a large variety of instruments. There are eight jalolu playing the kora, three on the balo, three on the konting. A *bolon* player has been included as well. The four heavy rawhide strings of his large arched harp add a bass sound to the ensemble. Even though this instrument is tuned differently from the other stringed instruments, and they in turn are not tuned to the pen-equidistant seven-note tuning of the xylophone beyond matching the fundamental, these differences are overlooked in favor of the new "orchestral" sound. Two men and two women, all renowned for their fine voices, are standing in front of the group, swaying gently as they sing, with great power in their voices. During the performance, people often come up with gifts of money for the jalolu, signs of special appreciation for the words sung or the excellent style. A public address system is used for the speeches, eliminating the need for the shouting voice of the jali to convey the dignified messages of the leaders, but he is still there, now functioning as translator to present the speeches in at least one other language for the many ethnic groups assembled.

Scene 5.

A kora jali has been given a fifteen-minute slot on a radio program. The engineer has noted that he should remove the metal plate attached to the bridge, for the gentle buzzing of the rings threaded around the edge will interfere with the clear broadcast of the melody. Then, as the tape is set in motion, the jali must begin on command and be ready to finish when told to do so as well. True, he will be paid a fixed rate for his time, and he may even reach some of his distant benefactors over the airwaves, but how will he measure up to the other kora players whose playing the radio audience has already heard?

In contrast to these scenes of jaliya are the following scenes from the realm of the drummer. While very similar scenes of jaliya might be seen in any part of Manding (hence no specific locations were mentioned), drumming styles and occasions tend to be more regional. Thus all of the following scenes are set among the Mandinka, in the western region of Manding.

SCENES WITH THE DRUMMER

Scene 1.

From the *bantaba* or town square comes the sound of *Nyoboring Julo*, the drum beat for wrestling (*nyoboringo*). It is time for the latest match in the regional tournament. Today it is between the Mandinka and the Fula. Each team has hired a drum troupe to assist them, and, as often turns out, both troupes are Mandinka, each troupe playing three open conical drums. The troupes play simultaneously but independently, from opposite ends of the square. Two drummers sit with each team while the leader of each remains standing, moving into the ring with each new contestant and playing for him as he challenges an opponent, wrestles with him, and returns, either in victory or defeat. But with often two or three pairs of contestants in the ring at once, the drummers are hardly noticed. All eyes are on the matches, and a winner is often surrounded by admirers who rush out to give him pennies.

Scene 2.

It is Boxing Day (December 26), and the streets of Banjul are alive with children dressed in homemade masks, parading around as their friends beat on boxes and tins. They are imitating the *Kankurang* who is there also, a full grown, muscular young man, his head, face, and torso covered with strips of red bark, with leaves at his elbows and waist. The Mandinka drum trio is there too, playing *Kankurang Julo* as he dances and moves down the street, brandishing his bush machete and short stick and demanding coins from onlookers. Today the young people's club is sponsoring him as they do on various occasions, but formerly he was seen only during boys' initiation activities. He served as a protective figure, chasing evil spirits, making sure bathing areas were safe, and dancing at the coming out celebration. Today he is mainly a source of colorful and amusing entertainment on festive occasions, but small children still flee from him. Once again the drummers would surely be missed if they were not there, but they are hardly the center of attention.

Scene 3.

The village *Kanyeleng Kafo* (Women's Fertility Club) is staging a dance. A young newlywed of two years is joining in hopes of improving her chances of conceiving, using the various medicines and cures the club offers. The club members, many of them older, and only some of them still childless, have put on crazy hats or men's clothing, and festooned themselves with jewelry made of shells, seeds, bottle caps, and other metal and plastic trinkets. The drummers have been called to play and they are performing *Nyaka Julo* (Girls' Initiation Beat), *Musuba Julo* (Matronly Woman's Beat) and other women's pieces as the club members clown and sing humorous and licentious songs.

Scene 4.

It is a month or so since the rainy season began. The rice planted in a fertile patch near the village is sprouted and ready for transplanting to the swampy field where it will grow to maturity. This is women's work and since hoeing the swamp in the hot sun is not particularly enjoyable, they have decided to hire the drummers to play for them. The work will go faster, not because the drumming synchronizes the work, but because it lightens the burden by providing accompaniment for some of the songs and something to think about besides the sun above. The drummers go right into the field with the women, playing *Nyaka Julo* and *Daba Tantango* (Hoe Drums) for the occasion.

Scene 5.

Since the drummers are in town, having played in the rice fields earlier in the day, they are staging a dance tonight for everyone's enjoyment—the popular *Lenjengo/Seruba*. In the late afternoon they go to the bantaba and begin their preparations. Two drummers sit on stools or chairs at the edge of the square, and the leader stands beside them. He drums out a greeting that announces the beginning of the dance: *Bantaba, i wurala! Bantaba, i wurala* (Greetings to the Bantaba. Good evening to the town square!) The greeting continues, "We have come to play and dance. We have come, not to fight, but to have a good time. Greetings to the town square!" Lenjengo attracts men, women and children to the square, but the principal participants are girls and young women, married or not. When enough people have gathered in a wide circle, the dancing begins. As the drummers begin the Lenjengo beat, a woman enters the ring and dances before the drummers. She bends deeply at the waist and, stamping her feet flat on the ground, throws her arms to the back and up. The women and girls in the circle clap vigorously in hemiola rhythms, and the lead drummer blows furiously on a police whistle as he plays. After a few seconds, the first dancer stops, and another takes her place. The drummers and dancers watch each other for cues—a different dance step calling for a different beat and vice versa.

After a break for dinner, the Lenjengo dancing starts up again, but before long the Seruba portion begins. At this time, a fourth member of the troupe sets up a small table and empties out some coins on it, and a fifth member takes his place in the center of the circle. He is the Seruba singer, and from here on there is little dancing, except what he might do as he sings. The drummers switch to the quieter rhythms of Seruba, and the singer begins with a well-known verse that is quickly answered by the drummers and the crowd. He soon begins extemporizing new verses, and each one is answered in turn by the crowd. Eventually people begin giving him pennies as a sign of admiration or appreciation for a particular verse, or they might request that he compose a verse for someone as they give him their penny. As his handful of pennies grows, he deposits them with the man at the table, then continues his performance. People in need of small change instead of their larger coins go to this man in turn. The only limits on the performance are the imagination of the singer and the enthusiasm of the crowd, neither of which is usually expended much before midnight. Unlike the songs of the jali, the Seruba songs are not about famous people or the glorious past, but about the ordinary people themselves, standing there in the crowd.

Lenjengo/Seruba, a form of entertainment in itself, is performed on many occasions, even some of those associated in the scenes with jaliya. If a family's social position or musical tastes do not warrant the invitation of the jali to their kulio or wedding, drummers will be invited instead. For the wedding in particular, other drum beats are used at different times in the festivities.

Apart from this overlapping of the realms of the jali and the drummer, it is apparent from these ten scenes that the occasions for jaliya and those for drumming are quite distinct. Those for jaliya—especially Scene 3, the sumungo or evening visit—invite comparison with an evening of chamber music in the home of an eighteenth-century patron of the arts. The drumming events—especially Scene 5, the Lenjengo/Seruba dance—while clearly not the type of performances that just anyone would be able to give without training, remind one more of a rural peasant dance that might have taken place at the same time. An even more apt comparison might be made between the presidential patronage of music in the United States in the early 1960s and a heartily-singing, hand-clapping crowd enjoying a folk music festival or gospel concert.

Music in Africa is usually thought of in terms of the gospel or folk concert or the European folk dance—a festive, even boisterous good time in which everyone participates and through which a unity of spirit is generated and expressed. But the more formal approach of private patronage is equally common and in fact predominates in the heavily Islamic savannah region of West Africa between the coastal forest and the Sahara desert.

What does seem to be less common in Africa is the coexistence of these two approaches within the same culture. But as the scenes above show, they are both present in the Manding culture and thus afford an unusual opportunity for observation.

To begin this study of what appears to be an African instance of the classical and folk coexisting just as they do in many other parts of the world, we shall investigate the broad socio-historical setting in which the opening scenes take place.

THE SOCIO-HISTORICAL SETTING

The term Manding refers to a broad culture area united by a common language family and a common history. The languages of the Manding people form a sub-group in the vast Congo-Kordofanian family of languages that stretches from Senegal to South Africa. The Manding languages are more or less mutually intelligible depending on their geographical proximity, but different enough that distinctions between people are made on the basis of what language they speak as well as where they live. Thus the Gambians in the drumming scenes and their neighbors in southern Senegal speak Mandinka and are known as the Mandinka (or less accurately, the Mandingo). Other groups include the Maninka (or, in most French writings, the Malinké) in Guinea and Mali, the Bamana (or Bambara) in Mali, and the Dyula in Ivory Coast. All of these groups claim a common descent from the ancient state of Mali, which became a great empire with the ascendance of Sunjata Keita in 1234 A.D. Because of the close affinity of all the groups, much of what is said about any one in particular will usually apply to the Manding in general as well.

For today's descendants of the Mali Empire, remembered history begins with Sunjata. Sunjata ruled Mali from his capital at Niani, a small town on the Sankarani River near the border between the modern nations of Guinea and Mali. The area unified under him was some 300 miles in diameter. After his twenty-year reign, the empire grew steadily, until at its height in the mid-fourteenth century, it stretched west to the Atlantic Ocean between the mouths of the Senegal and Casamance Rivers, and east to Niamey in present-day Niger. Its northern boundaries encompassed Walata in Mauritania, and Kidal and Timbuktu in Mali, and the southern limits included the upper reaches of present-day Guinea, Guinea-Bissau, Ivory Coast, and Upper Volta.

The people of Mali who settled along the Gambia River established smaller states with allegiance to Niani and eventually became known as the Mandinka. The Mandinka states became kingdoms in their own right after the central Mali Empire had fallen. Warfare between these Mandinka kingdoms and between the Mandinka and neighboring peoples was common well into the nineteenth century, sometimes over the question of land, but more often, especially in the last century, over the question of Islam. The coming of the British and French colonial powers stopped the wars eventually, and the British converted the kingdoms along The Gambia into provinces under the colonial government. Still today the legislative districts of The Republic of The Gambia bear their original kingdom names, and are governed by descendants of the original kings. Thus, among the Gambian Mandinka there are actually two aspects to their history: the legacy of old Mali—the original empire from which they sprang—and the recent history of the Gambia River kingdoms to which nearly every person living today can trace a not-so-distant relative. Manding of different regions share this situation, and we have seen that historical content—especially that of a regional nature, is one of the principal features of the jali's entertaining. Who exactly is the jali and what is his relationship to other people in Manding society?

The Jali in Society

The jali (also written dyali, dyeli, jeli) is the Manding version of the person known as the griot in many writings about West African societies—a professional verbal artist with specific roles in each society where he is found. His presence is one of the trademarks of the hierarchical social organization common to many West African cultures of the savannah region from Senegal to Nigeria. These hierarchies ascribe social rank and specific roles to the members of the society according to their family heritage.

The basic division in the traditional Manding social hierarchy is between the freeborn (horo) and the slave (jon). In the past, when slavery was inherited. imposed on war captives, or decreed as punishment for severe crimes, this was an important distinction.[3] Today slavery as an institution is of course long gone, but the factor of slave descent is still important in selecting suitable marriage partners.

Further social distinctions are made within the freeborn category. The basic division here is between the sula and nyamalo. By sula is meant anyone—farmer, merchant, soldier, urban job-holder, politician, religious leader, member of royal lineage—who follows no specialized craft or profession. The nyamalo, on the other hand, is a craft specialist, deriving all or part of his or her support from the practice of the craft. The traditional nyamalo categories provide further steps in the hierarchy. They are the numo, or smith, the karanke, or tanner, the jali, or verbal artist, and the fina, another type of verbal artist. The gawulo, a verbal artist of the neighboring Fula people, is also usually included because of his close association with the Manding. It is important to note at this point that the drummer is not among the nyamalo. He is a sula. The following chart represents these features of the Manding hierarchy:

I. Horo (freeborn)
  A. Sula (non-specialist)
  B. Nyamalo (craft specialist)
    1. Numo (smith)
    2. Karanke (tanner)
    3. Jali (verbal artist, instrumentalist)
    4. Fina (verbal artist of Koranic hadiso)
    5. Gawulo (Fula verbal artist, instrumentalist)
II. Jon (slave)

Strict endogamy was observed between all of the crafts and between the nyamalo and the sula in the past. This is hardly the case today, but contemporary social distinctions still tend to be made on the basis of these subdivisions.

For the performing artists, the hierarchy is still very significant. The jali, for example, relies upon certain wealthy and/or influential sula families for his support. The fina in turn, in addition to performing for sula families, counts the jali among his patrons, and the gawulo may approach anyone above him for support. His preferred patron is actually the jali. The jali is thus both craftsman and patron, but since we are concerned here with the practice of his craft, we shall look more closely at the sula/nyamalo relationship in general.[4]

Many attempts have been made to characterize the difference between the sula and the nyamalo. Most early writers described the nyamalo as a caste. However, as early as 1912 Delafosse pointed out that the only significant prohibition between the nyamalo and the sula was one of marriage, and that other prohibitions associated with intercaste relationships, such as physical contact, friendship, and acceptance of food and drink, did not apply (1912: 115).

Pollet and Winter, in *La société Soninké* (1971: 206), have attempted another explanation, noting that both the sula and the nyamalo should be regarded as castes within the freeborn class, both equally concerned with preserving their purity through endogamous marriage. In this view, the slave is regarded as constituting a separate class, but not a caste. Pollet and Winter feel that a significant difference between the sula and the nyamalo is that the sula is devoted to furthering communal agricultural goals, while the nyamalo is concerned more with the rapport between him and his patron.

In another interpretation, Sory Camara, himself a Manding, divides Manding society into three groups, regarding each as a separate caste: the freeborn, the nyamalo, and the slave (1969: 68). Camara points out that the freeborn and the slave are both subject to caste mobility. In the past, the former could be subjected to slavery as punishment for serious crimes, or as a result of becoming a war captive, or out of destitution. (The last of these is still a voluntary possibility.) Likewise the domestic slave could expect that his offspring would be free within four generations according to Manding custom (Labouret 1934: 107). A nyamalo, on the other hand, while sharing some features of both the other castes, enjoyed a stability that they did not by virtue of his incontrovertible and unchanging status as a nyamalo. This characterization does not coincide with information given by Labouret and also collected by the present author to the effect that a nyamalo *is* a freeborn, but distinguished from the sula freeborn on the basis of his profession. It does agree, however, in the characterization of the nyamalo, and especially the jali, as a person with unique social attributes which set him apart from either the horo or the jon.

Interpretations aside, the term "casted bard" is still commonly used today
to refer to the jali, presumably justified by the endogamous marriage rule.
But endogamous marriage is itself becoming a thing of the past. According
to Suntu Suso, a leading Gambian jali who has just recently taken a non-jali
as a wife, eyebrows are rarely raised when a jali man marries a sula woman,
and a sula man may take a jali wife without fear of debasing his status in
any way (Personal Communication, 1982).

In view of this, it would seem wise to adopt an approach proposed by
Robert Launay at the First International Congress of Manding Studies in
1972, which is to abandon the concept of caste and distinguish between the
sula and the nyamalo on the basis of a "craft status" that the latter enjoys
and the former does not (1972: 3). Although caste may disappear along with
endogamous marriage in the future, it seems likely that the craft status
enjoyed by the nyamalo (especially the jali) today will continue to be a part
of this profession in the future, whether actually inherited or not. Let us
look further at the meaning of craft status today, and in the past.

A nyamalo does not necessarily stand out readily or strike the casual
observer as someone special. Nor is the term nyamalo in common use. But
upon closer observation of Manding society, it is clear that the nyamalo is
regarded as a special person, sometimes even believed to be endowed with
supernatural powers, and always entitled to certain privileges associated
with his status. In spite of these things or, more likely because of them, as
we shall see, he is ascribed a low rank in the Manding social hierarchy.
Presumably if we were able to go back far enough in the history of the
Manding we would find a time when social ranks did not exist. But it is
reasonably apparent, both from the oral tradition and from early observers,
that in the past the low rank of craft status was no burden to the craftsmen,
for they were the only source of manufactured goods of iron, wood, and
leather. The jali held the only records of genealogy and history, and was the
only one who knew and could perform the music called for on important
occasions. The people who most often employed the services of these people
were in a position to provide ample recompense in the form of lodging,
cattle, clothing, and other manifestations of wealth. For the jali who, by
virtue of the verbal nature of his art, was always on more intimate terms
with his benefactors than others of craft status, this meant that he was
virtually assured of a permanent patronage. There was a great deal of social
and political importance associated with being a nyamalo. As one jali has
put it, "The jali was king," meaning that he needed concern himself only
with his profession, for all of his necessities and more were provided for him.

It remains to explain in more detail the jali's relationship to his patrons
today and how this relationship differs from earlier times. His fine clothes
and close association with top political leaders show that his craft status is
still no real burden, but why does it exist at all and how might both his
status and his roles have changed over the centuries?

The Arab geographer Ibn Battúta visited the Manding people in 1353 at the height of the Mali Empire and observed the jali in his principal role as a verbal artist, serving as public speaker, interlocutor, and praiser at Mansa Sulayman's court. He also noted his performance on the xylophone (the earliest mention of this instrument in Africa) but nonetheless referred to him as the "interpreter" rather than the "musician" at the court, thus suggesting the subordinate role that music played in his duties (Battúta 1939: 325-328).

The jali's role as an oral historian and genealogist is exemplified by the several versions of the epic of Sunjata, Mali's first emperor, and other historical narratives that are frequently told by jalolu. Within these epics, and especially in *Sundiata: An Epic of Old Mali* as related by Djibril Niane, we find many examples of the jali's prominent role as counselor, diplomat, master of ceremonies, praiser, and entertainer (Niane 1965). It is apparent from all accounts that the jali in these times commanded a high degree of respect.

Today there are some jalolu who continue to emphasize the historical and other verbal aspects of their profession, but most today regard themselves primarily as singers or instrumentalists. This shift in emphasis over the years reflects changes in the social context of the jali's work. The most significant of these changes was the introduction of colonial rule in the late nineteenth century. At this time, chiefs and other leaders were given government salaries instead of being allowed to derive their support directly from their constituents. For most, this meant that they could no longer afford to keep a jali and his family under their personal care in return for the jali's services, and the jali was forced to find a wider base of support by traveling more and seeking many patrons. Towards this end, he found that music and, in certain respects, instrumental music more than vocal music, had a more immediate and wider appeal than the historical side of his profession and thus gave it more of his attention.

The jali traveled in the past too, but it was always a festive occasion when he did. A large family group traveled together and spent several days visiting each patron. The women of the group sang, both as soloists and in chorus, and the men played their instruments and narrated stories. An elderly jali muso describes the way she and her husband used to travel:

We would stay two or three nights in one place, and move on, spending from two weeks to two months altogether, staying largely in the Kombo District, before returning home. We didn't always go to visit just one person in the town. Often we would arrive with a bag of *kola* nuts which we gave to our host, asking that they be distributed to all of the families in the town. This was a way of greeting the townspeople and showing our respect. Later we would perform in the town square for the benefit of everyone. Naturally we had to lodge at one man's house, but by this method, he alone was not responsible for our welfare while we stayed there (Nyali Jebateh, Bakau, 1970)

Today the practice of jaliya is less leisurely, and more an individual endeavor. Whether a jali is only making the rounds of the capital city or going on a more extended journey, his family usually stays at home. The itinerant nature of jaliya today has prompted some of the older jalolu to describe it as "galloping-horse" jaliya.

The shift in emphasis to the musical aspects of jaliya and the proliferation of jalolu relying on it for their support have given rise to a new image of the jali in recent years. As Djibril Niane notes in his preface to the Sunjata epic, "Nowadays when we speak of 'griots' we think of that class of professional musicians fashioned to live on the backs of others. When we say 'griot' we think of those numerous guitarists who people our towns and go to sell their 'music' in the recording studios of Dakar or Abidjan" (Niane 1965: vii). The hint of scorn evident in this remark is a far cry from the picture of the respected court interpreter given to us by Ibn Battúta, and yet Niane is hardly the first to have made such a remark. As early as 1623, when Richard Jobson sailed up the Gambia River, he noted that the musicians he met were held in such low regard by the people that he and his men were caused to:

. . . neglect and especially in their hearing to play upon any Lute or instrument which some of us for our private exercise did carry with us, in regard if they had hapned [sic] to see us, they would in a manner of scorne say, hee that played was a Juddy [jali] (Jobson 1623: 108).

It is this attitude of scorn or disdain towards the jali, dating from at least this time and becoming especially evident in nineteenth-century writings, that causes most of the puzzlement over the jali today. We might be able to brush off some references to this attitude as exaggerations by inexperienced writers overawed by the strangeness of the culture in which they found themselves, but beyond this the explanation hinges on at least three factors: rank, separation, and privileges.

The low social rank of the jali is often the cause of much consternation on the part of outside observers, since the jali seems to be such an important figure in the society. But it is not so strange when we consider the low social rank of so many great names in the history of European art music whose music was nonetheless widely appreciated. Franz Josef Haydn, who, with his musicians, wore a uniform marking him as one of the servants at Esterhaza, is the best-known example. If we accept legends as evidence, the subordinate rank of the jali is as old as the institution itself. According to legend, the "original jali" was a disbeliever-turned-devotee of Mohammed who in his ecstasy turned to praising the prophet and announcing his presence wherever he went. The same theme of verbal service rendered to a great person is reflected in other legends that tell how certain jali family lines were founded. In these stories a man turns to praising his brother either out of gratitude or admiration, and thereafter devotes all his time to this for their mutual benefit. The praiser is held in disdain as the one who didn't quite make the grade in ordinary pursuits (Zemp 1966b).

The social separation that prevailed in Manding society in the past is a second factor contributing to the non-jali's disdainful attitude. With the strictly endogamous marriage patterns of the past, there were certain things the jali could not do, simply because he was a jali. For example, he could not be fully initiated into Manding society, nor was he allowed to fight in battle. It is not unusual to hear a jali explain that even today being a jali is almost like belonging to a separate "nation" or ethnic group from the Manding, even though you are a Manding yourself. The scorn that members of one group may hold for another group is familiar enough, so little more needs to be said on this point.

The third factor contributing to society's attitude towards the jali is at once the most important and the least obvious. This is the factor of special privileges. These privileges have doubtless belonged to the jali since time immemorial, but the ways in which they have been exercised have changed in response to social changes over the years. The answer to why the jali was looked upon with such disdain in the seventeenth century and yet apparently knew of no such attitude in the fourteenth century probably lies in the manner in which he was exercising these privileges. They may be defined as the privileges of solicitation, criticism with impunity, specialized knowledge, and the privilege of power.

In the days of empire, solicitation, which is achieved even today always through the profession—by performing for someone who is then obligated to pay for the performance—was rarely, if ever, exercised out of necessity, since the jali was supported totally by his permanent patron. As the greatness of the empire waned, so too did the greatness of individual patrons, and solicitation through the profession became more and more a necessity. The result, of course, was the increased potential for resentment on the part of patrons who were disadvantaged by the necessity of paying the jali even though they were not able to do so.

In like manner the other privileges probably had little effect on the ordinary man in the days of empire when the jali's affairs and sphere of influence were confined mainly to the network of leaders holding the empire together. But as his audience widened, the exercise of his privileges affected more and more people. Today, a jali often uses his privilege of making critical comments, usually couched in an oblique expression or proverb, the subtlety of which makes it even more effective than an outright statement. In so doing, he can endanger a person's reputation as much as he can enhance it with praise. His privileged knowledge of specialized information on lineages and genealogies means that he is often called in for settling disputes and questions of succession. The privilege of power derives from his role as the adviser or deputy to a chief or other leader, and it means that he will very likely have a strong influence on important decisions.

The ordinary person can easily feel vulnerable or threatened if these privileges are working against him. But this is where the jali's low social rank comes in. The person who feels threatened by these privileges can seek refuge in his higher social rank and defend himself with a disdainful or distrusting attitude towards the jali. As the jali exercises more privileges, the non-jali increases his disdain. The privileges and the scorn serve thus as a system of social checks and balances. The jali exercises his privilege to solicit support from others, but the mere act of doing so reaffirms his subordinate status to them. For most jalolu today this is still an acceptable state of affairs. Any wise jali will note that even though he might travel widely and earn fine clothes and other signs of wealth for himself, he would never think of adopting any other attitude than subservience and dependency towards an old and trusted patron, for to do so would only invite the loss of any future support from that person. For the same reason, even in today's more relaxed social atmosphere where a patron might very well take an interest in learning to play the kora, for example, most likely his jali will not agree to teach him, reasoning that once the patron has learned to play for himself, he will no longer invite the jali over to perform.

It is likely that this patron/jali relationship will continue for some time, until alternative means of support, such as organized public concerts, radio programs, or national touring ensembles begin to play a larger role. In the balance, the jali enjoys far more respect through his profession than he suffers scorn. His patrons are generally his best friends, his music is an indispensable part of all important events, and his knowledge of the history of Manding civilization is of great interest to oral historians and cultural archivists. These things assure him a role of continued importance in the society.

The Drummer in Society

The privileged status of the jali, his association with royalty and other people of influence, and his flamboyant dress all combine to make him a highly visible figure in Manding society. This is not so with the drummer. He has gone virtually unnoticed in comparison to the jali. Ibn Battúta mentions only one drumming event from his visit in 1353, and even it does not resemble today's events, being a group of about thirty youths at the royal court, each playing a small drum slung from the shoulder (Battúta 1939: 328). Mungo Park frequently mentions the jali (Jilli Kea or singing man) in his late eighteenth-century narratives, but refers only occasionally to drumming, in one case describing a wrestling match animated by a single drum played with a crooked stick (most likely an hourglass drum called *tama*), and in another mentioning "the *tangtang*, a drum open at the lower end" (Park 1954: 31, 213).

These sparse references are hardly decisive evidence for the absence in earlier days of the many drumming events that are common today, but they do seem to indicate that at least the drumming events were less obvious than the activities of the jali. Contrast Park's minor remarks on drummers to one of his statements on the jali: "One or more of these may be found in every town" (Park 1954: 213).

Clearly the greater visibility of the jali has been a major factor in our knowledge of him. But, in spite of the relative lack of information on the drummer, some distinct impressions may be formed from what has been written. One is that, compared to jaliya, which consists of basically the same events today as it did in the past, drumming events and styles have changed. The drumming described by Battúta is no longer known, and two drum trios are used for wrestling today instead of the single drum mentioned by Park. Although recreational dancing is mentioned by various authors, whether it resembled Lenjengo/Seruba remains an open question.

Another impression given is that drumming was more closely allied to jaliya in the past than it is today. In Battúta's account, the drummers, together with a group of women playing musical bows and singing, are accompanying a performance on the xylophone by Mansa Sulayman's jali. Some of Mungo Park's observations lead one to believe that the drum was even a jali's instrument, for some of his many references to the "singing man" mention the drum as his instrument (Park 1954: 183).

Hugo Zemp does report that the tama hourglass drum is the only instrument of the Malinké jalolu living among the Dan in Ivory Coast (Zemp 1967: 88), but it is much less common—even rare—in the Manding area proper. This still leads one to believe that it may have been a more common jali's instrument in the past. Perhaps Battúta's "small drum slung from the shoulder" was the tama. The tama is not the tantang, however, and it is unlikely that the jali ever played the latter. The tantang jali is called "jali" only because as a performing artist he is associated in people's minds with the jali, not because he is one.

Apart from an actual performance, there is no way to single out a drummer from anyone else of a similar economic standing. As noted earlier, drummers rarely come from jali families, nor are they people of nyamalo status for any other reason. Family backgrounds of drummers sometimes show evidence of slave descent, but most are from non-craft-status freeborn families (sula) of modest means. Members of the Manding aristocracy do not usually take up drumming.

There is no hallowed body of praise names, no family lineages or town histories to keep track of as a drummer, and thus the endogamous marriage patterns that insure the preservation of such things within the jali families are unknown among drummers. A drummer belongs to no special social group by virtue of being a drummer. Quite often a member of a drum troupe will have another job besides his drumming, although if the troupe travels to overnight engagements, this can present problems.

We have seen that the jali is born into his profession and remains a jali for life. He may discontinue singing or playing his instrument as he advances in age, but older jalolu, both men and women, are well known for their relating of historical narratives and genealogical facts. There is no such permanence associated with drumming. Most drummers are young and will give up drumming at least by middle age, although some older men continue to play.

Part of the reason for the predominantly youthful complexion of a drum troupe is the strenuous nature of their activities. From the introductory scenes it is evident that drummers are essentially up for hire, and since the events they play for are common occurrences, they are kept busy moving from town to town at least five or six days out of the week. This schedule means a lot of traveling, a heavily calloused playing hand, and much socializing with other young people. For example, three out of the five opening scenes (Nyoboringo, Kankurang, and Lenjengo/Seruba) are generally staged by young people's clubs and involve primarily young people performing with the drummers. The troupe leader is of necessity older than the others, usually married and with a family, but the younger members of the troupe greatly enjoy the adoring popularity they receive from their audiences.

As noted in the opening comparison of the realms of the jali and the drummer, drumming events are decidedly popular in nature, appealing to a wide segment of the population. In a rural setting the arrival of the drum troupe is comparable in entertainment value to a major film coming to the local theater, or a rock concert staged at a high school auditorium. In an urban setting such as Banjul or any other city in the Manding area, a drum troupe does in fact compete against such events, but even here the drummers have a good following.

In hiring themselves out to perform for events where not they, but the people who hire them will be the center of attraction, such as for Nyoboringo, Kankurang, and Kanyeleng Kafo, the drummers differ significantly from the jali. Nothing the jali does, barring his participation in western-style stage productions designed primarily for export, could be regarded as being hired out to accompany some other entertaining event. When a jali performs, he is always the entertainment. In fact, if he senses that this is not so, he will more likely stop performing than take a subordinate role. But the drummer is not so proud. He knows that his events are for the common man and makes no pretexts about their importance or the depth of their content. He also knows that one of his roles is to accompany many other types of entertainment.

PERFORMANCE PRACTICE AND THE JALI

Instruments

In the opening scenes, the major musical instruments of the Manding have been introduced. If there is one instrument that represents the Manding unequivocably, it is the kora, for it is unique to them. Similar instruments, smaller and with fewer strings, are played by the Dogon in Mali (the *gingiru*) (Zahan 1950), the Akan in Ghana (*seperewa*) (Nketia 1962: 96), some of the hunting associations within the Manding (*donso konni*) (Rouget 1972: 1), and the Dan, Senufo, Baoulé, and Guéré in Ivory Coast (Zemp 1974: 372; 1965; 1966a-b; 1967: 84; and 1971). These instruments are in limited use today—for mystical healing ceremonies among the Dogon, and for light entertainment in the other areas—but they are clearly the ancestors of the kora, which the Manding regard as their youngest instrument. The first written reference to the kora was made in 1799 by Mungo Park (1954: 213).

The kora and its lesser relatives are harps by virtue of their playing technique (both hands plucking) and the perpendicular plane of their strings in relation to the soundtable of the instrument, but they are also lutes by virtue of the construction of the body and the use of a bridge to hold the strings out from the body. Thus, they are commonly referred to as harp lutes, which may be interpreted to mean lutes with prominent harp features, distinguishing them from conventional lutes, which have the string plane parallel to the body and are played with one hand while the other stops the strings.

The 21-string kora has a range of just over three octaves and is tuned to one of three (or in western Gambia, four) tunings, the choice being governed by which song is to be performed (See Example 1). The kora is played

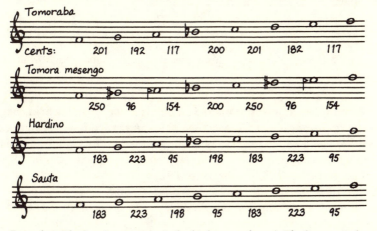

Example 1. The four kora tunings (only third octave shown). The first one is the principle tuning in western Gambia, but is not used in the eastern region of Manding. (Generalized examples adapted from King, 1972:133). The sign ♯ means ca. 50c. sharp, and the sign ⸕ means ca. 50c. flat.

all over the Manding area, but the greatest concentration of players is in The Gambia. This, and the fact that many songs known to have originated on the kora are about Gambian or at least Mandinka heroes, suggest a Mandinka origin for the instrument.

The second stringed instrument played by the Manding jali is the *kontingo*, or *ngoni*. It is a slender plucked lute with a skin sound table and five strings, three of which are drone strings. It also may be tuned to several different tunings, the choice of which is also determined to some extent by what song is played, and also by rules governing the use of two different tunings when two people are playing together.[5] It is most commonly found in Senegal and Mali, and the same type of instrument is played by musicians of the neighboring Wolof and Fula people as well. In fact, sharing of songs from each other's repertoires is common. The construction of this instrument shows it to be related to the lutes of ancient Egypt, and Farmer has shown that it was introduced into North Africa and the savannah region south of the Sahara by pre-Islamic migrations (Farmer 1928: 27). Gold and silver-covered instruments of this type were noted at the royal court of fourteenth-century Mali by Ibn Battúta, along with the xylophone mentioned earlier (Battúta 1939: 326, 328).

The xylophone, *balo* or *balafon*, is regarded by the Manding as their oldest instrument. It consists of seventeen or nineteen keys of African Rosewood tied to a low frame and played with a rubber-tipped beater in each hand. Suspended beneath each key is a resonating gourd fitted with a mirliton that modifies the tone of the wooden key to create a bright, metallic sound. The tuning of the balo, as measured by Rouget (1969) exhibits a clear tendency towards equidistance (See Example 2). As with the

cents: 165   175   169   173   171   172   170

Example 2. One octave of a balo tuning in the range corresponding to the kora tunings in Example 1. Adapted from Rouget (1969:51), his instrument No. 2, beginning on the fourth key from the bottom (actual pitch, F#+10 c.).

other instruments, the balo is played throughout the Manding area, but the strongest traditions are in Guinea. The balo figures prominently in the epic of Sunjata, being the instrument played by Sunjata's own jali, and one that Sunjata's main adversary, the sorcerer king of Sosso, Sumanguru Kante, also possessed (See D. T. Niane 1965: 39).

Each of these instruments has a repertoire of songs associated specifically with it but the musicians, though they play only one instrument, have also borrowed extensively from each other, so that a core repertoire of songs known throughout Manding is shared by all of them. The kora is the most versatile at playing songs originally conceived on the other instruments.

All of these instruments are played only by men. The jali muso plays only one instrument—the tubular iron bell called *ne* (iron) which is tied across the palm and struck with a thin iron rod. Women devote their efforts in jaliya to singing, and in this they excel. Women are regarded as the best singers, and it is a great honor for a man to have a voice quality or singing ability "as good as a woman's."

Outside the realm of the jali but still very closely related, both in style and in function, are two other musical traditions and their associated instruments. These are the hunter's music and the warrior's music. The instruments in each case are harps that bear a certain resemblance to the kora, except their necks are curved instead of straight, and in place of a bridge standing on the skin face, they have a bridge-like string holder mounted in similar fashion. The principal difference is that the strings are attached to it rather than passing over it. The hunter's instrument in Gambia is called the *simbingo*. In common with its close cousin, the diminutive harp lute mentioned earlier (donso konni), it has six strings. The hunter's musician, a hunter himself, plays the simbingo to accompany songs and stories about clever animals and foolish humans. The instrumental part is a short and simple ostinato, while the vocal line is mostly in a rambling, narrative style not unlike one of two vocal styles used by the jali, to be discussed below.

The warrior's instrument is the *bolon*. In making this instrument, only a small portion of the large gourd used for the body is cut away and the goat-skin stretched over the opening is left with the hair on rather than removed. The player sits before the instrument and drums a steady rhythm on the gourd with his fists, picking out a melodic pattern on the three or four heavy rawhide strings with his thumbs at the same time. The style is more intense and varied rhythmically than that of the simbingo, but the vocal line is also predominantly in a narrative style. This instrument also figures prominently in the Sunjata epic: the bolon player goes to the battlefield himself with the warriors, encouraging them to fight bravely by singing songs of their ancestors' prowess (Niane 1965: 10). The bolon player provides domestic entertainment today in much the same way as the jali, but his repertoire of songs rarely overlaps that of the jali.

In the past, hunting and fighting had a much more central role in Manding life than they do today, and music for and about the hunters and warriors would have been much more commonly heard. Just as the simbingo, the bolon, and the smaller harp lutes are clearly related to the kora, the praise songs and basic style of entertainment associated with them closely resemble the professional activities of the jali, only directed at a different audience. It seems more than likely that any search for folk-like elements in today's urban jaliya or even the ultimate origin of the jali's profession will lead to either or both of these closely related traditions. (For a further discussion of the relationship between the hunter's musician and the jali, see Bird 1972.)

Musical Organization and Aesthetics of Jaliya

There are four basic elements to a performance of jali music, regardless of the number of performers or the instruments used. These basic elements are the *kumbengo*, or instrumental ostinato; the *birimintingo*, consisting of variations, ornamentations, and expansions or deviations from the kumbengo; the *donkilo* or basic vocal melody; and the *sataro*, vocal lines sung in a rambling, declamatory or recitative style. A parallel can be seen between the kumbengo and the donkilo, the two basic parts. But they are not parallel in importance. Whereas the kumbengo is fundamental to the entire performance and must never be neglected for an overly long birimintingo passage, the donkilo (which in a more general sense also means simply "song" as opposed to speech) is only a stepping off place. The donkilo is a relatively short and easily recognizable melody consisting of one, two, or three phrases (See Example 3). As in a strophic song, several lines of text are

Example 3. The donkilo (basic melody) for Kelefaba ("Kelefa the Great").

usually sung to this melody, which bears a specific rhythmic and melodic relationship to the instrumental kumbengo. A singer usually begins a performance with the donkilo and returns on occasion to sing other lines throughout the performance. If a chorus of singers is involved, it is the donkilo they sing. But the fine singer devotes most of her (or his) efforts to the sataro rather than the donkilo, for it is here that one's real abilities can best be demonstrated (See Example 4).

Example 4. Sataro phrases from a performance of Bakariba. (Barlines mark the repetitions of the instrumental kumbengo, but vocal note values are often unmeasured.)

The songs of the Manding jali are basically commemorative and laudatory. The title of most songs is the name of a person, usually a very famous person, and the purpose of singing the song, beyond its entertainment value, is to perpetuate the memory of him and praise his deeds. Only in recent years have less important people such as local acquaintances or girl-friends become the subject of jali songs, and the traditionally oriented jali still looks down upon these songs as frivolous and a discredit to the dignity of the profession.

When the jali sings the name of a past hero, he views what he is doing as waking him up, bringing him back to life (*M b'a wulindila*). To bring his own message about the man to life demands clear diction and a deliberate playing style, for these give the listener time to understand the words being sung. If in the end the listener can say of the music, *Wo le dunta n na* (It has entered me), then the desired effect will have been achieved.

In the present day, a considerable variety of styles can be heard, but the jalolu who know and respect the older ways note that in the past, jaliya was always slow and deliberate, or literally "cool," as opposed to some of the more flashy or "hot" styles of today: *Folo folo, jaliya sumayata nun, bari sayin, a kandita le* (Before, jaliya was cool, but now it is hot). According to the jali, slow playing turns one's mind to the past, and thus he employs it if he has something significant to say about the past.

There is general agreement among singers that the most important qualities in their profession are, in order of importance: (1) courage, (2) the ability to talk (meaning a command of words) and a knowledge of the proper words, and (3) a good voice. Courage is regarded as most important because jaliya often involves standing up in front of a large crowd of people and talking or singing, often extemporizing to fit the occasion.

The requirements of knowledge and speaking ability are next in impor-tance. Again, over a good voice, a jali muso is appreciated for what she sings. This means knowing not only the standard text of a donkilo or the various standard praise lyrics for one's patrons, but also knowing how to extemporize texts that will please listeners by their immediacy and appro-priateness. It means knowing how to say things with sentiment (*balafa*)—things with which listeners can identify because of personal experience or their ancestry.

Another important technique that is stressed often by jalolu is the necessity of speaking (or singing) the words with clear diction, spacing them out so that they are understood easily. A jali who mumbles words or "speaks them inside one another" (*kumolu fola nyo kono*) will not be properly appreciated.

The Mandinka do not speak much about the actual traits of a "good voice," the third major requirement for being a good singer, so the concept must be deduced from the voices of female singers who are known for this. They exhibit a hearty and penetrating voice quality, one which Rouget has aptly described as a "rather acid timbre" (1972: A-1). Both this acid timbre and the relatively narrow range (usually about one and a half octaves) are the result of a vocal technique involving a tightening of the pharyngial muscles at the back of the tongue. This restricts the upward (thinning) motion of the larynx and results in the use of chest resonance rather than head resonance. In the western Manding area vibrato is used only minimally, if at all, but in the eastern area it is more common and sometimes even elaborate. An important characteristic of the singing style throughout Manding is that the ends of phrases are not dropped, but pushed off with a slight increase in intensity. Rouget has shown this trait to exist even at the level of every note sung (1970: 684). The ability to sing loudly and to project well are also traits shared by the best singers.

When all of the traits that make a superior singer are found in one woman, she is called a *ngara*. The following statement, made by a ngara, summarizes what she feels to be the essence of her profession:

A ngara is a woman who is not afraid of crowds, not afraid of anything, except God. She can stand before a crowd with all eyes upon her and not become confused (*kijo fara*). She can shout (*feten*), literally 'split' the air with her voice, but do it with feeling (*wasu*) and sentiment (*balafa*), so that people will sympathize with her. She sticks to her forte (*taburango*) in performing, never jumbling the words together (*faranfansandi*) so that they are unintelligible, but choosing words which contain the essence of her message (*sigirango*), words which all listeners will agree are true (*sahata*) (Nyulo Jebateh, Sambatako, 1970).

We have seen the importance of the kumbengo in the performance of this music. It follows that the first necessity in good instrumental technique is the mastering of the kumbengo. This means being able to play one kumbengo for twenty to thirty minutes at a time without sounding repetitious and boring. It involves knowing a great number of small alterations in rhythm and melody and knowing how to insert longer variations where appropriate. The kumbengo regulates everything else in a performance. As one jali explains, "Holding the kumbengo is essential for good jaliya. If you know your kumbengo well, you will have no trouble with birimintingo because good birimintingo depends on leaving and returning to the kumbengo smoothly" (Nyama Suso, Bakau, 1970). The basic importance of knowing the kumbengo is contained in the proverb, "Before you get angry over your load, tie it properly; then it won't scatter if it falls" (Example 5).

Example 5. The kumbengo, two different birimintingo passages, and the kumbengo again for Mamadu Bitiki, as performed on the kora.

It is also important that instrumental music be infused with the same qualities as found in vocal music. The kumbengo must have balafa (sentiment),
just as does the vocal line, and this is achieved by a clean, deliberate playing
technique. The same concept is sometimes called *nijio* (breath). The music
"breathes" if it is not too fast or agitated.

Fast playing has its place in jaliya too, but heavy emphasis on it generally
speaking is a more recent phenomenon. Many kora virtuosos today rely on
fast playing and a great deal of birimintingo to impress their audience. This
usually eliminates the possibility of women singing with them, for this is not
the jali muso's customary style, nor is it conducive to good ensemble
between the instrument and the voice. Still, technical facility and the ability
to play birimintingo are important in assessing an instrumentalist's excellence. As one jali notes, "The mark of a good (kora) jali lies in his ability to
tune, how he plays the kumbengo, and how good he is at birimintingo"
(Karamo Suso, Sotuma, 1970).

If it is a vocal performance, birimintingo must be confined to instrumental interludes and not played over the singer. It should not dominate
over the singer's role in the performance. The kumbengo and the birimintingo represent the visceral and the cerebral in Manding music, and the
proper balance between them is comparable to the balance that one strives
to achieve between interpretation and virtuosity in the west. As the jali
expresses it, "Good kumbengo playing is done by the ears (good listening)
and the heart, while good birimintingo is something your hands give you,
plus your intelligence" (Nyama Suso, Bakau, 1970).

Learning

Jaliya, as with the other nyamalo crafts in Manding, is learned through
apprenticeship. For the boy, who will most likely learn the instrument his
father plays, this means between seven and ten years spent with a recognized master—usually from about age ten, and usually not with his father,
since a non-family member can deal more strictly and objectively with a
student. For the girl, learning jaliya is more a part of her everyday training
in womanhood than a special discipline, since singing is regarded as coming
almost naturally. In the words of one jali, "You can learn singing by sitting
near a singer. The voice is not controlled by any teacher. It is natural. Some
voices are good, others are not" (Bai Konteh, Brikama, 1970).

When a man gets married, he is usually several years older than his bride,
so he usually continues to train her himself, and she gains her courage for
performance by performing with him. The following statements by two
leading jali women show this clearly:

As children, when people visited our compound and our parents had to entertain,
we would sit nearby and listen. They would ask us to dance to the kora. We danced,
and the people would smile and give us money and encourage us to continue

learning the profession. Later we learned singing, corrected by our parents until we were good at it. By the time we were qualified, we were ready for marriage. Once married, our husbands continued to coach and encourage us as we worked together. Sometimes the coaching involved force, for an impatient husband might beat his wife to get her to overcome her timidity (Fili Sakiliba, Sotuma, 1970).

I was embarrassed to sing at first; but the first time I went out to perform with my husband, he threatened to cane me if I didn't. The women of the compound where we were performing would not interfere, saying that as a jali I needed to sing. So I did, and I have ever since (Sira Sakiliba, Sotuma, 1970).

In the past, the boy's apprenticeship was strict and demanded complete subservience to his master. He did many chores and was denied all privileges. Slow learning was punished. But at the successful completion of his studies, at least in the case of a kora jali, his teacher built him an instrument and presented it to him in a special "wedding" ceremony, releasing him to go with his "kora wife" (kora manyo) and seek his fortune. Learning today is less rigorous, with peers often providing the instruction, but there are still many young jalolu who take their profession quite seriously.

The actual instruction on an instrument is done by observation and imitation, although if it is the balo, the teacher may reach over the student's shoulders to guide his hands on the keys. Structured lessons, exercises, and practice are largely foreign to the tradition. Instead the student is encouraged to participate in actual performances in any way he can. At first it may be only singing or tapping a rhythmic pattern on the back of his teacher's kora, but later will include performance on the instrument as well. Instruction is usually limited to the kumbengo, or basic ostinato, but through participation, the student quickly learns the basic birimintingo technique. In an advanced student, this skill leads to the eventual composition of new pieces, something again that is not formally taught but grows out of the creative element of performance.

The most striking feature of the learning process, on both the kora and kontingo, is the question of tuning. It is quite common to see a young kora student playing happily on an instrument that is totally out of tune. Furthermore, even a reasonably accomplished apprentice will still give his instrument to his master for tuning. There are two reasons for this seeming neglect of an aspect of music that is indeed very important to the kora player. First, by disregarding the tuning altogether initially, the student is made to concentrate on the rhythmic and tactile aspects of playing. He knows the melody—he has heard it many times. The question is, can he coordinate his fingers and make them move in rhythm? By the time he is playing more than just the kumbengo and singing as well, his teacher will have given him a tuned instrument. But why not teach the advanced apprentice how to tune? Naturally any young jali who has paid attention and applied himself to his studies will have developed a good ear and observed the tuning process many times. He will know the different tunings and their usage, but giving him an actual lesson on how to tune the instrument is regarded as the final key to his independence. This lesson is therefore withheld from him until his master feels he is fully qualified to embark on his own career.

The Content of Jaliya

In singing his songs of praise and commemoration, the jali perpetuates the memory of the glorious past and encourages the continuity of the Manding traditions. In addition, many of the lines he sings reveal his important function as advisor and counselor on a variety of moral, religious, and philosophical issues. In other lines the relationship between him and his audience is clearly portrayed.

The style of commemoration is exemplified in the song for Kelefa Sanneh, a song traditionally used to begin instruction on the kora: "Kelefa the Avenger, Kelefa from Badora has died, His spear is lying at Bariya" (See Example 3). Another example is found in the song for Mamadu Bitiki, a well-loved merchant and patron of music: "Good Mamadu has become famous, Mamadu the shopkeeper has become famous." Phrases such as these are usually part of the basic donkilo of a song.

Praise takes many forms in jaliya, but the most common types are called *jairo* and *jamundiro*. The first type, jairo, is simply praise in general for deeds or characteristics that are appreciated. It too is usually sung in the donkilo section of a song. Some examples: "The brave man knows not running." "You have equalled your parents in achievement," "You are beloved by God and will not suffer," "Times were good under Maki, giver of slaves and horses." The second type, jamundiro, is praise associated with a surname and either includes the name or refers to events associated with it in the past. Jamundiro is usually sung in the sataro style. An example may be found in the song for Bamba Bojan, another beloved and generous merchant, where the places known for the Bojans who live there are enumerated: "The Bojan-Jari clan is at Kafuta, the Bojan-Sankaranka clan is at Brikama, the Bojan-Tamba clan is at Manduware, Yundum, Lamin, Bakau-Komani, and Sabiji-Dembadu."

The connection between some jamundiro phrases and the name they commemorate is not always as obvious as in this case. In the standard jamundiro for the names Sonko and Sanyang, the names are not mentioned at all: "The well near the timber palm tree produces bitter water, but the women who carry it are beautiful." This is clearly a reference to some event or place in the past, but the explanation for it is lost—only the connection remains.

The jali's role as advisor, counselor, and commentator on life in general is revealed in two other types of texts called the *jali kumolu* or jali words, and the *mansalingo*, a metaphorical or semi-metaphorical proverb. Neither of these is usually associated with any song in particular, and every jali has a large stock of them which he inserts at random in a performance, again, usually in sataro style, thus helping to maintain continuity between the basic texts of the song and other texts that he may improvise to suit a given audience. They cover a wide range of subjects, as the few examples included here show:

Islam—Advocation of Faith

There is one moon, one Mohammed; one sun, one Mohammed. Mohammed was first and he is last.

Your enemy can give you a bad name, but God will remove it in due time.

Islam—Predestination

Blessedness begins on creation day, foolishness does also.

A jali is born to do jaliya.

Every morning has its sunrise, every word its time and place; every king has his time to rule.

Islam—Fatalism

Before God created life, he created death.

Death will not leave you alive, but it cannot miss a good name.

All things standing must one day lie down.

Moral judgments by comparison

Someone who doesn't know people will say they are all equal; they are not the same at all.

The talkative kings are plentiful, but men of great deeds are few.

The horseman and the pedestrian are not walking mates.

A warrior and his men are not the same as a ruler and his people.

Misery is hard on a woman, shame is hard on a man.

Moral judgments and advice

Three people have carefree lives in this world: the rich man, the king, and the shameless person.

Excess pride is from lack of traveling; so is self-scorn.

Big size doesn't make an elephant; big deeds do.

What you did, what you said, people will talk about it after you've gone.

There is nothing in this world without patience and endurance.

Ungratefulness is a serious thing.

Your birthright goes unknown in a foreign land, but your character doesn't.

The ambitious do not rest at all.

The world is ever-changing. If someone doesn't know your past, don't tell him your present affairs.

Observations on life in general

It is difficult to make secret arrangements.

Life is nothing without conversation.

The liar and the thief can never be friends.

Familiarity strengthens on parting day.

There are not many who benefit from momentous events.

Observations on wealth

Wealth will disappoint the greedy man.

Water doesn't clean a man; it's wealth that cleans a man.

Wealth is not a tonic for life; wealth is to save you from disgrace.

The wealthy will talk of wealth.

The wealthy inherit the wealth.

A man with followers is a wealthy man.

If a man doesn't have money (friends, gold) he's a slave to the one who does.

Finally, there are those lines in the jali kumolu and the mansalingo that reveal the jali's reliance on his patrons. The inclusion of such lines as these is often a gentle hint to the listeners not to be stingy about rewarding the jali for his performance.

Every word has a place to be said, every action its time to be done; every child has his father, every jali has his host, every woman has her loving man.

A jali owner and one who has none are not the same.

If you say "fighting king," many kings will answer.

I know the good persons; every jali has his benefactors.

It is we who know the kings and they in turn know us.

The jali of the inheritor of wealth is not happy (A man has to have earned his wealth to know how to manage it).

Getting a hundred is not easy if you don't see a big-hearted person.

A Manding jali is not ungrateful.

If you do something for your jali, you're not doing it for a silent jali, nor for an ungrateful jali.

For the person who puts one hundred in my hand, I will give him a hundred-worth praise with my mouth.

The great carrier of loads has put me on his back—the elephant never tires of carrying his trunk.

I'm following my father's trade, just as all jalolu do. The jali and his patron should both do as their fathers did.

Patron of the jali. Not everyone can support a jali. The wicked man will not have
a jali at his side.

Hear the great song. Not everyone understands its value. The one who has re-
nounced his heritage doesn't understand the great song.

If you see the weaver bird in the cotton tree, he is there to visit the millet below. (If
you see someone at another man's house, that other man is the reason he's there.)

Two birds have collided in mid-air; one has lost his wing. (Of these two great men,
one has been shamed.)

If you see a chicken following the woodcutters to the forest, it didn't see the
women pounding millet in the compound.

Just as the chicken in the proverb knows there is more food around the
mortar than there is around the base of a tree, the jali knows where the
wealth lies in a village or city, and no matter how popular or widely known
his music becomes, he will never lose sight of the wealthy and the influential
as his true benefactors.

PERFORMANCE PRACTICE AND THE DRUMMER

Instruments

In the opening scenes we saw the same set of drums used on several
different occasions. These drums are the "tangtang" mentioned by Park.
There are other drums in Manding, such as the now rare tama, or hourglass
drum, and in the eastern region of Manding, the *jembe*, similar to the open
conical tantang, but larger. In Gambia there is also a set of three cylindrical
two-headed drums used for a performance called *siko*. Their technique and
repertoire are rudimentary since the group only came into existence with the
advent of party politics in the 1960s and is still primarily associated only
with rallies and other political functions.

The tantang drums are the principal drums of the Mandinka of Gambia
and Senegal. They are single-skin conical drums, open at the lower end
where the cone shape flares back out slightly. Two are short (about 17" and
13" [43cm and 33cm] in height) with heads of 10" (25cm) and 7" (18cm)
respectively. The third is longer (26"-28" or 66-71cm), but very slender, also
with a head of about 7" (18cm) in diameter. The heads are of goatskin, held
in place by pegs and further tightened by lacing attached to the pegs. All of
the drums are played with the fingers and palm of one hand (usually the
left) and a slender stick in the other, but the players of the short drums dis-
card the stick in favor of pure hand drumming for Seruba. On the left wrist
of each drummer is tied a pair of small iron pellet bells in the shape of a
rolled leaf (*jawungo*) and this jingles with the motions of that hand. The
two short drums are known individually as the *kutiriba* and *kutirindingo*
(large and small *kutiro*). The long drum is called *sabaro*.

Musical Organization and Aesthetics in Drumming

The basic technique is the same on all three drums. It consists of four strokes that may be expressed verbally by mnemonic syllables. The syllables greatly facilitate learning and memory, but are not used in actual performance. They are as follows (published previously in Knight 1974: 28):

kun is an open hand stroke, produced by striking the head with the forward half of the palm (just how much depends on the size of the drum) and all of the fingers held together and flat. The fingers bounce off the head, allowing it to ring.

ba (pronounced with a glottal stop) is a damped hand stroke, produced by striking the head with the fingers only, still held together and flat, but slightly inclined down towards the head. The fingers are pressed against the head, damping the vibration.

din is an open stick stroke, produced by dropping the hand towards the head and slightly rotating the wrist. The stick is held lightly between the thumb and forefinger or middle finger so that it bounces off the head.

da (pronounced with a glottal stop) is a damped stick stroke, produced with the same arm motion as for *din*, but the forefinger slides down the stick over the thumb and the other fingers grip the stick more firmly as it strikes the head. This presses the tip of the stick to the head and damps the vibration.

All of the different drum beats played by the troupe (Lenjengo, Kankurang, Nyaka Julo, etc.) are based on two tightly interlocked and/or overlapped rhythms, one played on each kutiro drum. The characteristic sound of the composite rhythm is as much a function of the pattern of different timbres created by the two drums as it is of the rhythms themselves. To begin with, the rhythms played on each drum generally utilize all four basic strokes in an aurally satisfying sequence that is equivalent to a well-thought-out melody on a melodic instrument. When the two kutiro parts are combined, still using only the four basic strokes, there are twenty-four different sounds that can be made: eight single sounds (four strokes on each drum), plus sixteen combined sounds (each stroke on one drum played simultaneously with each stroke on the other drum), as shown in the following diagram:

Kutiriba

Kutirindingo		K	B	D	d
	K	KK	KB	KD	Kd
	B	BK	BB	BD	Bd
	D	DK	DB	DD	Dd
	d	dK	dB	dD	dd

Legend

K = kun
B = ba
D = din
d = da

The composite rhythmic patterns as played by the two drums are not long enough to accommodate all twenty-four of these sounds, but whether they are long or short, the patterns make maximal use of the various sounds and contain very few if any repetitions. The six rhythms notated in Example 6 show this clearly:

Example 6. Six kutiro rhythms. A dot indicates a silent pulse. Repeated sounds are marked with an asterisk where the repeat occurs.

```
rhythm            drum              notation              sound

Lenjengo 1:       kutiriba:  |K  .|D  .|d  .          kun-din-da
                  k-dingo:    .  B|D  .  d  K         (start with the K:) kum-ba din-da

Lenjengo 2:       kutiriba:  |K  d  K|D  B  d         kun da kun dim ba da
                  k-dingo:    .  B|D  .  d  K         (same) kum-ba din-da

Nyaka Julo:       kutiriba:  |K  .|D  d |B  D         kun-din da ba ding
                  k-dingo:   |d  B|D  D |K  K          da ba din ding kung kun

Kankurang:        kutiriba:  |K  .  D  .|B  d  .  d|B  .  D  .|D  d  .  d
                  k-dingo:   |D  .  D  .|B  d  .  d|D  .  D  .|K  .  K  .
                                                *                          *
Chingo:           kutiriba:  |K  .  d  B|d  .  K  D|B  .  d  K|D  .  B  d
                  k-dingo:   |d  .  d  B|D  .  D  K|d  .  d  B|D  .  D  K
                                                *
Daba Tantango:    kutiriba:  |K  .  d  B|.  K|D  .  .|d  .  d
                  k-dingo:   |K  d  .|B  D  B|K  d  .|B  D  D
                                                *              *
```

Naturally the individual drum parts, unless they are only four strokes long, must use any or all of the four basic strokes repeatedly. But if the two parts are considered as a composite whole, the picture changes. The first three (six-pulse) patterns in Example 6 contain no repetitions at all. The sixteen-pulse pattern for Kankurang (actually only eleven attacks considering both drums together) incorporates three repeated sounds ("da" on both drums, "din" on both drums, and "da" on kutiriba only). Each is marked with an asterisk at the second occurrence. Chingo, another sixteen-pulse pattern with twelve attacks, contains only one repeated sound ("da on both drums). Daba Tantango contains two repeated sounds since the kutiriba part is silent in both places where "din" and "da" are played on the kutirindingo.

These examples also serve to point out the uncomplicated nature of the rhythms on each drum. Sometimes even their combination is quite straightforward, as in Chingo, where both drums move in the same rhythm throughout. Thus the timbral patterns are a very important feature of the style.

All of the drummers utilize several other strokes once they have advanced beyond the beginning stage, but the sabaro drummer has a still greater vocabulary than the other drummers. Being the leader of the group, he plays a part which is highly improvised and communicative. Although words or verbal meanings are often assigned to many of the drum rhythms, much of the sabaro part consists of actual translations into drum sounds of spoken phrases, commands, and names. By duplicating the tonal and rhythmic patterns of Mandinka speech, the sabaro drummer transmits messages such as the "Greeting to the Bantaba" used to open a performance of Lenjengo/Seruba, or shorter messages inviting dancers to join in or to stop and give the next person a chance. He also incorporates signals to his kutiro drummers to stop, start, or change patterns, and the rest of the time keeps up a rapid succession of patterns of his own that contribute variety to the performance.

Drummers, unlike the jali, have very little to say about what constitutes a good performance, but one thing they do say is that improvisation is important. This extends to the kutiro drummers as well as the sabaro. Although the primary responsibility of the kutiro drummers is to maintain the basic rhythms of a piece in recognizable form so the dancers can follow them at all times, this does not preclude variations or even momentary departures from the rhythms. Indeed, it is clear from the above examples that many repetitions of these short ostinatos would be quite uninteresting without variations. The ability to create a personal style around the basic rhythms is greatly admired by listeners and other drummers alike. When a drummer remarks about the outstanding ability of another member of his troupe or another troupe, he is usually referring to this ability. The extreme of "grandstanding" on the other hand, where a kutiro drummer detracts from the attention on the sabaro by overzealous playing or moving around the dance circle instead of staying seated, is not desirable and is frowned upon by other drummers.

Skill at improvisation extends to the Seruba singer too. His ability to extemporize lines that are amusing or clever and draw the audience into the performance is the key to the success of Seruba. It is on this point that lesser-known troupes usually fall down when people compare them to their favorite group.

The openness and participatory quality of drumming events is most obvious in Seruba, but it is an important feature of all of them. Thus if a drumming performance should be anything, it should be inviting. Unlike jaliya, which invites one to listen and be moved by what one hears, drumming encourages one to take part, without regard for dancing or singing ability. A performance that falls short on this point is bound to be judged inferior.

Learning

Even though drumming is not regulated by family traditions, an apprenticeship is required for membership in a troupe, and the troupe's busy schedule usually requires a full time commitment to drumming once one has started. Thus, although one is not "born to do drumming," and will most likely not continue it for a lifetime, it is a full time profession while one is doing it.

A drumming apprenticeship might begin when a boy is a teenager. By the time he is in his early twenties, if he has shown great promise, he will most likely be in a position to take over the sabaro for short periods at the beginning of a performance, and he will have mastered all of the rhythms of both kutiro drums. A student begins on the kutirindingo. Of the two kutiro drums, this smaller one is played with less variation than the other, and in performance it is the drum that usually starts the rhythm, the kutiriba coming in afterwards. Both of these factors make it easier to master as a beginner. The beginning drummer will spend all of his time for the first few years on this drum. As with the learning of jaliya, structured lessons and practice sessions are virtually unknown, but early participation in actual performances builds confidence quickly, and the student soon learns how variations may be introduced. Thus flexibility is learned simultaneously with the basic repertoire.

Once the kutirindingo has been mastered, the student moves to the kutiriba. The deep tone of this drum stands out more in performance than the kutirindingo, but because the apprentice has learned the basic techniques on the small drum, he is able to reach a public performance standard quickly, and can then devote his efforts to developing his own personal style of performance.

Playing the sabaro of course requires the greatest skill, not only because of the greater vocabulary of strokes to be learned, but because the sabaro drummer is the leader of the troupe and must have complete confidence in everything he is doing in order to keep the music flowing and responsive to what the dancers, maskers, wrestlers, or his own Seruba singer are doing as well. The advanced apprentice is given the opportunity to practice the skills of sabaro drumming frequently. The sabaro player is usually five to ten years older than his kutiro drummers, and, at least in Lenjengo/Seruba, is treated much as the star of the show, overshadowed only by the Seruba singer when he comes out. Thus, he never appears right at the beginning of a performance. Instead, one of his kutiro drummers, usually the kutiriba player, takes his place and gets the drummers and dancers warmed up. Only after fifteen or twenty minutes of this does he take over, usually causing a noticeable increase in tempo and excitement. This arrangement allows apprentices to take their turns at the kutiro drums, and when they are advanced enough, to learn the sabaro as well.

A major difference between the apprenticeship of jaliya and that of drumming is evident here. Even though both encourage participation in actual performance from an early stage, the ultimate aim of the jaliya apprenticeship is to prepare the *jalindingo* for his release to an independent career as a *jaliba*. The drumming apprenticeship, on the other hand, moves a drummer up through the ranks of his troupe, ultimately rewarding his ability and devotion, not with release from the troupe, but with the promise of eventual leadership within it instead.

The Content of Seruba Songs

If we think of the basic purpose of jaliya as being entertainment through commemoration and praise, the basic purpose of Seruba singing is entertainment through honorable mention and thanks. Much of what the jali sings about happened in the past to great men long since passed away. In contrast to this, much of what the Seruba singer sings about happened to his next door neighbor just yesterday.

The Seruba singer has a stock of standard verses that he has either composed or learned elsewhere, and he extemporizes new verses each time he performs. True to the participatory nature of his performance, he relies heavily on his audience to influence the direction of the singing. He may notice someone he would like to sing about in the crowd, or a woman may come up to him with a penny and request a verse for someone, as we have seen in the opening scene. After he initiates a verse, the audience and the drummers join in to complete it with him. If they seem to enjoy it very much, he will probably repeat it immediately. If they don't he may drop it as fast as he composed it. Especially successful verses will become part of his stock of standard verses. These he uses in the same way the jali uses his jali kumolu, to fill out the performance as he extemporizes his next new verse (see Example 7).

Example 7. A verse of Seruba singing. The translation appears in verse No. 1 below. The other verses shown (except No. 9) are also sung to this basic melody.

The following lines of Seruba singing have been excerpted from a single performance, representing perhaps ten or fifteen minutes out of an evening of entertainment by one of Gambia's leading Seruba singers, Bakary Marona. The topical and popular nature of Seruba will be evident from them.

1. Oh, the people of Njo Sidibe's place at Wasulunkunda
   Ah, the "twenty-five" givers
   The people of Njo Sidibe's place, Wasulunkunda.

2. Oh, August has come, the month of no money, but Fatu has not failed me.
   The people of Fatu Bajana's place have come to dance.
   August is here, but Fatu has not failed to pay me well.

3. Who are the good citizens of the town? I will tell all of you
   Bori Jasi (a woman) is in charge of everything. She takes responsibility for the
      town
   I will tell you who are the good citizens of this town.

4. Oh, Queen of Gunjur, I say Big Tuti Jammeh
   The Gambian flag flies at your place
   Queen of Gunjur, I say, Big Tuti Jammeh.

5. Oh, if I leave Samban, I'm going to Dankunku (both in Nyamina District)
   Oh, take me to the people in Nyamina
   If I leave Samban, I'm going to Dankunku.

6. Oh, you should all give Bojan beautiful things
   Manyima of Jambanjele, oh
   You should all give Bojan beautiful things.

7. Oh, I danced at Lamin, didn't the people tell you?
   Near the pump house, at the young people's place
   I danced at Lamin, didn't the people tell you?

8. Oh, people should be kind to Mama of Jambour
   Yes, Malanding's new wife
   People should be kind to Mama.

9. Oh, sing praise to Allah
   All those standing will one day lie down
   The ground holds you forever
   All the big trees have fallen
   Aren't all the great people gone?
   The pens are all broken
   Yes, the ink is all gone (The marabouts are gone).
   Everybody say "Dabo from Kunkali "(a marabout)
   Who has instructed the people of Kunkali
   They called him Seku Sadibu.
   Oh dear, Seku Sadibu, our prayers have been answered.
   I have leaned against the trunk of the bantang tree
   Yes, nothing can touch me (I am protected).

10. Oh, the crocodile's hope lies in the river.
    Mr. Knight, come and take me.
    I said to him, "What about America?"
    The white man is studying (drums).
    I give thanks to God.

11. Oh, Dembo Marong's place, Bakary Marong's place
    Yes, Little Omar, beat the drum for me
    The beautiful girls are dancing, the girls are dancing
    Yes, at Bakary Marong's place.

In this representative sample, the emphasis is clearly on mentioning and
thanking women that have sponsored his performances in various towns
(No. 1-4, 6, and 8). Other verses remark on recent events (Nos. 5 and 7) or

current events (Nos. 10 and 11). In No. 9, longer than the others, the content is notably similar to the jali's. The person for whom the lines are sung is obviously highly respected by the singer, but he is also dead. Suddenly the mentioning and thanking changes to commemoration and praise, and the singer strikes a philosophical pose, noting the transient nature of life and the inevitability of death—both familiar themes in jaliya. Although the inclusion of these lines emphasizes the shallow nature of the other lines by comparison, it also shows the parallels between the two.

SUMMARY AND CONCLUSIONS

In comparing the jali and the drummer in Manding society, we have noted significant differences in the social setting of their performances, the nature of their audiences, the style of their music, and the content of their songs. At the same time, we have speculated on the possibility of a drumming jali in the past and have seen in the Seruba singer's lines some evidence of affinity with the jali. Before we reach any final conclusions, a final point of comparison can be made on the basis of their regard for one another.

In one respect the drummer regards the jali much as most sula freeborn people do—with considerable admiration for his special knowledge of family histories and genealogies, for his ability to tell these histories in a captivating style, and for his verbal and instrumental virtuosity. On the other hand, the hint of scorn that may enter into a sula's regard for the jali for the reasons detailed earlier, is not often part of the drummer's regard for the jali. The first reason for this is obvious: the drummer is a performer himself and is even called "jali" on occasion, as we have seen. A second reason is that people who take up drumming are not usually from families that the jali counts among his patrons, and thus they are not susceptible to his solicitation for support.

The jali, being the professional that he is, can hardly be expected to pay much attention to the comparatively trivial subjects that the drummer sings about. He may be entertained by the Lenjengo dance or any of the other drumming events, but he hardly takes them seriously, and almost never considers learning them. In fact, in the past, a young jali would have been strongly enjoined against having anything to do with drumming. Today, because of the changing methods of teaching jaliya, one occasionally hears of a young jali who has taken up drumming, or of another who travels around with the drummers because he likes the female company they attract, but even now such things are usually frowned upon by the older or more serious jali who might call the young man in the latter case a *muso jali* (woman's jali).

These attitudes reinforce the original characterization of jaliya and drumming as the art music and folk music of the Manding. One more look at

Seruba in particular makes the impression even stronger. The drummers themselves note that Seruba is the youngest of drumming events, and its style is still very much in a state of flux. Although several drumming events include singing, it is always spontaneous and led by one or another of the participants. Seruba stands out as the only event to include a lead singer—and virtually a professional at that. Do not the youth of this event, the inclusion of the singer, and the similarity of his songs to jaliya point to a clear case of borrowing? Seruba is jaliya for the common man.

In contemporary Manding society there are many popularizing trends that threaten the traditional styles of both jaliya and drumming and their claims to certain audiences. The radio recording session in Scene 5 was depicted as a mixed blessing. Jali Nyama Suso elaborates:

Jaliya in the future will be very difficult. The radio has made the music familiar to many people, and everyone knows what excellent kora playing sounds like. Not just anyone will be able to bluff their way through. Also, playing on the radio detaches you from your audience. They hear you as if you were there with them, but you are not, and thus your reputation rests solely on the sound of your instrument. Finally, if a man can hear you or somebody even better than you on the radio, why should he bother to pay you when you come to his house for jaliya? (Nyama Suso, 1972)

The popularity of the jaliya style as used by the Seruba singer tends to draw a potential audience among young people away from jaliya, and in some cases draws the young jalolu themselves towards it as a facile means of gaining an audience for their singing and playing. But the threat of competition can generate new and imaginative solutions. Before his death in the late 1970s, Mori Suso of the Casamance region of southern Senegal had fitted his kora with four extra strings, developed a playing style that was only possible with these strings, and composed his own songs in this style. He performed regularly for dances that were equally as popular as the local drumming events.

Since change is the only certainty of the future, we can expect to see more as time goes on. These events invite us to watch carefully the relationship of the jali and the drummer in Manding society. Perhaps their realms and roles will not be so distinct in the future.

NOTES

1. In Mandinka, the language of the western region of Manding and the one used in this study, the plural is formed by changing the final vowel to "o" (commonly done to indicate the definite article as well) and adding the suffix "-lu." Thus the plural of jali or jalo is jalolu. Mandinka and the other languages of Manding are tone languages, but the correct pronunciation of plural words may be approximated by stressing the penultimate syllable.

2. The letters "ng" in Mandinka words represent the homorganic nasal, always pronounced as a single sound—as in the English word "singer," for example, not as

in "finger." When this sound occurs at the end of a word its pronunciation will vary, depending on the next consonant. For example, it is pronounced "n" before "d," "j," or "t," "ng" before "k" or "g," and "m" before "b" or "p." Since many words end in this sound, a degree of economy in transliteration may be achieved by eliminating the "g" in such cases, as in *bolon, balafon, jon, feten*. This is the rule followed in this article, with one exception: words ending in "-ang," such as *tantang* and *Kankurang* are spelled with the "g" included, primarily because over long years of use they have become familiar in this spelling.

3. Two authors who have written extensively and carefully on the question of slavery in Manding culture are Mungo Park [1954: (1795-1806), 220 ff] and Henri Labouret (1934: 105ff). A contemporary focus is given by Matt Schaffer and Christine Cooper in 1980.

4. The reader will please forbear the use of only the masculine pronoun throughout this general discussion. The points made refer to both men and women, but the use of bi-gender pronouns seemed unnecessarily cumbersome. Extensive information on the role of the female jali in particular is given later in the chapter.

5. This subject is discussed in detail by Michael Coolen (1983).

REFERENCES CITED

Battúta, Ibn
    1939   *Travels in Asia and Africa, 1325-1354.* Translated and selected by H. A. R. Gibb. London: George Routledge and Sons Ltd.

Bird, Charles
    1972   Heroic Songs of the Mande Hunters. In Richard M. Dorson, ed., *African Folklore.* New York: Doubleday.

Camara, Sory
    1976   *Gens de la parole. Essai sur la condition et le röle des griots dans la société malinké.* Paris: Mouton.

Coolen, Michael
    1983   The Wolof Xalam Tradition of the Senegambia. *Ethno-musicology* 27(3): 477-498.

Delafosse, Maurice
    1912   *Haut-Sénégal-Niger (Soudan français).* Première série, Tome III (Les civilisations). Paris: Larose.

Farmer, Henry George
    1928   A North African Folk Instrument. *Journal of the Royal Asiatic Society.* 25-34.

Jobson, Richard
    1932   *The Golden Trade.* London: Penguin Press. (Originally published by Nicholas Okes, London, 1623).

King, Anthony
    1972   The Construction and Tuning of the *Kora. African Language Studies* 13: 113-136.

Knight, Roderic C.
    1973   *Mandinka Jaliya: Professional Music of The Gambia.* PhD dissertation (Music), University of California at Los Angeles. 2 vols.

Knight, Roderic C.
  1974   Mandinka Drumming. *African Arts* 7(4): 24-35.
Labouret, Henri
  1934   *Les Manding et leur langue.* Paris: Larose.
Launay, Robert
  1972   Les *clans et* les *castes mandingues.* Paper presented at the Conference
          of Manding Studies, London. A summary appears in the booklet
          Manding: Focus on an African Civilisation. Guy Atkins (ed.). Lon-
          don: School of Oriental and African Studies.
Niane, D. T.
  1965   *Sundiata: An Epic of Old Mali* (translated by G. D. Pickett). London:
          Longmans.
Nketia, J. H. Kwabena
  1962   *African Music in Ghana.* London: Longmans.
Park, Mungo
  1954   *The Travels of Mungo Park.* Ronald Miller (ed.). New York: Dutton.
          (Original text—Mungo Park, 1799: *Travels in the Interior Districts of
          Africa.* London: Nicol).
Pollet, Eric and Grace Winter
  1971   *La société soninké.* Bruxelles: Université de Bruxelles.
Rouget, Gilbert
  1969   Sur les xylophones équiheptaphoniques des Malinké. *Revue de Musi-
          cologie* 55(1): 47-77.
  1970   Transcrire ou décrire? Chant soudanais et chant fuégien. Jean Pouillon
          and Pierre Maranda (eds.). *Echanges et communications. Mélanges
          offerts à Claude Lévi-Strauss.* Paris: Mouton. 677-706.
  1972   *Mandinka Music, Guinea* (Collection Musée de l'Homme). Paris:
          Disques Vogue LDM 30 113.
Schaffer, Matt and Christine Cooper
  1980   *Mandinko: The Ethnography of a West African Holy Land.* New
          York: Holt, Rinehart and Winston.
Zahan, Dominique
  1950   Notes sur un luth dogon. *Journal de la société des africanistes* 20(2):
          193-207.
Zemp, Hugo
  1964   Musciens autochtones et griots malinké chez les Dan de Côte d'Ivoire.
          Cahiers d'études africaines 4(3): 370-382.
  1965   *The Music of the Senufo* (UNESCO Anthology of African Music).
          Kassel: Bärenreiter Musicaphon BM 30L 2308.
  1966a   La légende des griots malinké. *Cahiers d'études africaines* 6(24):
          Kassel: Bärenreiter Musicaphon BM 30L 2301.
  1966b   La Légende des griots malinké. *Cahiers d'études africaines* 6(24):
          611-642.
  1967   Comment on devient musicien (Quatre exemples de l'ouest-africain).
          In Tolia Nikiprowetsky, ed., *La musique dans la vie,* Vol. 1. Paris:
          Office de Coopération Radiophonique. 79-103.
  1971   *Guéré Music, Ivory Coast* (Collection Musée de l'Homme). Paris:
          Disques Vogue LD 764.

3

Berber Professional Musicians in Performance

Philip D. Schuyler

The ethnography of performance shows promise of providing a meeting ground for the various theoretical camps allied under the banner of ethnomusicology. Anthropologists, folklorists, musicologists, and others will no doubt continue to emphasize their respective areas of expertise, from the "cultural system" to the "music itself." But representatives of these fields have come to realize in recent years that music, both as organized sound and as a cultural phenomenon, is best examined as it takes place in performance (cf. Basgöz 1975, Blacking 1981, Fogelson 1971, Herndon 1971, McLeod and Herndon 1980).

Although interest in performance is of rather recent vintage in ethnomusicology, Malinowski's observations, from 1926, on the performance of folktales, are of equal relevance to the study of music:

The text, of course, is extremely important, but without the context it remains lifeless. . . . The stories or performances of music live in native life and not on paper, and when a scholar jots them down without being able to evoke the atmosphere in which they flourish, he has given us but a mutilated bit of reality (Malinowski 1948: 104).

1. THE "RWAIS" IN SOCIETY

The present study is concerned with professional musicians (*rwais*, sing. *rais*)[1] from the *tashlhit*-speaking region of southwestern Morocco.[2] The home territory of the *rwais* spreads across the western High Atlas and Anti-Atlas mountains, spilling over into parts of the fertile Sus valley between the two ranges and the pre-desert oases to the south of the mountains. The *rwais* are specialists in a society with few professions and little need of them. The *tashlhit*-speaking Berbers (Ishlhin) are sedentary peasants, organized into numerous tribes, many of which are no larger than a cluster of villages in a narrow valley. Isolated politically and geographically from each other as well as from the Arabized peoples of the plains and cities, the villagers have become self-sufficient in meeting many of their own needs, including music. The *rwais*, like well-diggers, tinsmiths and other craftsmen, must therefore be prepared to travel great distances, seeking work wherever and whenever there is demand for their services.

The *rwais* are well adapted to a life of wandering. Many have no strong family ties or capital to hold them in their native villages. Further, the ideal performer is complete in himself—composer, lyricist, singer, dancer, and accompanist all at the same time. Both history and legend (Chottin 1931: 18) confirm that all *rwais* were originally soloists, accompanying themselves on the *rribab* (monochord spike fiddle) or *loṭar* (a three- or four-stringed fretless lute).[3] Today most groups remain small and mobile, with an average of five performers; the stringed instruments are given rhythmic support by a *naqus* (lit., bell; usually a brake drum beaten with long nails or truck valves). A few short-lived groups have as many as fifteen members, with up to eight female dancers (*raisat*). Each musician maintains his independence, however, and reserves the right to leave a group at almost any time, to perform solo or with another ensemble.

Traditionally, the *rwais*, alone or in groups, have made long trips through the mountains, stopping at each village and country market (*suq*) on their itinerary for as long as they could find food, lodging, and other payment for their performance. Making a virtue out of what was once an economic necessity, the *rwais* still consider travel essential both as training and initiation for novice musicians, and as the major source of new material for songs.

By mixing music, poetry, and information heard on the road with their own experiences and compositions, professional musicians have been able to offer villagers not only a change from a steady diet of local music, but also news and opinion from the world outside their valley. In the days before good roads or radio, the *rwais* were valued primarily as journalists, historians, and moralists. Poets still point out that "We (I) have only our words to sell" (*is akka znz-gh awal*). Indeed, most *rwais* sell their words made to order, by acting as singers of praise. Their praise of a generous host, or criticism of a stingy one, can have an appreciable effect on an individual's reputation. Recognizing this, wealthy farmers and merchants, as well as local political and religious leaders, have always patronized the *rwais* lavishly. Until the early 1950s, a few *qaid-s* (tribal governors) even kept personal bands of professional musicians.

In the past, the *rwais* confined most of their travel to late summer and early fall, the season of feasts after the harvests, when leisure and relative wealth permit the Ishlḥin to organize large parties with hired entertainment. Late summer continues to be the busiest time of year for the *rwais*, as indeed it is for most Moroccan musicians; many count on the income from summer parties to carry them through the rest of the year. In recent years, however, the *rwais* have found more regular employment in the city. Based primarily in Marrakech, Agadir, and Casablanca, they retain easy access to their home villages and rural audience, but they live in the midst of a much more affluent market, the colonies of emigrant Ishlḥin.

Migration, both within Morocco and abroad, has long been a means of relieving population pressure and providing additional income for the poorer areas of the *tashlḥit*-speaking region. The Ishlḥin have exported themselves as farm laborers, religious scholars, and acrobats, and more lately as miners, factory workers, and merchants. In this century, temporary migration has become the largest single source of income in many tribes; in some villages it involves over 60 percent of the adult male population (Noin 1970: vol. 2, 184; Waterbury 1972).[4] To reach this audience, nostalgic for the mountains and wealthy enough to indulge the nostalgia, the *rwais* have expanded their itineraries to include not only northern Morocco, but the industrial cities of France, Belgium and Germany as well.

City life also brings the *rwais* in contact with many non-Ishlḥin. These encounters may supply the stuff of caustic moral commentary for village consumption. Under certain circumstances, however, non-Ishlḥin may just as easily be potential patrons whom the *rwais* must accommodate in order to earn a living.

The Elements of Performance

With only minor exceptions, the structural elements of the *rwais'* poetry and music remain the same wherever they perform. The *rwais* sing almost exclusively in Berber, although travel has enriched their poetic vocabulary with Arabic and French terminology, as well as a panoply of archaisms, regionalisms, and neologisms in *tashlḥit*. Both imagery (based largely on nature, agriculture, and hunting) and most themes (such as unrequited love, religion, and social commentary) are drawn from a traditional repertory of ideas shared by *rwais* and village poets. The basic formal unit of poetry is the distich line, which lends itself well to responsorial singing between antiphonal choruses in village music or between leader and chorus among the *rwais*.

Compound duple meters predominate in both village and professional music; the simultaneous or successive juxtaposition of binary and ternary rhythms in compound duple produces rhythmic tension that gives Berber music great vitality. Many pieces begin slowly in simple duple or triple meters, and asymmetrical rhythms, though rare, also appear in the repertory. As the tempo accelerates, however, the rhythm inevitably modulates to compound duple. Instrumental and vocal passages in free rhythm are a mark of virtuosity in both village and professional music.

Melodies are set, for the most part, in anhemitonic pentatonic modes, varied by the introduction of an occasional semitone. The tunes leap up and down in fourths and fifths over a range of an octave and a half. Melodic structure assumes a variety of shapes, but in the majority of cases, the melody is built of two to four parallel phrases, adding up to a total length of eight to twelve cycles of the chosen rhythm. Each melody generally corresponds in length to a single line of poetry.

The Form of Performance

While the underlying principles of poetry and music remain the same in every performance by the *rwais*, the musicians have no fixed format for their act, nor yet for individual pieces. Every piece is, in fact, an enchained series of formal segments, each an independent entity with no necessary connection to the segments which precede and follow it:

Amarg (lit., yearning, unrequited love)—Sung poetry. *Amarg* is literally the centerpiece of any performance, and the only indispensable element of the *rwais'* act. An individual poem is known as *aqsid* or *taqsiṭṭ* (from the Arabic *qasida*). In most cases, a single line form and melodic setting are repeated from beginning to end of the song.

Astara (lit., travelling, strolling, i.e., over the principal degrees of the scale)—An instrumental prelude or interlude, analogous in form and function to the Arabic *taqsim*. An *astara* serves to warm up both musicians and audience. It consists of a series of short phrases in free rhythm, centered on the main tone and other important pitches of a given mode. An *astara* may last as long as three minutes, or as little as three strokes on the main tone.

Ṭbil—A choreographed overture, in free or fixed rhythm (generally 4/4). A *ṭbil* is optional in some situations, and is reserved for use only at the beginning of performance. Each *ṭbil* is a collection of short melodies, arranged in a roughly predetermined order. The group leader, however, chooses *ad libitum* the specific melodies and variations to be performed, as well as the number of times each is to be repeated.

Tamsust (lit., movement, acceleration)—A bridge between two songs, or between *amarg* or *ṭbil* and *l-aḍrub*. Based on the song setting or final *ṭbil* melody, *tamsust* accelerates the tempo, and frequently modulates from simple to compound metric patterns.

L-Aḍrub (sing., *ḍḍerb*, from the Arabic for beat, strike)—A series of melodies, almost invariably in 6/8 time, used to accompany dance. A *ḍḍerb* melody may be used as a setting for *amarg*, and vice versa, but as accompaniment to dance, *l-aḍrub* are exclusively instrumental. The choice, order, and repetition of dance melodies are left entirely to the musicians' discretion.

Qṭaᶜ (from the Arabic for cut)—A cadential formula, four rapid rhythm cycles in length.

The *rwais'* act also includes spoken, unaccompanied prose: *mashkhara*, slapstick comedy; and *fatḥa* (from the Arabic *al-fatiḥa*, the prayer that opens the Qur'an), a simultaneous benediction and request for money.

The musical elements of performance fit loosely into the framework given in Diagram 1, which is the *rwais'* own model of performance. A number of *rwais* pointed out that a piece should begin with an *astara* and then move to *amarg*. At the end of the song text, the vocal melody (*rih*) accelerates into the *tamsust*, often shifting to compound duple meter, to lead into *l-aḍrub*. The piece is brought to a close with a short cadential formula, the *qṭaᶜ*. The *rwais* seldom mentioned the *ṭbil* section of performance without prompting. They did point out, however, that the *ṭbil* comes only at the very beginning of performance. When it appears, the *ṭbil* follows the same general format as *amarg*, preceded by an *astara*, and followed by *tamsust*, *l-aḍrub*, and *qṭaᶜ*.

Diagram 1

The Rwais' Model of Performance[5]

$$\#S + \begin{Bmatrix} T \\ M \end{Bmatrix} + TS + D + Q\#$$

S	Astara
T	Ṭbil
M	Amarg
TS	Tamsust
D	L-Aḍrub
Q	Qṭaᶜ
#	Boundary of piece
$\begin{Bmatrix} - \\ - \end{Bmatrix}$	Choose any one

The model of performance suggested by the *rwais* gives a good general idea of the order of segments in a piece, but it simplifies drastically the variety and complexity of forms in actual performance. The model does not include comedy or prayer, for example. Strictly speaking, these are verbal, not musical elements of performance; but in certain circumstances, they are the dominant elements, with a pronounced effect on musical form. Further, the musicians may choose to expand or eliminate any given segment; thus, the "same" piece may last from three minutes to forty-five minutes on different occasions. Finally, even the order of segments is subject to considerable variation.

In all, the *rwais* lend themselves well to an ethnography of performance. Their individualistic spirit leads to continual changes in both the personnel and the configuration of any group of *rwais*. As itinerant professionals, they perform in a wide variety of situations, before audiences of divergent ethnic and social make-up. Finally, the flexible formal structure of their music permits the *rwais* to vary their performance to suit each situation.

The remainder of this essay will examine the *rwais'* performance in four different sets of circumstances: the marketplace; private parties; commercial establishments; and the electronic media. The form of performance in each situation will be examined on two levels. The analysis will begin with an overview of the circumstances surrounding performance—the historical or cultural background of the situation, the physical setting, the nature of the audience, and so on. The second part of the discussion will trace the effect of these external factors on performance as it is more narrowly defined—group configuration, the quality of performance, and, above all, the selection and order of performance segments.

2. THE MARKETPLACE

The most common type of performance by the *rwais* takes place in the open air, at country *suq-s* and in urban marketplaces. In the simplest situation, the *rwais*—one or two at most—wander among the shops and cafés. They play short snatches of songs (if not waved away by the proprietor) in exchange for small coins. The same technique is used, door to door, in more remote villages in the mountains, in which case the musicians can generally expect no more than payment in kind—milk, butter, or grain.

More frequently, the *rwais* meet their audience on neutral territory. Both *suq-s* and cities generally have an area reserved for public entertainment. These open places attract all sorts of entertainers, not only *rwais*, but acrobats, magicians, fortunetellers, gamblers, and so forth. Each group or individual performer tries to form a circle (*ḥalqa*, pl., *ḥlaqi*, from the Arabic word for circle or throat; in *tashlḥit: lḥalqt*) of spectators who will provide both a backdrop for the action and the money to make it all worthwhile.

Jamaᶜ l-Fna

The most impressive assemblage of *ḥlaqi* can be found on Jamaᶜ l-Fna, a large open square which lies between the Kutubia mosque and the main market area of Marrakech. Like a country *suq* in the heart of the city, Jamaᶜ l-Fna is a place of mediation and transition, where rural Morocco becomes urban, and where North Africa meets Europe.

Nearly all of the inter-city taxis and bus lines which serve Marrakech have their terminals here, as do the municipal buses, taxis, and Victoria cabs. Half a dozen hotels, including the luxurious Club Méditerranée, line the perimeter of the square, and at least thirty more fill the narrow streets adjacent to it. A couple of these are solid three-star hotels catering to middle-class tourists, but most are modest, converted houses or the traditional, caravanserai-like *funduq-s*.

More often than not, buses, hotels, and the square itself are filled to overflowing, because Marrakech offers a wide range of urban goods and services within five minutes walk of Jama᷈ l-Fna. Off one end of the square are market streets offering everything from almonds and brassware to radios and wristwatches. Near another corner are myriad shops selling bed-frames and kitchen utensils, and wholesalers dealing in cloth and ready-made garments specifically designed for the rural market. For Marrakchis and inhabitants of the region, there is a still more potent drawing card in the nearby government buildings, where taxes are paid, disputes settled, papers validated, and passport applications filed.

While the outskirts of Jama᷈ l-Fna are devoted to serious business, the square itself is given over to diversion. The open area of the "square" measures about 100,000 square feet, divided into a rectangle and adjacent triangle. Merchants and prepared-food vendors operate out of small shanties and push carts along the edges of each section. These structures, shaky if not actually *démontable*, threaten to disappear overnight, like the tents of a country market. Indeed, it often seems that the only permanent feature of the square is the constant ebb and flow of humanity.

At first glance, the activity on Jama᷈ l-Fna seems chaotic. This disorder is sometimes real (e.g., the "disorderly conduct" of occasional drunks or fighters), but most often it is only apparent, like the disorder in nature which, on closer examination, turns out to be strictly patterned. Jama᷈ l-Fna might be likened to an ecosystem, such as a pond or estuary, which under-goes daily and seasonal cycles of change.

The square is never totally devoid of activity. Even in the hours between midnight and dawn, a few food and cigarette vendors remain open, pri-marily to serve—at inflated prices—arriving or departing travellers. In early morning, the pace is still slow; as merchants begin to set out their wares, entertainment is largely confined to snake charmers, storytellers, fortunetellers, public writers, and medicine men. By late morning one can choose between several groups of musicians, but during the early after-noon, activity falls almost to a late-night level. As the mid-afternoon prayer (*l-ᶜasr*) approaches, more performers begin to emerge; the daily life-cycle reaches its peak in the hours before sunset, when as many as forty or more *ḥlaqi* operate simultaneously. As darkness falls, most *ḥlaqi* begin to disperse, leaving the square to food vendors (who are at their busiest at this time), and a few storytellers, urban Arab musicians, and members of the Gnawa religious brotherhood.

This schedule varies during the course of a week or a year. In winter, rain and cold can all but eliminate the *ḥlaqi* from the square, and the heat of the summer extends the mid-afternoon doldrums. On Sundays and holidays, the *ḥlaqi* thrive on large crowds of spectators, but a concomitant growth in the number of parked cars consumes parts of the playing area. Religious holidays have a particularly radical effect on the ecosystem. Before ᶜAid el-

Kebir (the Feast of Sacrifice), ᶜAid eṣ-Ṣaghir (marking the end of Ramaḍan), and ᶜAshura (tithing day), many groups are displaced from their "natural habitat" on the rectangle to make room for temporary booths selling seasonal specialties. During Ramaḍan (the month of fasting) there are, of course, no cafés, restaurants, or cigarette sellers working during daylight hours. The ḥlaqi, however, are particularly active during the late afternoon, as a means of diverting the mind from the rigors of fasting. In a marked departure from the normal daily schedule, a number of ḥlaqi resume performance after the fast is broken at sunset, and, along with special food vendors, remain active until dawn.[6]

The pattern of activity on Jamaᶜ l-Fna is determined by natural forces, like the passage of seasons, and all-encompassing human events, like religious holidays. Within the larger system, the various organisms—that is, the ḥlaqi and merchants—behave in an equally predictable manner. Only a very few entertainers choose their spots at random, setting up in a different place on the square each time they perform. Most types of ḥalqa follow regular patterns of distribution. Public writers, for example, organize themselves in a neat line opposite a row of shops, while fortunetellers disperse themselves over the entire square. Some musicians are migratory, consistently occupying one area each morning, and another in the afternoon.

In late morning, a few solo rwais and small groups of three or four play near the middle of the triangle. These are usually younger musicians in need of experience, or men past their prime in urgent need of money. In the afternoon, more rwais come out to play at the very edge of the triangle. Here, in a relatively small space, two to five ḥlaqi of rwais gather along with other tashlḥit-speaking performers: two or three preachers and storytellers, a comedian or two, a couple of solo rwais, and, occasionally, an aḥwash drummer. Twenty feet away are the acrobats, also Berbers from the High Atlas. The Ishlḥin always crowd into this space even on slow afternoons when there is room elsewhere.

No one oversees the arrangement of groups. No space is marked out on the pavement; no permit is issued by the city, although that may come.[7] Yet day after day groups occupy exactly the same places. More remarkable still, they do so without obvious conflict between groups, even when there is barely enough space to move between ḥlaqi.

The secret to maintaining a position on the square is timing. It is understood that various groups have priority over certain spots, but they still must stake their claims well in advance for those hours, such as late afternoon, when space is at a premium. Thus, from about 2 P.M. on, musicians begin to mark their spots with small cairns of instruments or clothes. These possessions are secure; shopkeepers and other permanent denizens of the square keep a watchful eye on the piles, and, in any case, a musician's worldly goods offer little temptation to most thieves. As the mid-afternoon prayer approaches, however, novice musicians are sent out to guard not the instruments, but the spot, until the rest of the group arrives.

Each *ḥalqa* also has its own internal order. Viewed from above, the *ḥlaqi* resemble so many amoebae under a microscope. The audience, of course, forms the cell wall, whose shape changes constantly as spectators come and go. The *rwais* work continually to maintain a *ḥalqa* of ideal shape and density. When spectators are scarce, one of the musicians tries to close up ranks by pushing stragglers into a semi-circle. When the crowd is large, the *rwais* coax the inner circle to sit down, in order to make a firm boundary and allow those in back to see.

The musicians themselves are the nucleus of the cell. The size of the performing group varies widely from *ḥalqa* to *ḥalqa*. Some musicians demand complete autonomy, and perform most frequently as soloists. Others team up in permanent groups of two or three, travelling together and sharing both income and expenses. In order to cut down on competition and concentrate the crowd, soloists and small bands often form temporary alliance groups which may number up to fifteen musicians. Such agglomerations are inherently unstable, however, and generally divide into two or three new cells within a few days. The optimum performance group includes five to seven musicians, sufficient in number to handle all the different chores in the *ḥalqa* without having to split up the day's take into too many small shares.

Performance in the "Ḥalqa"

To open the *ḥalqa*, the *naqus* player (*bu naqus*) beats a rapid pulse as loudly as he can, the pattern known as *ti-n-lḥalqt*. The musicians take out their instruments and tune, and then check their tuning by playing an *astara*. The backup musicians may hold a drone to support the leader's *astara*, but just as frequently each musician warms up by playing his own improvisation in a different part of the circle. These sounds of preparation may draw a crowd of one to two hundred spectators in a matter of minutes.

When tuning is completed and a sufficient crowd has gathered, the *rwais* gravitate to the center of the circle, and confer on a *ṭbil* with which to begin their act. The *ṭbil* accompanies a sedate circle dance, in which the *rwais* move in and out from the center, and back and forth around the edge of the circle. As the music changes from *ṭbil* to *l-aḍrub*, the symmetrical group-dance gradually evolves into a soloistic dance (*rkkẓa*, from the Arabic word for stamping, or pounding mud bricks), in which the *rwais*, singly or in groups, race across the *ḥalqa*, stamping out different rhythmic patterns with their feet. Each *rkkẓa* pattern ends when a *rais* leaps and lands on the beat, right in front of the *naqus* player. In a playful mood, the *rwais* may take a kick at *bu naqus*, or tumble into him. *Rkkẓa* contests or races also provide the opportunity to introduce the dramatis personae. The musicians are identified by name and tribe as they come forward, and each reveals a bit of his professional personality in his dance style and in the wisecracks offered between heats.

After several *l-aḍrub*, sometimes interspersed with *qṭaᶜ* (the closing formulae), the sung poetry (*amarg*) begins. The *rwais* form a line on one side of the *ḥalqa* (usually the east, facing the setting sun) while the lead singer stands opposite them. According to the *rwais'* own model, this should be the heart of the performance. In fact, however, the *ḥalqa* imposes a different set of priorities.

The opening of the *ḥalqa*, from the beginning of *ti-n-lḥalqt* through the first song, takes about fifteen to twenty minutes. It is the longest uninterrupted stretch of music in the afternoon's performance. Indeed, even this section can hardly be said to be uninterrupted, because the lead singer is never allowed to finish that first song, or any song for that matter.

After the leader has had a few minutes to spin out his song, one or two of the other *rwais* often find a pretext to stop him, by criticizing the song text, interpretation, or style. This interruption, which may arise out of real disagreement about procedure, is actually a calculated entrée into *mashkhara*, the comedy routine.

RAK: "Why are you standing like that? Is that any way to run a *ḥalqa*?"

ROR: "What do you know? Listen to how it would sound if you were in my place (playing out of tune)." And so on, until they start slapping each other around, pushing and chasing. MyL comes between them to try to break up the fight, and they both start to beat up on him. He is driven out of the circle, and comes back pushing a spectator in front of him for protection. But RAK and ROR pay him little attention, except for a few swats, and return to chasing each other around, coming finally to LTZ, the ostensible leader of the group. ROR hides behind him, asking for protection and mediation. But it is decided that ROR is somehow at fault (perhaps he is not yet a Muslim, i.e., circumcized) and is carried around by RAK, MyL, and AAR, arms around the shoulders of two, and feet held up by another. At this point, LTZ plays alternating semitones, imitating an ambulance or police siren. Others proclaim his imminent circumcision. He is eventually let down, and MyL comes in for a few more swats with a slipper. After his first beating, MyL had felt it necessary to slump down next to a seated spectator, with his head on the man's shoulder, catching his breath. Now he staggers around the *ḥalqa*; warned of the presence of a woman seated on the opposite side (he had almost backed into her earlier), he deliberately falls backward into her lap.[8]

The comedy routine, whatever the pretext, usually escalates from what seems to be a normal piece of *ḥalqa* business into some kind of exaggerated physical confrontation. The humor, obviously dependent on heavy slapstick, is often frankly bawdy or, at the very least, rich in double entendre. Both the profanity and the violence provoke smiles or outright laughter from the audience. It might be argued, however, that the primary effect is to ease the transition from music to speech, and hence pave the way for a pitch for money.

The audience contributes to the spectacle in a number of ways. There is, of course, the unmeasurable "audience input" which informs and inspires any public performance. Given the proximity of musicians and audience in a *ḥalqa*, that input can be intense. As the example above shows, the spectators have a more dramatic contribution to make. In the normal course of events, they serve as both backdrop and boundary for the playing area. When the performance turns to comedy, they become straight men and stage properties. In general, only the poor and unemployed have the time or the inclination to stand around watching the *ḥlaqi*, so the *rwais* have few reservations about manhandling members of the audience, or making them the butt of their jokes. But even tourists or the occasional wealthy Moroccan spectator are considered fair game for the musicians' humor, should they linger at the edge of the circle. It must also be noted that the spectators, for their part, are willing victims, enjoying the excitement and attention. In short, the *rwais* are willing to try anything to involve the audience in their act, in order to soften spectators up for the pitch, and elicit a more tangible contribution—money.

The request for money is always couched initially in religious terms; indeed, the pitch is called *fatḥa*, from the Arabic *al-fatiḥa*, the brief opening chapter (*sura*) of the Qur'an. The *rais* who "reads" the *fatḥa* calls on all present to hold out their hands and join him in prayer. He then goes through a long invocation to God, asking for blessings upon the King, his family, his army, and upon all believers. After each burst of blessings, the audience is asked to clap hands in unison, once, twice, three times, sealing the blessings as they come down from the sky. As this is going on, the leader or another member of the group begins to patrol the perimeter of the circle, looking for donations. At this stage of the afternoon (still only a half-hour into the performance), it is not necessary to pressure the crowd much, and four or five people make offerings before the collector gets half way around the circle. If a contribution is large enough (over 10 *ryals* or about 11¢),[9] the donor merits a special prayer, particularly if the musicians know the person or his family.

The *rwais* claim that they are not seeking money, only the blessings (*baraka*) that money can provide. When presented with payment in kind, however, the *rwais* use it as the subject of a brief, impromptu sermon to vary the *fatḥa* and enhance the object's value; then they try to convert the gift back into cash.

(A woman donates a candle.)

RMB: Ah, *rwais*.

All: Yes.

RMB: (Takes candle and tries unsuccessfully to stand it up on the ground.) Look at this candle. A woman has given it to us. Look there. (Points to the Kutubia minaret, where a light has just been lit to announce prayer time) It is sunset, the *maghreb*. The light on the mosque shows us the way to prayer. This candle is light. The woman has given us light. The Prophet is light, leading us to God. The King is light. This candle has light; it has *baraka*. The woman has given us *baraka*. What do you say, *rwais*? Rais Lahsen?

RLS: God help her.

RMB: Rais Mohamed?

RMM: God bless her parents. (And so on.)

RMB: Now, who wants to buy this *baraka*?[10]

Another device used to garner more contributions is to count the money gathered, announce the amount, and then ask the audience to round out the figure by adding a few *ryals* to make an even two *dirhams*, or five, or ten. The suggestion is that if the money is collected, the music will proceed, though that is by no means always the case.

The *rwais* push the *fatḥa* to the limits of tolerance, sometimes running it out for forty minutes at a time. In spite of that, a popular group seldom takes in more than 100 *dirhams* in an afternoon, and the normal take for a lesser known group is under 20 *dirhams*. If money is slow in coming in, the *rwais* take a hectoring tone, and the audience diminishes. Indeed, it is the dispersing audience more than the amount of money taken in which turns the *rwais* back to music. At times, they push their luck too far, and must start up again almost from scratch, or pack up their instruments and go home.

After the first introductory stretch of music and the first long *fatḥa*, the *ḥalqa* performance is a pastiche of music, comedy and pitch. Often, all three go on simultaneously. *Astara*, *amarg*, and *l-aḍrub* may be injected into performance, independent of one another. Only at the very end of the afternoon, as darkness falls, do the *rwais* again play a straight twenty minutes of music, relatively uninterrupted.

Usually, the *rwais* cannot resist a final pitch, but the last benefits may not be theirs alone. By general consent, as the *ḥalqa* draws to a close, beggars may come in and demand their share of the take. Though the musicians may initially try to resist or delay the incursion, they often end by making their pleas on the beggars' behalf, and allowing the invaders to take all the proceeds. In similar fashion, at a *suq*, a performer may distribute a share of his take directly to a group of assembled beggars.

Diagram 2 illustrates the flow of events in a *ḥalqa*. Performance is continuous, and may last for three hours or more; conversely, it may be rained out in five minutes. The line of characters indicates the normal progression through the first half hour or so of performance, by which time all performance elements have been introduced. It is significant that the *fatḥa* comes last, because, for the *rwais* at least, all events seem to build up to the

Diagram 2

Performance in the Ḥalqa

$\#H + S + (Q) + T + TS + D + Q + (S) + M + ((TS) + (D) + (Q)) + (C) + F\#$

H	Ti-n-lhalqt	(rapid pulse beat on naqus)
S	Astara	(instrumental prelude in free rhythm)
Q	Qtaᶜ	(short cadential formula)
T	Ṭbil	(dance overture in slow duple time)
TS	Tamsust	(accelerating bridge between sections)
D	L-Aḍrub	(rapid dance melodies in compound duple)
M	Amarg	(sung poetry)
C	Comedy	
F	Fatḥa	(prayer/plea for money)

( ) Optional segment

⌐⌐ Option to repeat segment

$\underline{\quad}_n^o$ Sequence of $\underline{n}$ different examples of same genre

$\left[\dfrac{-}{-}\right]$ Co-occurring segments

$[-]_n^o$ Simultaneous occurrence of $\underline{n}$ different realizations of same genre

$\emptyset$ Silence

$\underline{\quad}/$ May be accompanied by following segments

$D = D_n^o$

$D_n^o = D^1 + ((Q) + ((\emptyset) + (S))) + D^2 \ldots .D^n$

$M = M_n^o$

$M_n^o = M^1 + (TS) + ((D) + ((Q) + (S))) + M^2 \ldots .M^n$

$H = \underline{\quad} / \begin{bmatrix} \text{Tuning} \\ \\ [S]_n^o \end{bmatrix} \qquad F = \underline{\quad} / \begin{bmatrix} [S]_n^o \\ M \\ D \end{bmatrix}$

pitch. Parentheses indicate optional segments. For example, as we have seen, it is normal procedure to break from the first song directly to comedy or *fatḥa* (Diagram 2a, Sample Realization 1). From the *fatḥa* it is possible to return to any of the segments indicated by arrows, and begin the series of options again (Diagram 2a, Sample Realization 2).

Diagram 2a

Sample Realizations of Ḥalqa Performance

1. $\#H + S + T + D^1 + Q + D^2 + Q + \emptyset + S + D^3 + Q + S + M + C + F \ldots \#$

2. $\# \ldots F + \begin{bmatrix} F \\ D \end{bmatrix} + \begin{bmatrix} F \\ S \end{bmatrix} + M + D + Q + F + \begin{bmatrix} F \\ M \end{bmatrix} + D_5^o + Q + F\#$

Square brackets signify co-occurrence of several segments, as, for example, during the beating of *ti-n-lḥalqt*, when the musicians tune up and play separate *astaras*; or, again, during the *fatḥa*, when the group may play unrelated scraps of music while one *rais* gives the pitch. The sections marked M (*amarg*) and D (*l-aḍrub*) may themselves be broken up into a sequence of distinct musical segments. The composite nature of M and D is indicated in the rewrite rules below the diagram. The rules for enchaining and embedding *l-aḍrub* and *amarg* can apply in every performance situation. Indeed, it is customary to enchain as many as a dozen *ḍḍerb* melodies to extend a performance; the introduction of *qṭaᶜ* and, particularly, an *astara* between two *ḍḍerb* melodies usually signals a change in solo dancers. The enchaining of two songs, on the other hand, is quite rare in the *ḥalqa*, since the *rwais* do not want to give the audience too much music in return for the meager take.

While the outline of performance in Diagram 2 gives a good idea of the options open to the *rwais* for structural improvisation, it cannot convey completely the fragmentation of performance, which sometimes seems to border on musical anarchy. The music which accompanies the *fatḥa*, for example, is sometimes well coordinated and played by all members of the group while one silently takes up the collection. The pitch can, however, be as tiresome for performers as it is for listeners. To relieve the boredom, the *rwais* often converse among themselves, and occasionally one or more musicians may start practicing separate melodies. At other times, several musicians may strike up a song over the *fatḥa*, as a signal that they think the pitch has gone on long enough.

The *rwais* do not consider these random interjections a part of public performance so much as private communication between members of the group. Yet fragmentation is clearly inevitable given the nature of *ḥalqa* performance. The *ḥalqa* is in many ways the most challenging situation faced by the *rwais*. Their performance must be continuous and varied, lest the crowd dwindle. At the same time, the musicians must take time to organize the spectators into an orderly group, spaced as aesthetically and comfortably as possible. Above all, the *rwais* must persuade the audience, often as poor as the musicians themselves, to pay for the spectacle. Operating simultaneously as producers, directors, and performers in their own show, the *rwais* could scarcely avoid a certain amount of disorganization in their music.

The fragmentation of performance is also part of a conscious effort to create suspense and manipulate the audience. By playing on audience expectations, the *rwais* keep the crowd in suspense, all with a view to increasing their take. When a song is cut off, the response is to ante up immediately (if at all) so the musicians will get on with the show. Experienced *halqa*-watchers know that that is not a likely eventuality, and may begin to drift off as soon as the *fatha* begins. A random *astara* thrown into the *fatha* can stay this drift, by suggesting that the *rwais* are preparing to recommence. More often that not, that promise is not kept, but it may keep the crowd around until the musicians have exacted their toll.

Fatha and comedy are such a dominant part of the *halqa* that some *Ishlhin* (non-musicians) have suggested that *mashkhara* is actually the main attraction, and the audience does not expect to hear much music. Certainly the performance includes far more talk than music. In any case, while it must be admitted that the *halqa* often offers amusing drama, real aficionados of *amarg* must look for their entertainment elsewhere.

3. PRIVATE PARTIES

Starting with a naming ceremony seven days after birth, a number of events in a Moroccan's life are celebrated with private parties. Subsequent rites of passage include circumcision, engagement, marriage, the return from the pilgrimage to Mecca, and death. Annual events, such as national or religious holidays, or the felicitous resolution of personal crises, like recovery from illness or success in an important examination, may also serve as occasions for parties.

The particulars of each feast vary according to the event that motivates them, but the general characteristics remain the same. The parties are as large and lavish as the host can afford—and often somewhat more so. Most of the budget goes for food, including as much meat as possible, preferably from animals sacrificed for the occasion.

The celebrations require the participation of a person's entire alliance group; not just close family and friends, but the greater part of a village, or a tribal segment, or urban neighborhood. A marriage, in particular, is not the joining of two individuals to create a new family, but rather a new bond between two extended families which already exist, and which are very likely already linked. Indeed, for maximum size and economy, several weddings, or simultaneous weddings and circumcisions, may be organized jointly.

Ideally, the events should be sanctified by the recitation of the Qur'an by a group of *tolba* (religious scholars), though in fact the *tolba* are indispensable only at a funeral. On happier occasions, music plays a key role in the success of the party. Since many feasts are actually made up of a series of parties, spanning a period of several days and a distance of many kilometers, there can be several types of music, amateur, professional, or both.

The choice of entertainment depends less on the nature of the event celebrated than on the social context, urban or rural, surrounding the party. The urban-rural dichotomy in this case is not so much a matter of geography as of the background and taste of the host and guests. Recent immigrants to the city—particularly those living in shantytowns on the outskirts of town—tend to hold onto their country ways, while back in the village a school master or an emigrant laborer recently returned from Europe likes to exhibit his urbanity.[11] Thus, a "country" wedding can take place in the city, and vice versa.

The *rwais* are equally at home performing in the city or the country. However, under the influence of other groups of musicians with whom they share the limelight, the *rwais* modify their performance to suit the different audiences. In the country, an *ahwash* is the expected entertainment at any feast given by the *Ishlhin;* the *rwais* appear only when an *ahwash* is impossible, or when the host wants to display sophistication or conspicuous consumption. Among urbanized *Ishlhin,* the *rwais* are the preferred form of entertainment, but their music may be mixed with that of other professional groups from the Middle Atlas and the Atlantic plain. Since the *rwais* have been influenced by both the village music of the *tashlhit*-speaking region and the professional music of other areas, it is appropriate to examine briefly these contrasting styles.

"Ahwash" and Rural Parties

Literally, *ahwash* means "a dance" (from the *tashlhit* verb *hush,* to dance). Usually, however, the term is used to describe a complete piece, with successive emphasis on sung poetry, choral song, dance and drumming. More broadly, *ahwash* can be understood as an entire evening of music, or even music in general.

More than mere entertainment, *ahwash* is an integral part of a feast, and of village life in general. Participation in the dance is a way of expressing group unity. At the same time, it provides the opportunity to resolve social conflict. Feuding factions and individuals can argue the greater good in poetic duels (*abaraz*), and deviant behavior can be obliquely criticized. The dance also offers a suitable occasion for courtship, at least as much as courtship can be pursued under the eyes of several hundred relatives and guests.

The rules governing performance style and participation in *ahwash* change noticeably from village to village, yet there are certain elements of performance common to *ahwash* everywhere in the region. Performers may number as many as one hundred fifty or more, though somewhat smaller groups are more usual. The singers divide into two antiphonal choruses.

When both male and female villagers participate in the same *ahwash*, the choruses are sexually segregated.[12] The accompanists, from two to thirty in number, join in one of the lines, or form a third group. At the core of the participants is a group of specialists, sometimes called the *ait uhwash* (people of the *ahwash*), known for their passion for the dance and their skill as poets, singers, and drummers.

The principal (and often the only) accompanying instrument is the *tallunt*, a frame drum, sometimes equipped with a snare (*adinan*; cf. the Arab *bendir*). Other instruments may include the *bengri*, a side drum borrowed from the Gnawa brotherhood; *tiqarqawin* (Arabic: *qaraqeb*), metal double castanets, also borrowed from the Gnawa; the *naqus*; and the *tag^wmamt*, a six-inch, end-blown flute.

In many respects, *ahwash* and the music of the *rwais* are polar opposites. Though *ahwash* performers may be rewarded with special servings of food, gifts of clothing, or even cash, the *ait uhwash* are basically local amateurs, who perform only under inspiring circumstances. The *rwais*, of course, are professionals, most often brought in from outside the community. A minimum of fifteen performers is required to generate the collective energy necessary for *ahwash*. *Amarg*, in contrast, is an individualistic art; the *rwais* can barely sustain a performance with more than a dozen musicians. With the exception of the flute, an *ahwash* is accompanied entirely by instruments of percussion, particularly membranophones. The *rwais*, on the other hand, rely primarily on chordophones; the professionals almost never use drums in the *halqa* or rural weddings, and include the flute in their ensembles only in occasional recording sessions. In fact, the *naqus* is the only instrument truly held in common by the two styles.[13]

Despite these differences, however, *ahwash* is the principal source of the professional repertory. Without exception, the *rwais* are of rural origin, and grew up hearing and performing village music. *Ahwash* has provided a model for both the form and imagery of the *rwais'* poetry, as well as the basic elements of their musical style—responsorial melodic form, pentatonic modes, and compound meters. Although many *rwais* have now settled in the city, young musicians are still advised to travel extensively in the mountains, collecting melodies and scraps of poetry to weave into their own compositions. The influence of village music is most evident in *astara* and *l-adrub*, forms which the *rwais* attribute to the flute players of the Haha tribe. But professional musicians have borrowed widely from the village music of other tribes as well, fusing the diverse elements into the only style shared by all *Ishlhin*.

Ahwash has another, more subtle influence on the *rwais'* performance. The transmission of ideas between village and professional repertories is not unilateral. The *ait uhwash* listen to the *rwais* with special care, hoping to expand their own repertory with tunes and poems composed by the *rwais* or brought by them from other tribes. In any case, as poets and musicians themselves, villagers constitute a knowledgeable and enthusiastic audience. As a result, rural parties elicit from the *rwais* their most inspired performance.

An *aḥwash* is difficult to organize in the city. Few urban houses are sufficiently spacious for the requisite numbers of dancers and spectators. Further, while Agadir, Casablanca, and Marrakech all have substantial numbers of *Ishlḥin*, it is hard to assemble a large group from a single village, and nearly impossible to gather anything resembling the *ait uḥwash*. Finally, long-time residents of the city often lose their interest and ability to perform village music as they acquire some urban sophistication and a taste for other kinds of entertainment. Better then, they reason, to bring in groups of professionals to provide proper entertainment.

"Sheikhat" and Urban Parties

In the course of a single evening at a party in Marrakech, for example, one can hear several genres of music. A set of *amarg* may be followed by one of Middle Atlas music (*izlan*), and then music from the plains north and west of Marrakech (*ᶜaiṭa*). This mixture reflects both the mixed origin of the guests and the catholic taste of urban residents exposed to different kinds of music.

Though *amarg, izlan,* and *ᶜaiṭa* are all from different regions of southern and central Morocco, the three styles have much in common. The aspects in which *amarg* differs from village music—status of musicians, group size, and instrument type—are exactly those features which it shares with *izlan* and *ᶜaiṭa*. The *shiakh* (sing., *sheikh*; lit., old man, leader) of *izlan* and *ᶜaiṭa* are professional musicians of rural origin. Like the *rwais*, they are often itinerant and perform in small groups. *Izlan* and *ᶜaiṭa* are accompanied by a variety of drums, including the *bendir* (frame drum), *taᶜarija* (6-8 inch, single-headed hourglass drum), and *derbuga*. But the principal accompanying instruments are the *kaman/kamanja* (European violin or viola, played vertically), the *ginbri* (a three-stringed lute, similar to the *loṭar*), and sometimes the *ᶜud*. These chordophones, while not identical to the *rribab* and *loṭar*, at least correspond in type to the *rwais'* instruments.

Conversely, the elements of performance which *amarg* shares with *aḥwash* are precisely those which distinguish it from *izlan* and *ᶜaiṭa*. *ᶜAiṭa* is sung in dialectical Arabic, *izlan* in *tamazight* (Middle Atlas Berber); both languages are related to, but quite distinct from, the High Atlas dialect *tashlḥit*. The *shiakh* also use different musical languages. In contrast to the wide-leaping pentatonic melodies of the *Ishlḥin*, the melodies of the *shiakh* move sinuously through the neutral intervals of an Arab-influenced scale. Seldom exceeding an ambitus of a fifth, or at most an octave, the long phrases seem to make up in time what they lack in space. Though *amarg, izlan,* and *ᶜaiṭa* are all set primarily to compound duple rhythms, the Middle Atlas and rural Arab styles make frequent use of additive and asymmetrical patterns.

The separate influences of *ahwash* on the one hand, and ᶜ*aita*, above all, on the other, are reflected in the *rwais'* technical vocabulary. The terminology for music and poetry (e.g., *amarg, astara, tamsust*) is drawn primarily from *tashlhit*. In contrast, the term *rais* itself is an Arabic word, meaning leader (analogous to *sheikh*). The *rwais'* slang term for themselves, *lmherfin*, is similarly derived from the Arabic word for professional. More significantly, the names for the *rwais'* instruments have been borrowed directly from Arabic, and the terms *rribab* and *lotar* can be traced to a Persian origin. In short, it might be argued that the *rwais'* style originally developed as a composite genre, its content derived from Berber village music, and its instrumentation and organization provided by ᶜ*aita* or some similar style in the Arabo-Persian tradition.

In recent years, ᶜ*aita* and *izlan* have had a more direct influence on the *rwais*. Wealthy patrons may hire two or three separate groups, but hosts of more modest means seek both variety and economy. Thus there has been an increasing tendency among musicians to broaden their repertory to accommodate a variety of instruments and musical styles; as a purely practical consideration, such versatility increases the *rwais'* opportunities for employment. For example, one group of four musicians included two *rwais*, playing *rribab* and *lotar*, backed up by a *naqus* player and a decidedly non-traditional *derbuga*. In a set of *izlan* or ᶜ*aita*, the *bu naqus* assumed the role of lead musician, playing the ᶜ*ud*; the *derbuga* player retained his instrument; one of the *rwais* retuned his *lotar* in fourths to match the ᶜ*ud*; and the other *rais* played *bendir* or *naqus*, according to his mood.

Bi-musicality has had little effect on the content of *amarg*. A few examples of poetry have been translated into Arabic for the benefit of non-Ishlhin, and occasional snatches of diatonic melody may be injected into performance as a mark of virtuosity. For the most part, however, while the musicians have been acculturated, their traditional repertory has not. Thus, in a sense, when the *rwais* switch instruments and language to perform another kind of music, they cease to be *rwais*.

Certain external aspects of performance have, however, been affected by the association of *rwais* with other groups of professionals. In an urban context, as we have seen, drums have become an accepted part of the *rwais'* ensemble. But the most striking example of the influence of *izlan* and ᶜ*aita* is the use of female singers and dancers. Among the *Ishlhin*, these women are known as *raisat*, elsewhere as *sheikhat*.

In the Arabic-speaking tribes of the Atlantic plain, *sheikhat* are the most highly-valued entertainers. Male musicians (*shiakh*) are needed to form a back-up band, but women do most of the singing and drumming themselves. Arab *sheikhat* also improvise poetry and a few at least preserve esoteric knowledge of little-used musical forms. Among the *tamazight*-speaking Berbers of the Middle Atlas, professional musicians fall into at least two categories: the *Imdyazn*, who, like traditional *rwais*, are exclusively male, and combine high-minded religious and social commentary with slapstick comedy (Roux 1923 and 1929); and the *shiakh* of *izlan*, generally regarded as a lighter genre. The *shiakh* often perform alone, but *sheikhat* are indispensable for a full performance. In fact, in both the Middle Atlas and the Atlantic plain, female dancers are so important that ⁽aiṭa, *izlan*, and related styles are known generically as *sheikhat*.

Female dancers (*raisat*) are less essential to the *rwais*. The *rwais* themselves, as the performance in the *ḥalqa* demonstrates, are quite capable of putting on a complete spectacle of music and dance. At country weddings, too, the *rwais* often perform alone. Contrary to the beliefs of many of my village informants, the *raisat* are by no means all engaged in prostitution, but their frank use of sexual enticement in performance renders them unsuitable for appearance in many village situations. Among emigrant *Ishlḥin* in the city, on the other hand, the moral constraints that operate in the village become more relaxed. Further, since not all members of an urban audience understand or appreciate *amarg*, *raisat* broaden a group's appeal. Even the best *raisat* today compose no poetry, and so must depend on a *rais* to provide them with texts as well as accompaniment.[14] But many *raisat* sing well, and a few rank among the real stars of *amarg*.

The performance of the *raisat* suggests strongly that they are a product of Arab influence. During the performance of a song, the *raisat* dance in line, supporting the *naqus* beat with finger cymbals (*nuiqsat*, lit., little bells). Occasionally they move forward and back in line, bending deep at the waist with arms dangling, swinging their heads and shoulders in imitation of some *aḥwash* steps. The most important dance of the *raisat*, however, takes place during *l-aḍrub*, when the women move out from the line in pairs. They approach each other from opposite ends of the performance area, doing suggestive shimmies and rolls with their hips. After several passes in this fashion, they go down on their knees, facing each other. Arms akimbo, they shake shoulders and hips, and gradually arch their backs until they touch the floor, gyrating their pelvises in imitation of the sexual act. These steps—and the dancers themselves—could be substituted in a performance by the *sheikhat*. Indeed, while the *rwais* are inevitably *Ishlḥin*, a few *raisat* at least are natives of Arabic- or *tamazight*-speaking communities.

Private Parties: The "Rwais'" Performance

Private performance usually takes place in the courtyard of a house, or, in a village, on the threshing ground or other open area (*asarag*). Five to seven musicians is again the ideal size for an all-male group, allowing for four to six musician/dancers in addition to the lead singer and *bu naqus*. When *raisat* appear there may be six or eight dancers; three, or at most four, male musicians are considered sufficient for the back-up band. An all-male group is physically arranged just as in the *ḥalqa*. When the ensemble includes *raisat/sheikhat*, the women dominate the dance area; the men refrain from dancing, and cluster together off to one side.

Guests sit on benches, rugs, and mats laid out around the edge of the enclosure. At a men's party, urban or rural, the men spread out around the center of action, while women are tucked away in an inaccessible corner of the court, or, more usually, given an overhead view from the upper levels or roof of the house. At their own parties, women take ringside seats; in principle, no adult males are present, except the musicians, the host, and a few other men needed to help run the affair.

Performance is divided into sets, each a half-hour to an hour in length. The first set may consist entirely of *ṭbil* and *l-aḍrub*. Subsequent sets are made up of long, uninterrupted songs, interspersed with equally long passages of *l-aḍrub* and dance. The party may last until dawn, but between sets musicians are allowed to relax over tea, cookies, and a full meal.

Private performances are the *rwais'* main source of income. During the season of feasts in late summer and early fall, a competent group works at least several nights a week. At a good wedding, every member of the band can make 100 *dirhams* or more in a single night; musicians, and especially dancers, rely on their summer's earnings to help them survive months of unemployment in the winter or to pay off debts from the previous year.

Since the musicians are generally guaranteed a certain sum of money for private performance,[15] it is no longer necessary for them to "read" a *fatḥa*, nor yet to withhold music from their audience. Quite the contrary, the *rwais* are aware that the spectators may reward them for outstanding musical performance, but not for preaching and entreating. Thus, the *rwais* extend each piece to great lengths, often enchaining two or more songs.

Frequently, having completed a precomposed text, the *rwais* begin to improvise verses dealing with recent events of general interest, or with the party itself. These improvised verses can prove a fertile source for supplementing their guaranteed income. The lead singer, with the help of a member of the wedding, if necessary, sings several lines about each guest, mentioning him by name, and discussing the nobility of his parents, children and profession. Often these are mere formulaic lines, with slots for the subject's name, village, and so on. A good poet, well acquainted with his subject, makes his description more precise. Whenever inspiration fails, however, the poet returns to his stock phrases, over and over again.

The praise-singing (known as *tashajiᶜt*, from *shjiᶜ*, the Arabic word for encouragement) recalls the days, as recently as twenty-five years ago, when the more powerful Berber *qaids* (tribal governors) kept personal troupes of *rwais* or *raisat* to entertain and sing of their master's ancestry and exploits. The *rwais* still reserve their most effusive praise for their most generous and powerful supporters, but any guest at a private party may be the subject of *tashajiᶜt*. In return, of course, the honored guest is expected to become the singer's patron, at least for the moment. In fact, the *rais* will continue to sing about a spectator until the latter comes forward with a bill, a coin, or some other symbolic contribution. In this way, the *rwais* can more than double the amount of money promised them by the host. Indeed, during the winter, when jobs are scarce, a group may agree to perform at a party for no fee, counting on the revenues from *tashajiᶜt* to make their appearance worthwhile.

For the connoisseur of *amarg*, *tashajiᶜt* is a more pleasant method of extracting money than the *fatḥa*. Praise songs would not, however, bring good results in the *ḥalqa*. *Tashajiᶜt* depends for its effectiveness not on the satisfaction of the subject alone, but on the effect that the praise (or threat of criticism) makes on other listeners. Each new name is greeted with cheers from the audience, though whether this is out of agreement with the sentiments expressed by the *rais*, or from pleasure at seeing an acquaintance put on the spot is not always clear. In any event, the subject cannot disappear into the crowd, as he might in a *ḥalqa*. Peer pressure forces some sort of contribution, even if the donor has to borrow the money to do so. The better known the *rais*, the greater must be the gift. However, success is never a foregone conclusion, even for the most famous musicians; sometimes an individual, or an entire audience, may turn a reluctance to pay into a negative judgment of the performance as a whole.

The *raisat* have their own methods of gathering extra money for the group. Since they are not generally poets or improvisers, songs of praise fall outside of the repertory of most *raisat*. The best singers may be rewarded spontaneously by exuberant guests, simply on the strength of their performance. Most *raisat*, however, rely on the dance. By dancing up to a likely guest and going down on one knee in a shimmy, a *raisa* virtually guarantees herself a tip. Just as in *tashajiᶜt*, it is considered bad form for anyone singled out for this treatment to reject the suit.

The *raisat* also soften up their patrons between sets, sitting among them, with much hand holding and nuzzling, a technique which usually earns them larger tips, or at least a few free cigarettes. This behavior is tolerated, if not always sanctioned, by everyone present at the party. Those who feel they cannot (or dare not) participate in such extra-musical activity, for moral or financial reasons, have the sense to withdraw from the front line of spectators.

A *fatḥa* may occur—particularly in the country—right after the opening set, as part of the introduction of performers, or at the very end of performance. In this context, however, the primary recipients of both blessing and profits are the host and the object of the feast, the newlywed couple, newborn child, successful candidate for the baccalauréat, or whatever. At a country wedding, some sort of *fatḥa* is part of the ritual, and a specialist—not one of the musicians—is called in to handle it. The take may be phenomenal, running into thousands of *dirhams*; the proceeds help to defray the cost of the feast and, if anything is left, to give the young couple a start in life.

Comedy has a place in private parties, but here again speech is isolated from musical entertainment. Except for occasional crashes into *bu naqus*, the random slapstick which characterizes comedy in the *ḥalqa* is limited. For the most part, however, comedy at a party is the province of specialists.

If one of the *rwais* happens to be a *baqshish* (comedian) as well, he may be given the chance to do his routine between sets of music.

Similarly, a village often has its own amateur theater group, which may perform during an evening of *ahwash*, or between sets by the *rwais*. These presentations are more elaborate than the comedy routines of professional musicians. Costumes are made in advance, and half a dozen or more men and boys dress up as women, Jews, old beggars, thieves, urban merchants, and other characters (including *rwais*) despised or feared by villagers. These little plays enjoy a suspension of shame, and, like *ahwash*, serve as a vehicle for working out tensions within society (Berque 1955: 252).

Diagram 3 outlines the format of the *rwais'* performance at a private

Diagram 3
Private Performance

$$\#(H) + S + T + TS + D^o_n + Q\# \quad (F)$$

$$\#S + M^1 + (((TS) + (D)) + ((Q) + (S))) + M^2 \ . \ . \ .M^n + D^o_n + Q\# \quad (C) \quad (F)$$

H	Ti-n-lhalqt
S	Astara
Q	Qta^c
T	Tbil
TS	Tamsust
D	L-Adrub
M	Amarg
C	Comedy
F	Fatha

( )	Option to eliminate segment
$\_^o_n$	Sequence of $\underline{n}$ different examples of same genre
$\left[\overline{}\right]$	Co-occurring segments
$[\overline{}]^o_n$	Simultaneous occurrence of $\underline{n}$ different realizations of same genre
$\emptyset$	Silence
$\_/$	May be accompanied by following segments

$$D^o_n = D^1 + ((Q) + ((\emptyset) + (S))) + D^2 + \ . \ . \ .D^n$$

$$H = \_ \ / \ \begin{bmatrix} \text{Tuning} \\ [s]^o_n \end{bmatrix}$$

party. All the elements of the *halqa* are present in private performance, but the act progresses in a more orderly fashion. Additional boundary markers (#) indicate that private performance may be divided into sets, unlike the *halqa* which proceeds in a continuous, if choppy, flow. At the same time, each set lasts up to forty-five minutes or an hour, which is longer than any stretch of music in the *halqa*. The expansion of performance by the enchaining of songs and *l-aḍrub* is a key feature of private parties. At urban parties, *amarg* and *l-aḍrub* are balanced, with perhaps a slight emphasis on dance music. At a country party, the classic example of private performance, the focus of attention is on *amarg*. This emphasis is represented in the diagram by placing the rewrite rule for M_n^o in the main sequence of segments.

Fatḥa and comedy, the main detours from *amarg* in the *halqa*, have been relegated to optional status. Strictly speaking, they are no longer a part of the *rwais'* act, since they are frequently eliminated, or performed by people other than the musicians. Even if performed by the *rwais*, comedy and *fatḥa* are isolated from the rest of performance. They take place during clear breaks in the music, rather than being linked directly to it.

The gradual change of emphasis from *amarg* in a rural situation to dance in an urban context is indicative of deeper changes in the lives and music of the *rwais*. Performance of *aḥwash* in the country uncovers the roots from which the *rwais* have sprung. The use of *raisat/sheikhat* and the mixture of styles at a wedding in town show the directions in which the *rwais* have been branching out.

4. COMMERCIAL ESTABLISHMENTS

Performance by the *rwais* in the *halqa* or at a private party remains much as it was a half century ago or more. However, under the French Protectorate (1912-56) there arose new performance situations which would have been impossible without twentieth-century technology and the social and economic changes brought by colonialism. The most obvious technological change was the development of broadcasting and recording techniques, whose impact will be discussed below. In this section, we are concerned with another legacy of colonialism—the commercial exploitation of music.

Four different types of commercial establishment offer performances of Moroccan music, including *amarg*: 1. cabarets; 2. tourist restaurants; 3. tent theaters; and 4. cinema/concert halls. Performance in these establishments, even more than at an urban wedding, is characterized by the use of *raisat/sheikhat* and by the mixed ethnicity of both audience and performing groups. The distinguishing feature of these performances, however, is the alienation of musicians from the audience. Not only is the physical and social distance between performers and audience greater than in traditional situations, but the flow of money and the reciprocal flow of blessings which linked musicians and spectators has largely been diverted through a third-party intermediary, the entrepreneur.

Cabarets

Some *rwais* claim that performance in night clubs, and the concomitant use of *raisat*, goes back only to the 1960s. A few older *rwais*, however, can recall working in *quartiers réservés*, such as BuSbir Jdid in Casablanca, as early as the 1930s. Prostitution was, of course, the raison d'être of these legal redlight districts. The French administration was prepared to tolerate prostitution as a necessary evil, even during a period when it was forbidden in France, for the benefit of colonial troops and entrepreneurs, as well as the new wave of immigrant laborers from the countryside. Song and dance were meant to set the proper mood, and allow the women to display their charms.

The *quartiers réservés* are long gone, and prostitution is illegal in independent Morocco, but today's cabarets are left-overs, in spirit if not in fact, from colonial days. The cabarets are most numerous in Rabat and Casablanca, European-style cities par excellence; but wherever they are found, the cabarets are inevitably located in a new quarter of town, one of the areas designed and built (with Moroccan labor) by Europeans and for Europeans. Today a typical cabaret audience consists almost entirely of urbanized Moroccan men, but alcohol and women remain the principal enticements.

In order to attract the ethnically diverse urban audience, a night club show offers a variety of acts, including Middle Eastern style music, western-influenced popular bands, folk-revival groups, or popular folk musicians like *rwais* and *sheikhat*. In all, relatively few cabarets employ *rwais* on a regular basis—half a dozen in Casablanca, two or three in Rabat and Agadir, and one or two (intermittently) in Marrakech. Yet almost every *rais* seems to pass through the cabaret circuit at one time or another. A few find the situation to their liking, and end up working permanently in one cabaret or another. Most, however, find conditions unsatisfactory, and, after a month or two, leave to seek their fortune elsewhere.

The pay in a cabaret is adequate if not generous. In 1976, one top *rais* received 75 *dirhams* a night for a limited engagement, and one or two others could command 50 Dh a night, seven nights a week for a year or more. Such high fees are rare, however, and most musicians average about 20 Dh a night, with dancers making somewhat less.

Praise-singing produces limited results in a cabaret, where most spectators are unknown to the *rwais*, but performers do have ways of supplementing their fixed salaries at the expense of the audience. Between acts, dancers, and to a certain extent musicians, are expected to mix with the audience. The *raisat/sheikhat* in particular act as B-girls, encouraging customers to drink, and getting a few (watered) drinks for themselves.[16] For every drink they consume, the dancers receive a percentage of the take at the bar.

If the customer is a *tashlḥit*-speaker, the *raisat* may try to learn his name, to feed it to the *rwais* for later use in *tashaji^ct*. In any case, a customer singled out for attention from a *raisa* may also be expected to hang a bit of money on her as she dances. The combination of wine, women, and song sometimes proves overwhelming. An emigrant worker on the way home from France, a man with a month's pay in his pockets, or someone just out to paint the town red may want to express his appreciation for the performance by indulging in conspicuous consumption. Fifty or one hundred *dirham* notes may find their way into a *raisa*'s belt or bodice, or tucked under a *rais'* turban. On one occasion, I saw a man in a Casablanca cabaret decorate four *rwais* and six *raisat* with a total of 1900 Dh (about $400). His act was not quite as generous or foolish as it first appeared: there is an understanding that the musicians will keep only 10 percent of such outlandish tips, and return the rest during a break in performance.[17] With money and alcohol flowing so freely, however, some miscalculations are inevitable. When the man went to recover his money, he came up short by some 200 Dh. In this instance, the *rwais* were innocent of deliberate deception; either the man had not kept a proper count, or several of the thirty-odd bills had fallen off the *rwais* and gotten lost in the shuffle. In another case, however, a young *rais* reported that when a spectator came to collect his change for 300 Dh, the leader of the group patted him on the back, and, saying, "I'm glad you enjoyed the show," walked off with the money.

Ultimately, even these windfalls are small recompense for the hazards of cabaret performance. The musicians are seldom in immediate physical danger, though an inebriated spectator can cause some unpleasantness. The schedule, however, can be taxing. While each group only puts on about four sets, a half-hour to forty-five minutes in length, the entire performance lasts from 10:00 in the evening until 4:00 or even 6:00 in the morning. In time, the hours, the drinking, and the general atmosphere have a corrosive effect. During the winter months particularly, musicians and dancers run constant risk of illness, or worse.

RLI: Have you heard about Raisa Khadija? She died, poor thing, right in the middle of the cabaret.

RLS: Really? God have mercy on her, poor thing. What happened?

RLI: Well, she was singing, and she grabbed her chest and fell down. They took her in the back room, and then drove her to the hospital, but she was dead. Her heart, they said.

RLS: God have mercy on her. Whisky and cigarettes, that's what ruins all those *raisat*. Have you seen FT lately? Her voice is gone. A year ago she had the best voice around, but smoking and drinking have spoiled it. And *look* at her, it's terrible. She'll be the next to go.

Tourist Restaurants

Working conditions in a tourist restaurant are far less deleterious to a musician's health, if not his art. Like other stops on a guided tour, tourist restaurants offer a taste of Moroccan life which is neither too raw nor too spicy. Architectural design and music are meant to enhance the impression of a meal in a Moroccan home, but all along the line concessions are made to European preferences. The decor is traditional but sterile; most tourist restaurants are located in converted bourgeois houses; others are in hotel dining rooms or contemporary restaurants decorated with traditional tile, plasterwork, and carpets. Customers sit on *banquettes* around low, circular tables, but they eat their individual portions with a knife and fork, rather than dipping bread in a communal bowl. The food itself is an imitation of Fes cuisine, washed down with wine and *eau minérale*. Indeed, the music served up to the tourists may be the most unadulterated item on the bill of fare, but it, too, has been diluted for the occasion.

More than any other situation, a job in a tourist restaurant demands versatility at the expense of virtuosity. In hopes of maintaining the attention of uninitiated foreigners, some restaurants even try to duplicate the musical diversity of the Marrakech Folklore Festival. At the same time, managers are loath to hire more musicians than are absolutely necessary. Thus the Marrakech Casino, for example, offers up to a dozen different acts (including belly dancers, acrobats, *rwais*, *izlan*, ᶜ*aiṭa*, *gedra* from the Sahara, and communal music from the Atlas mountains) all drawn from a pool of three groups of musicians. None of the group line-ups is precisely traditional, but of course the tourists do not know the difference.

The audience's lack of understanding does not preclude a favorable response to the music, nor does it necessarily dampen the *rwais'* enthusiasm for the job. Some performers, in fact, consider the audience as one of the rewards of working in a tourist restaurant, and delight in recounting anecdotes of colorful touristic behavior. The musicians came to entertain, and were themselves entertained. Furthermore, though the musicians rarely receive the extravagant tips offered at weddings or in night clubs, they sometimes pick up 10 German Marks or even 50 French Francs for posing for pictures; they also have the occasional opportunity to sell a musical instrument or article of clothing for a handsome profit.

Pleasant working conditions in tourist restaurants help to compensate for the relatively poor salary, from 10 to 25 Dh a night. Moreover, the early performance time (8:00-12:00 in the evening) often permits the musicians to play at a wedding once they have finished their regular job. Indeed, many *rwais* feel that a tourist restaurant offers ideal working conditions; they complain about the job only when the management falls behind in payment, or when working hours come in direct conflict with a more interesting and lucrative private party.

Tent Theaters

Tent theaters (*sirk*, cf. the French *cirque*) first appeared as side-shows in the Franco-Algerian circuses of the nineteenth and early-twentieth centuries. Though they can still be found adjacent to more usual carnival attractions, like octopus rides and wheels of fortune, the theaters are under independent management, and often travel alone. They are most frequently set up near large country markets and, particularly, at religious and secular fairs, like the *musem* (saint's festival) of Mulai Brahim in the High Atlas, or the Taroudant district craft and agriculture fair.

The *sirk* is a hybrid, a small concert hall with the mobility of a *ḥalqa*. The structure itself is a rectangular enclosure made of wood-framed metal panels, with a bare floor and a roof of canvas and plastic. The entire edifice can be struck in an hour and loaded on the roof of a bus for transport to another site. What the *sirk* lacks in stability and elegance, it makes up for in fanciful decoration. Large murals, inside and out, depict dancing girls, musicians, famous landmarks, and *trompe l'oeil* courtyards and gardens. The paintings are usually muted and worn from extended travel, but a freshly painted theater is truly stunning.

The theaters hold about one hundred people, seated on folding chairs or narrow benches, but they rarely seem filled to more than half capacity. Low ticket prices (50 centimes to 2 Dh) make a *sirk* almost as accessible as a *ḥalqa*. Country markets, and especially fairs, attract many visitors from the city, but most theater customers are countrymen. Unlike the cabarets, however, it is at least possible for a respectable woman (accompanied by children or female friends) to enter without compromising her virtue.

Performance conditions in a *sirk* are less than ideal. The stage, elevated about three feet off the ground, measures approximately 10 feet by 20. For a group of four *rwais* and six *raisat*, that leaves barely enough room to stand in comfort, and dance movements are necessarily restricted. Each act is allotted ten to twenty minutes per show. If a group seems to be going overtime, the master of ceremonies cuts the performance short by running across the front of the stage, dragging the light curtain behind him. Between sets, the band retires to a little cell of a dressing room next to and under the stage, where there is barely enough room for the whole group to sit down, much less to entertain friends and admirers.

All in all, the *sirk* offers a bargain show to its customers. The performers, however, come out badly in the deal; for as little as 5 Dh a day (and no tips), they must do an average of one set an hour for up to ten or twelve hours on end. Not surprisingly, the rigors of the show are reflected by the performers who display, by turns, indifference, giddiness, and exhaustion.

Cinema/Concert Halls

Concert performances by the *rwais*, though rare, are the embodiment of the alienation common to all commercial performances. Understandably, with ticket prices ranging from 5 to 20 Dh or more, audiences do not flock to hear music which could be observed elsewhere in more exciting or less expensive circumstances. The concert stage creates a literal gulf between performers and audience, a gap which the *rwais* at least are ill-prepared to bridge.

Concert tours, within Morocco or for emigrant laborers in Europe, are generally built around popular recording stars with a national following. These are, for the most part, Egyptian-influenced popular singers, such as Abdelwahhab Doukkali and Abdelhadi Belkhayat, or western-influenced folk revival groups, such as Nass el Ghiwane and Jil Jilala, whose entire production is geared to a mass audience. Such groups sing almost entirely in dialectical Arabic, the most widely understood language in Morocco; they draw from both foreign sources and from a variety of styles within Morocco, so their appeal is not limited to any single ethnic group. The singers, and the genres they represent, are known primarily through records, radio broadcasts, and television appearances. They make live appearances on occasion at private parties for the wealthy, or in the more exclusive night clubs of Casablanca, but the majority of their fans, young city-dwellers, can see them perform live only in concert.

Audiences expect lengthy concerts of up to four hours, and to satisfy that demand, promoters bring in a long string of warm-up groups, including comedy teams, *sheikhat*, *rwais*, or other regional groups. The *rwais* may broaden the appeal of the concert in Europe, where emigrant *Ishlḥin* might be equally attracted by modern styles as well as by their own traditional music, and where the entire audience might welcome any act as a reminder of home. Within Morocco, however, there is little overlap between fans of the *rwais* and fans of the modern popular groups; even the greatest *rwais* are essentially unknown outside *tashlḥit*-speaking communities. Thus, in a mixed concert, they are passed off as "folklore," a colorful relic of Morocco's past, a symbol of cultural nationalism with no intrinsic interest of its own. This intellectual concept holds little appeal for most concertgoers, who feel that such acts only delay the awaited appearance of the featured performer. Arab *sheikhat* can command the attention of the crowd with their racy lyrics, and Middle Atlas groups at least use familiar instruments. The *rwais*, however, are unique in their language, melodic settings and instrumentation, and thus have little hope of reaching an audience of non-*Ishlḥin*.[18]

The *rwais* have difficulty reaching the audience in a more literal sense as well. Like other popular folk groups, they simply do not produce a large enough volume of sound to fill a hall of five hundred or one thousand seats; the amplification systems available to most small groups are barely acceptable in a cabaret or tent theater; in a large hall, the poor amplification renders the music so incomprehensible it might as well be inaudible. Much of the music is inaudible anyway, since accompanists frequently have no microphones for voice or instruments. Dance survives the transition to the concert stage somewhat better, though not without undergoing some changes. The proscenium arch collapses dance patterns from three dimensions to two, and the subtlety of some dance movements is lost in the shadows of poor lighting, just as the subtlety of melodic variation is buried in the cacophony of poor electrical connections.

The physical setting of a Moroccan concert hall (almost inevitably a movie theater rented for the occasion) does not inhibit audience behavior. Quite the contrary, the audience behaves as much as possible as though the performance were private. Comments on performance are frequently shouted out over a continuous hum of conversation. The audience, bored and anxious to get to the main act, can be merciless to an unknown warm-up group; but each song by a favorite performer is greeted with cheers and cries of encouragement. Yet even in those concerts actually organized as private parties to celebrate national holidays (cf. Waterbury 1972: 86-88), where tea and cookies are served to warm the atmosphere and the *rwais* receive a favorable response, neither the audience nor the musicians can completely overcome the separation imposed by the stage.

The Alienation of Performance

In any commercial establishment, the *rwais* are doubly alienated from the audience. They are either isolated up on a stage, or separated from the audience by a symbolic barrier of tables. More important, in most of these situations, *Ishlḥin* make up at best a minority of the audience. In the tourist restaurants, most customers are not even Moroccan. Yet the young, urban audiences at cabarets and concerts are often no less estranged from the music: the *rwais* most often do not represent the places from which they have come, and certainly do not point in the direction they would like to go.

The lack of rapport between musicians and audience is exacerbated by the financial arrangements in commercial establishments. Aside from occasional gratuities, money moves from spectator to performer in two discontinuous steps; the customer pays an entrepreneur, and the entrepreneur pays the musician. That in itself breaks an important bond between musician and spectator, and makes the entrepreneur the most important member of the audience. Often, however, the entrepreneur is reluctant to complete the second step, and the performers may not be paid for months, if at all. The *rwais* can expect little redress in such situations. Most cannot afford to go to court, and if they quit or strike, they may lose not only their jobs and back pay, but also the opportunity to work in other commercial establishments. The *rwais* can express their dissatisfaction only through their performance, which thus often reflects both indifference towards the customers and hostility towards the management.

Commercial Performance

The exigencies of performance in a commercial situation bring about a restructuring of the *rwais'* act. The *rwais* have only a limited time (generally less than half an hour) to complete each set, and the audience expects a tightly organized spectacle. Thus, for example, musicians tune up before stepping out in front of the audience; since their presence alone signals the beginning of performance, *ti-n-lḥalqt* is no longer necessary. Slapstick routines are barred from the act; comedy, when not inappropriate to the situation, is performed by specialized troupes of actors or comedians. The *fatḥa* is likewise eliminated; it would be ineffectual in a concert hall or tent theater, and simply ludicrous in a tourist restaurant or cabaret.

Amarg, too, is sharply curtailed in favor of dance. Where other aspects of the *rwais'* performance seem foreign to non-*Ishlḥin,* the dances of the *raisat,* so reminiscent of the *sheikhat,* strike a familiar note. Even tourists can understand the highly colored costumes and suggestive movements. Indeed, the *raisat* dominate performance to the point that *ṭbil,* whose accompanying dance is sedate and masculine, may be eliminated.

These changes are reflected in Diagram 4. The form of performance is

Diagram 4

Performance in Commercial Establishments

$$\#(S + T + TS + D + Q) + S + M + TS + D^1 + ((Q) + ((\emptyset) + (S)))...D^n + Q$$

S	<u>Astara</u>
T	<u>Tbil</u>
D	<u>L-Aḍrub</u>
Q	<u>Qṭa^c</u>
TS	<u>Tamsust</u>
M	<u>Amarg</u>
$\emptyset$	Silence
( )	Optional element

$$M^o_n \longrightarrow M^1 + (((TS) + (D)) + ((Q) + (S))) + M^2 \ldots M^n$$

much the same as in private parties, but with a different emphasis. It is still possible, for example, to enchain several different songs (M^1, M^2, . . . M^n), but since the songs are no longer the featured part of performance, the enchainment has been reduced to a rewrite rule. On the other hand, the enchainment of *l-aḍrub,* which accompanies the *raisat's* dance, has been elevated to the main sequence, since it may take up as much as two-thirds or more of performance time.

In the end, the effects of the commercial situation can be felt more in the quality of performance than in its form. As a result of the alienation in commercial establishments, performance tends to be perfunctory. Dancers often go through the motions of performance with very little spirit, and sometimes even refuse to do solos. While the leader sings, the *raisat* may pull at each other's clothes and make private jokes, and they are frequently out of tune in their responses. The musicians, too, may be out of step or out of tune with each other. All of these failings may occur from time to time in other situations as well, of course, but when musicians have more reason to please the audience, they take more care with their performance. In any case, the responsive atmosphere of a private party encourages the musicians to make corrections, while in the *ḥalqa* the flaws are easily integrated into a comedy routine. In commercial establishments, on the other hand, the flaws are literally spotlighted; worse, the indifference or hostility of the audience gives the musicians little reason to correct their mistakes. In short, the tightest of all live performances in form, commercial performance, is also the most haphazard in execution.

5. THE MEDIA

Electronic media play a small but influential role in the musical life of Morocco. Three media—phonograph discs, radio, and cassette tapes— provide at once the rarest and most common performance situation for the *rwais*. This apparent paradox is, of course, not at all contradictory, since the electronic preservation of sound allows the infinite reproduction of music without the presence of musicians. Indeed, the most prominent characteristic of media performances, beyond the limits imposed by a common technology, is the complete isolation of performer from audience, and of the experience of performance from the experience of listening. The influence of the media, however, is not confined to the recordings alone, because the very existence of recordings has altered the concept, content, and execution of live performance. In broader terms, the media have affected the attitudes of the general public towards the *rwais*, and the *rwais'* own ideas about themselves.

The three media are interrelated technologically, sociologically, and economically, but they have all had different effects on the lives and music of the *rwais*. Therefore I shall sketch briefly the institutions behind each medium before examining their influence on musicians and audience.

Records

By all accounts, the first commercial recordings of the *rwais* were made in 1931. The honor of precedence usually goes to el-Hajj Belaid ((Blᶜid) (Chottin 1933: 15; Galand-Pernet 1972: 171). With his group, Hajj Belaid accompanied the Sultan Mohamed V to Paris for the 1931 Colonial Exposition, at which time Belaid apparently recorded several songs for the Franco-

Lebanese label, Baidaphon. At any rate, one of his earliest recordings *amuddu s bariz* (the *Trip to Paris*, Baidaphon 98809/10; Galand-Pernet 1972: 46-50) has that trip as its subject. If Belaid was indeed the first, he was quickly followed by others, including Mohamed Sasbo, BuBker Azaʿri, BuBakr Anshad, and Rzuq. These early recording artists are still regarded as the finest *rwais* of this century, if not of all time.

Belaid's *Trip to Paris* indicated a path, literally and figuratively, for other *rwais* to follow. For the next twenty-five years, the production and distribution of records were controlled by European (mainly French-based) companies: Pathé, Polyphon, Gramophone (His Master's Voice), Baidaphon, and Philips. The Moroccan (Algerian?) company Boudroiphone may have been founded in the early 1950s, but basically the local record industry did not get its start until after Independence (1956), when business opportunities opened up for Moroccan entrepreneurs.

Since the late 1950s, most, but by no means all of the primary production of records has been done in Casablanca. The development of the 45 rpm record, with a lower cost per unit and greater playing time than the old 78s, undoubtedly helped the growth of the local industry. The cost of records remains relatively high (in 1977, 5-7 Dh for a single 45 rpm disc of medium-poor quality), however, because mastering and pressing continue to be done in France.

Until the mid-1970s, there were perhaps two dozen small record companies based in Casablanca, with names like Boussiphone, Casaphone, Atlassiphone, and Ourikaphone. (Since 1977, most of these companies have switched to cassette production, or have gone out of business; there has been virtually no new production of disc recordings.) Generally, these companies have been named for the home territories of their owners (e.g., the Atlas Mountains, the Ourika Valley), or simply for the owners themselves (e.g., Ahmed Boussif, the artist and repertory [A & R] director for one of the first French labels to record in Morocco, and the founder of Boussiphone). Most companies specialize in one kind of regional music, though they are open to diversification.

Since the mid-1960s, the dominant force in the Moroccan record market has been SMEDIP—the Sociéeté Marocaine d'Edition et Distribution de Phonographes—exclusive importer and distributer of many Middle Eastern and European labels. A SMEDIP subsidiary, Koutoubiaphone, is the largest locally owned record company in Morocco. With its organized distribution system and corporate resources, the company has established a virtual monopoly over the top performers of *amarg*.

Koutoubiaphone offers a fee of 1500 Dh per song to its most popular singers; less known *rwais* settle with smaller companies for 250-500 Dh per record. From that, the leader must cover the cost of sidemen, though the record company may pick up travel expenses. The fees are not high by western standards, but they do constitute relatively generous pay for a day's work, since a group usually records several songs in a single session.

A recording date thus pays better than all but the most lucrative private party.

In discussing their recording careers, however, the *rwais* often seem less concerned with pay than with prestige. The number of records to a *rais'* credit is an important criterion in determining his status within the society of professional musicians. The prestige also brings financial benefit which endures long after the initial recording fees have been spent, since a well-known *rais* can expect frequent, high-paying jobs at private parties.

The *rwais* perceive these and other blessings as flowing directly from a single source—the producer or A & R director for the company. The producer is the *rwais'* most powerful and exacting patron. He chooses both the personnel and the material (usually love songs) to be recorded. He may have contacts at the radio station and on the cabaret circuit, to guarantee air time for his product, and regular employment for his protégés. For favored clients, the producer may provide loans or advances against future recordings. In short, the producer has a good deal of control over a musician's personal and professional life. Small wonder, then, that the *rwais* are careful to cultivate good relations with record company executives. As a mark of respect, the *rwais* may wear full performing garb in the recording studio, when performing before a handful of technicians and executives, and thousands of unseen future listeners. More important, to ensure continued favor from producers, many *rwais* have been willing to cede residual rights, or even part of the advance, to the producer or his company.

A *rais'* involvement in a record essentially ends when he leaves the studio. He has had the aesthetic satisfaction of performing before a few connoisseurs, and he has already received most of the money he will get from the record. Later, the existence of the disc may add considerably to his stature, but little to his pocketbook. Sales determine who will be asked to record again, but most *rwais* have earned little or nothing from royalties. Indeed, until 1977, only one of my informants claimed to have received any royalties at all, and these payments seem to have been more in the nature of an informal retainer, to guarantee his loyalty to the company. Copyright organizations have only recently begun to attract wide interest among the *rwais*. One *rais*, for example, had recorded over fifty songs before he applied for membership. Ironically, his application came just at the time when cassette piracy forced companies to cease production of new records of *amarg*.

The Radio

Radio broadcast facilities were established in Morocco during the early years of the Protectorate, but not until the coming of Independence did the radio begin to speak for Moroccan national interests rather than for those of the French administration. With the appearance of transistorized portable radios, the medium extended to villages in the deepest reaches of the High Atlas, while short wave carried Moroccan broadcasts to emigrant workers in Europe.

The Radiodiffusion-Télévison Marocaine (RTM) has three principal networks, which operate 18-20 hours a day. In addition, there are numerous local stations which broadcast over the national network, or on local frequencies for at most a few hours a day. All are government controlled. Of the three networks, one broadcasts entirely in Arabic, one in French, and one in a variety of languages—English, Spanish, and three Berber dialects. The government maintains Berber-language broadcasts to serve—and to placate and propagandize—the Berber-speaking population, but government support for the broadcasts (or any manifestation of Berber culture) cannot be too generous lest it provoke opposition charges of sectarian and neo-colonialist policy.

Programming in *tashlḥit* has increased considerably since the 1930s, when, according to one RTM employee, there was one fifteen-minute news summary each week. Today, the daily *tashlḥit* broadcast from Rabat runs from 8:00 P.M. till midnight. The local station in Agadir offers a few additional hours of programming, alternating between Arabic and *tashlḥit*. Not only is the Berber broadcast limited in time, vis-à-vis French or Arabic, it is also limited in budget and technical assistance. Both stations are received with difficulty, and sometimes disappear from the airwaves for several days in succession. As one mountain man put it: "Berbers have the same rights on the radio as a bicycle on the highway."

In spite of limited facilities, the radio is important to the government, to the *Ishlḥin* in general, and to the *rwais* in particular. As part of the Ministry of Information, RTM is an educational-political vehicle, broadcasting the government's version of the news, and offering several public service broadcasts, like *Sn tamazirt-n-k, iᶜadl a-t-tsint* (know your country, it is good to know about it) which explains Moroccan history, geography and economics, or *isseqsitn ddin* (Questions on The Religion, i.e., Islam). One weekly broadcast (*Abaraz n Ait Umarg*, the battleground of the people of *amarg*) is devoted to news of the *rwais* and analysis of their songs. Produced by Ahmed Amzal, *Abaraz* is a mixture of new releases, interviews, critiques, and biographies of various *rwais*, as well as letters and poems from listeners, and even an occasional contest.[19]

Public service programs present the royalist view of the world, and seek to integrate Berbers into the general national culture, while at the same time attempting to purify Berber dialects by eliminating regional expressions and Arabisms. When possible, radio functionaries try to use music to further these institutional goals. The budget provides for honoraria of up to four or five hundred *dirhams*, to pay for occasional songs praising the King and his family on such holidays as Independence Day and the Feast of the Throne. In exchange for the commission, RTM reserves the right to dictate themes and even specific words to be used in the song text. The radio archives contain enough songs of praise to fill the broadcast hours during the week surrounding any national political holiday.

For country Berbers, the radio provides entertainment and education. At the same time, it is a reminder of home to urban and emigrated *Ishlhin*. By offering such services as song dedications (often to or from relatives in Europe) and appeals to missing persons, RTM actively helps to unite the dispersed population of *Ishlhin*.

For the *rwais*, the radio has been both a proving ground and a barometer of public opinion. Until very recently, original RTM recordings and interviews with young musicians often created demand for a *rais'* music, and thus helped launch a recording career. Then, air play, especially on *Abaraz*, could determine the commercial success of the record. Finally, in the long run, repeated exposure and favorable comment on a *rais'* output can still help establish a musician's general reputation.

Like record producers, radio programmers and announcers have power disproportionate to their numbers. For the most part, RTM personnel exercise this power very conservatively. Young, western-oriented Berber groups have been discussed at length on the *tashlhit* broadcast, but the programmers refuse to sanction the acculturated groups by giving them air time.[20] RTM personnel are equally conservative in their views of traditional music; several announcers privately prefer *ahwash* to the *rwais*, and old *amarg* to new.

The bulk of the radio play list is drawn from a relatively small selection of commercial records; many of these are old 78s. RTM is frequently approached by *rwais* offering new *amarg*, but the programmers, bound by both personal taste and bureaucratic restrictions, seem reluctant to capitalize on these opportunities. Indeed, throughout the mid-1970s, announcers frequently lamented the apparent death of *amarg*, taking as evidence the dearth of new commercial recordings. RTM personnel were well aware that the moratorium on new releases was instituted by the record companies themselves, for economic, not artistic reasons. Yet announcers reserved their criticism for the *rwais*, without recognizing publicly the real cause of the companies' decision: the undermining of record sales by pirate cassettes.

Ultimately, *tashlhit* programming on the radio may be hurt nearly as much as the record industry by the growth of cassette recording. Young musicians seem as eager as ever to have exposure on the radio; but by 1980, when new production of *amarg* had been almost exclusively on cassettes for more than two years, RTM still had no cassette playback facilities. Meanwhile, aficionados of *amarg* have been turning more and more to the new medium, which gives them more control over the music they hear, both old and new, without the prohibitive expense of buying records.

Cassettes

In 1970, there were scarcely any cassette tapes or recorders commercially available in Morocco, outside the cosmopolitan markets of Tangier, Rabat,

and Casablanca. By 1975, cassette recordings had practically driven discs off
the market. Sales of urban music were hurt, though records by folk revival
groups and Egyptian-oriented popular singers continued to turn a profit.
Cassettes met with such success in rural markets, however, that record sales
fell to nothing, and the companies felt obliged to suspend new production of
rural popular music.

Cassette machines were apparently first imported to the mountains by
emigrant laborers returning from Europe. Introduced to tape recording
abroad, the emigrants saw the machines as a way of carrying a bit of home
back to their jobs after vacation. Arriving *en masse* from France, Belgium,
Holland, and Germany, the emigrants brought tape recorders to capture the
ahwash, which is not readily available on record. Today, an *ahwash* seems
almost incomplete without a small Stonehenge of recorders in the middle of
the dance-ground, to immortalize the performance. Cassette machines, particularly the popular *combinaison* of recorder and radio, also made ideal
gifts, permitting taped correspondence between parents, often illiterate, and
their scattered children.

The *rwais* make no strong objection to the presence of tape machines at
their own performance. The musicians realize that these amateur recordings
may cut into their commercial sales, but they do not want to alienate any
guests. Besides, by turning the audience's attention to a tape recorder during
a round of *tashaji⁢t*, a *rais* can usually exact a good tip from the owner of
the machine. But while these recordings are almost always of such poor
quality that they pose little threat of commercial exploitation, they do
inhibit a singer's poetic expression. Connoisseurs are aware, even as they
preserve a performance on tape, that the performance may suffer from their
efforts:

PDS: How did you like HMLD tonight?

BBS: There were too many people at the wedding, too many outsiders. Some of us
didn't even get anything to eat.

HUB: That's the way it is with him. Everybody wants to see him . . .

BBS: But he didn't say anything new.

HUB: What do you expect? With all those cassette recorders, he won't say anything new, and he won't say any strong words.

In other words, knowing that his performance was being taped, the *rais*
limited his considerable powers of poetic improvisation. He "said" (sang) no
new songs for fear that other *rwais* might learn the songs and record them
commercially before he did. And he uttered no "strong words" (i.e., songs
of moral or, particularly, political commentary) lest the recording reach the
wrong ears and lead to repercussions.

A more serious problem, from the *rwais'* point of view, has been the
growth of cassette piracy. Early in the 1970s, one or two electronics shops in

Tangier, run by Indian merchants, began offering tape copies of European and Middle Eastern records to their clients, mostly foreigners and affluent Moroccans on holiday from inland cities. Within three years, stacks of pirate recordings (primarily of Moroccan music) were being sold openly on street corners and in shops. These tapes often include a cover photo, copied from the jacket of one of the pirated discs, complete with serial number and company logo.[21]

In many cases, record stores have become little more than cassette factories, filling tapes with recordings selected by individual customers. This practice has become so widespread that the largest record shop in Imi n Tanut (in the High Atlas), which carries an exhaustive catalogue of *amarg*, refused to sell me any discs, preferring to keep only one copy of each record for duplication on tape. By charging roughly a *dirham* for each record copied, record dealers are able to clear the same profit as on the actual sale of a disc, without the inconvenience of maintaining an inventory. Even with the cost of a blank cassette (which yields additional profit to the dealer), a customer realizes substantial savings over the cost of buying individual records. Obviously the saving is still greater should the customer choose to record a new group of songs over a set no longer in favor.

The companies cut their losses by halting the production and distribution of records of many varieties of music, including *amarg*. The freeze, lasting nearly two years, was a particularly frustrating time for the *rwais*. Established musicians lost whatever royalties they had been earning, and rising young musicians lost the opportunity to boost their careers with new recordings.

At the same time, the *rwais* were also quick to see the advantages of the new medium. They roundly cursed the pirates, but they bought machines and tapes for their own use and enjoyment. Cassettes were clearly a powerful educational tool. The tapes permitted musicians to familiarize themselves at leisure with the songs of their well-known colleagues. By taping their experiments and new compositions, the *rwais* were able to evaluate their own work, and keep a record of their ideas. These same tapes could also serve as a medium of exchange, in the form of gifts to friends, family and patrons. For a time, it appeared that some *rwais* might go even further, and take commercial production into their own hands. With my assistance, one *rais* produced a master tape of one of his more popular songs (recorded for the radio, but unavailable commercially), and sold it to a record dealer for distribution on cassette. Another *rais* contemplated the possibility of setting up his own company to produce commercial cassettes.

Eventually, in the fall of 1977, several established companies re-entered the market with new, copyrighted material on cassettes. Encouraged by the low capital outlay required to produce cassette recordings (at a minimum, only two tape machines are needed), a number of new companies joined the competition; one of these, at least, was operated out of a small record store that had, until recently, been turning out pirate recordings.

Unlike a 45 rpm record, which could hold at most two songs, each new cassette release contained six or eight new pieces. Thus, though the established *rwais* had accumulated a backlog of unpublished material, they were often unable to keep up with the demand that had built up in their audience during the two years' drought. The competition, and the relatively low risk involved, persuaded many companies to bring out recordings by previously unpublished performers, both young and old. Within a matter of months, relatively unknown *rwais* had as many as twenty songs on the market, a feat that would have taken years under the old system, if it had been possible at all. Advances on recordings, even from the smaller companies, often rose as high as 10,000 Dh or more for each set of songs, thus proving competitive with Koutoubiaphone's old price of 1500 Dh per song. Furthermore, those *rwais* who had enrolled in copyright organizations began to collect regular royalties for the first time.

The boom in legal cassettes had already begun to fade by the summer of 1980. Legally produced tapes with copyright stamps range in price from 11 to 30 Dh depending on the label and type of music. Pirate producers, paying nothing for studio time, recording fees, or royalties, can copy the same material onto inferior tape, and sell their cassettes for as little as 5-7 Dh, the price of one 45 rpm disc, and less than half the going rate for legal cassettes. The *rwais* continue to talk enthusiastically of new compositions and projected new releases, but the pace of production has clearly slowed. Thus, cassettes, which have already brought the *rwais* famine and feast in turn, may once again bring famine.

The Listening Audience

Amarg can be heard crackling over small speakers in simple rooms in the Barbès neighborhood of Paris and the isolated oasis of Tata, in the shanty-town hovels and palatial villas of Casablanca. Wherever the *Ishlhin* find themselves, the disembodied voices of the *rwais* perform daily before audiences who may not see the musicians in the flesh more than once a year, if that. Indeed, listening to *amarg* via the electronic media is so commonplace that during broadcast hours, on certain streets in the old quarter of the larger Moroccan cities, the pedestrian can hear an entire song, relayed from shop to shop as he passes.

Given the size and scope of the listening audience, its members cannot be easily characterized in terms of their social or economic status. They must, however, include the *rwais'* most dedicated partisans. With the choice of at least three stations, tuning in to the *tashlhit* broadcast involves a conscious choice to listen to the *rwais*. The radio offers none of the visual spectacle of the *halqa* or tent theater to attract idle listeners strolling across the dial.[22] In other words, the non-*Ishlhin* who frequent live performances are filtered out of the radio audience. This is still more true of record and cassette buyers, who must pay to hear their choice of music without the additional inducement of alcohol or dancers.

Finally, just as the *rwais* often put on their finest clothes to record in the studio, so the listening audience often conforms to rules of behavior appropriate to a live performance. Specifically, rural listeners may segregate themselves by age and, above all, by sex. A mountain man explained this as he switched off the radio after the news:

There is probably no harm in listening to the song they announced, you're right. But you can never tell what the *rwais* are going to say. And with my sister and her daughter here in the room, it would be shameful for us to hear that sort of thing together.

Recorded Performance

The stages of production that come between an initial performance in the studio and the final product heard by the listeners inevitably affect the *rwais'* music in a number of ways. The capabilities and limitations of the recording studio itself, for example, directly determine group configuration. Most recordings by the *rwais* are made with only one or two microphones. Microphone placement favors the lead singer, and makes the chorus of three to four *rwais* or *raisat* sound remote. The possibility of rehearsal and multiple "takes" also benefits the leader by allowing each published song to approach perfection. For the sake of balance and clarity, the instrumental group is kept to a minimum, with no more than one *rribab*, two or three *loṭars*, and a *naqus*. In addition, the flute (*tag^wmamt*) appears on recordings by one or two artists, and a few other *rwais* have experimented on record with more exotic instruments, like the *ʿud* or violin. Because of tuning difficulties, especially between the *rribab* and flute, such innovations are rarely carried over into live performance.

A recording is the shortest of all performances by the *rwais*. The early 78s held only three minutes on a side; microgroove 45s carry twice that, but even two- or, more rarely, four-sided songs are shorter than most sets in live performance. The few long play or extended play records that have been produced do not begin to exploit the possibilities of a larger format. Short performances have been equally prevalent on radio and cassettes. Indeed, at one recording session for RTM, a group of young *rwais* stopped dead several times in mid-performance, and then resumed the same song, or started a related piece, after a short pause. As the musicians explained, "That is the way songs are on the radio." Apparently they did not realize that such breaks stemmed from time limitations of a disc, not the performance criteria of RTM or the limits of tape supply. While experience with cassettes has accustomed musicians (and listeners) to uninterrupted performances, the length of recorded songs has not increased significantly.

In fact, six minutes is usually ample time to convey those segments of performance which can and need to be included in a recording. A record is not a miniaturized abstraction or compression of live performance. Rather, it is a truncated version, with many of the appendages and trappings of live performances atrophied, or sloughed off altogether.

Diagram 5 outlines the format of one side of a record. This pattern may be repeated with variations up to four times, on the four sides of extended-play 45 rpm discs needed to hold a long narrative song. The same pattern

Diagram 5
The Recorded Song

$$\#(S) + M + (TS) + (D) + (Q)\#_4^o$$

S	Astara
M	Amarg
TS	Tamsust
D	L-Aḍrub
Q	Qṭa^c

( )   Option to eliminate segment

$\underline{\quad}_n^o$ Sequence of $\underline{n}$ different examples of same genre

:   Division between sides of a record

Sample realizations

1. $\#S + M^1 + Q : S + M^1 + TS + Q\#$

2. $\#M^1 : M^2 + TS + D + Q\#$

3. $\#S + M^1 + TS : M^2 + TS + D + Q\#$

can also be found in original cassette releases, without, of course, the break in performance between sides. All elements other than *amarg* are optional; when present, the additional segments are reduced to a simple frame for the song text. A recorded *astara*, for example, seldom exceeds thirty seconds. The prelude is shortened not only to allow more time for *amarg*, but also because it is no longer necessary to warm up the musicians. By the time the *rwais* have rehearsed and recorded a usable take, they are more than warmed up. Further, on record the *astara*, like the *qṭa^c*, is superfluous as a boundary marker; recorded performance has its own idiomatic framework in the spoken announcement of singer and company at the beginning of a record, and silence (or scratches) at the end. Thus, as Sample Realization 2 shows, *amarg* may stand completely alone.

The absolute limitations of time on a disc may lead to a break in the music at what would be, in live performance, a capricious moment. This brings to the fore another performance element—*tamsust*, the accelerating bridge between two songs (M¹ and M²) or between *amarg* and *l-aḍrub* (M and D). In recorded performance, *tamsust* often becomes a bridge to nowhere, and so takes on a bounding function more prominent than in its role in a live situation.

It might be argued, however, that the exigencies of time have had less effect on recorded format than has the isolation of the musicians from their audience. Recordings of extended instrumental passages, for example, have found little or no place in the catalogues of commercial record companies or on the playlist of RTM. One or two *ḍḍerb* melodies may be used to fill out a side of a record and give a suggestion of a complete performance, but *ṭbil* recordings are practically nonexistent. For the listener, instrumental music, unlike *amarg*, must always be incomplete in a recording, because the sound media cannot reproduce dance, its complement and *raison d'être*. Without the atmosphere and visual stimulation of live performance, the *Ishlḥin* do not care to listen to music without words.

The *rwais'* slapstick comedy must also be seen to be appreciated. The few comedy records available in *tashlḥit* have been made not by *rwais* but by comic specialists (*baqshish*). Even these, like comedy records everywhere, have met with little success, because good comedy depends on a kind of spontaneity and surprise (even if contrived) which seldom survives repeated playings of a record. Finally, the effectiveness of *tashajiᶜt* and, particularly, *fatḥa* depends even more than comedy or dance on direct interaction between performers and spectators. Both are pointless without the immediate inspiration and tangible response of a live audience.[23]

In short, a recording is the most tightly structured of all performances by the *rwais*, with none of the surprises, detours and silences which heighten the excitement of live performance. On first hearing, however, recorded performance is not always completely predictable. Sample Realization 3 represents the most typical pattern for a 45 rpm record, but the body of recorded music encompasses practically all the possible variations suggested by Diagram 5.

The current model of recorded performance imposed itself on the music only gradually. The early 78s, though shorter than modern recordings, actually bear more of the earmarks of live performance. The records were the result of as few takes as possible, so mistakes are not infrequently heard —coughs, or silence in the middle of a line when the singer or chorus forgets the text. Sides begin and end almost inevitably with *astara* and *qtaᶜ*, even when both sides are devoted to one song (Sample Realization 1).

The early 78s also include some performance elements which have long since disappeared from commercial recordings. Some early Odeon 78s, dating from 1931, apparently include two sides of *ṭbil* and three sides of *l-aḍrub* (Chottin 1933: 15). One *rais*, Mohamed u Draa, made a record for Gramophone with *amarg* on one side and comedy on the other. Another *rais* managed to close a recording with a line of *tashajiᶜt* for Ahmed Boussif, who had arranged the session. Even in the early days, such carry overs from live performance were never common, and as recording and marketing techniques improved, they were weeded out altogether.

Beyond Performance

Recordings have had relatively little influence on the form of live performance. The *rwais* do not try to reproduce a recorded song word for word or note for note; even those *rwais* who perform no songs of their own composition still give a personal interpretation to the borrowed melodies, and manipulate each text to serve the needs of the situation. In short, the *rwais* weave the song into the format appropriate to the occasion, with improvised lines, *l-aḍrub*, and a full dressing of other performance elements.

On the other hand, records have had a marked influence on the concept of performance. Recording jargon gives the *rwais* the means to describe the complete progression of performance from *astara* to *qtaᶜ*, a phenomenon for which no word exists in the musicians' traditional vocabulary. The term *disk* (cf. the French *disque*) or its loose Berber equivalent *tawriqt* (from the Arabic *warqa*, a sheet of paper or anything flat) is not limited to records alone. It can refer to a song text, or even to a single part of the text. One *rais* (HOW), for example, mentioned a *disk* he had composed in honor of a wealthy hotel keeper; when pressed for clarification, he explained that he had been talking about a few lines of *tashajiᶜt* attached to a longer song. On another level, after a performance the *rwais* frequently evaluated each other's performance, commenting first on the *disk* as a whole, then zeroing in on one element or another, the *astara*, the song text, and so on. Extending the analogy still further, when discussing a performance with two enchained songs, the first (M^1) was known as the *disk* proper, and the second (M^2) as *l-fas* (from the French *deuxième face*, that is, the second, or "flip" side). Finally, it is worth noting that the format for recorded performance corresponds most closely to the *rwais'* own model.

In still broader terms, the media have given the *rwais* a new history and hierarchy. Traditionally, the *rwais* have been ranked by their colleagues and their audience on the basis of their musical, poetic and choreographic ability on the one hand, and on their age, experience and moral rectitude on the other. Initially, the early recordings changed neither the relative ranking of the *rwais* nor the nature of the hierarchy. The prestige of some musicians was enhanced, but this only reaffirmed, and slightly exaggerated, their existing status. With the passing of years, however, the reputation of the early recording stars has continued to grow.

Professional genealogies, like the social/biological genealogies of mountain tribes, have always been shallow, rarely reaching beyond three or four generations. Hajj Belaid would undoubtedly be remembered today even if he had not been the first to record. Yet, coincidentally or not, the *rwais* cannot recall any notable musician before Belaid's time, except the semi-legendary Sidi Hammu (Johnston 1907), who may or may not have been a *rais*. Perhaps in the normal course of events, even a *rais* of Belaid's stature would soon fade from memory, fifty years after his peak, and thirty years after his death. The phonograph, however, has given the *rwais* a recorded history, insuring that Belaid will never be forgotten, at least as long as copies of his discs survive.

Many of the old songs remain in the *rwais'* repertory, and excerpts from them continue to crop up in "new" compositions. To judge from the songs of Sidi Hammu, this practice of reworking old poetic and musical ideas goes back well before Hajj Belaid's day.[24] The existence of recordings has given Belaid and others permanent claim on certain turns of melodic or poetic phrase, removing them from the public domain. Thus, though the *rwais* continue to recycle traditional material, no modern *rais* can hope to approach his predecessors' reputation for originality and inspiration.

The large-scale production of 45s during the 1960s and early 1970s added new criteria—wealth and popularity—to status ranking among *rwais*. Even the richest *rais* is poor by the standards of some Arab and Western popular singers, but a few recording stars have at least been able to invest their advance payments in property, thus enabling them to live at a standard unknown to their predecessors and most of their contemporaries. Others have accumulated capital in legends, by squandering their money with memorable profligacy. Similarly, even the most popular of the *rwais* has not attained a following comparable to that of his Arab and Western counterparts, yet some *rwais* are still content to measure success simply by the number of their songs on record or the number of requests for their music on the radio.

In sum, the media have vulgarized *amarg*, in both the English and French senses of the word. In the French sense, that is, to popularize, the media have disseminated the music of the *rwais* to a larger, more dispersed audience than would ever have been possible under traditional circumstances. Radio, in particular, has brought *amarg* to many listeners who often have neither the occasion to see live performance nor the means to buy commercial recordings. If the *rwais* have not always enjoyed the fruits of this popularity, some at least are wealthier than they might otherwise have been.

The media must also assume responsibility for the vulgarization of the *rwais* in the English sense—that is, their cheapening or coarsening. First, the marketing of a recording demands that the song be both short and non-topical. Exposure to Arabic and Western popular music via the media has also given both the *rwais* and their audience a taste for the explicit treatment of banal themes. The radio has undermined the *rwais'* entertainment value as the model of professional competence and the only alternative to a regimen of village music, by offering a vast smorgasbord of musical styles at the twist of a dial. Finally, RTM has also usurped the *rwais'* role of journalist and intermediary between tribes.

Over the past five years, the cassette tape has become the dominant medium in Morocco, and it seems likely to continue to dominate other media for the foreseeable future. The wide distribution of cassettes has brought the production of discs to an end, and drawn attention away from RTM as the main source for *amarg*. But the medium has been at best an ambiguous oracle. The introduction of cassettes has not put control of production of recorded *amarg* into the hands of the musicians, as some hoped it would; nor has the sale of pirate tapes totally deprived the *rwais* of royalties or the opportunity to record, as many still fear it might. Indeed, the position of the *rwais* in the media will remain uncertain until the problem of piracy, which appears to be on the increase around the world, has been resolved.

Ultimately, the effect of cassettes on the *rwais* cannot be reduced to simple economics. Like records, which have helped shape the *rwais'* concept of history, and like radio, which has usurped some of the musicians' roles, cassettes may have their greatest influence on the social organization of the *rwais*. Young performers have taken to cassettes enthusiastically as a study tool. This may result in a generation of highly competent musicians with unusually large repertories. But, by eliminating the need for a traditional, itinerant apprenticeship, it could also cut the *rwais* off from their roots.

6. SUMMARY AND CONCLUSIONS

Considering the four performance situations together (Diagram 6), it is clear that each one emphasizes a different aspect of the *rwais'* act. In the *ḥalqa*, verbal entertainment, *mashkhara* and *fatḥa*, is given the most play. Music and dance seem almost to be transitional interludes between rounds of comedy and pitch; songs in particular are kept to a minimum. At a private party, the *rwais* sing freely and at great length, performing songs which may be long to begin with, and which the musicians extend with improvised verses of praise. These long songs are balanced by equally long passages of dance music. Comedy and prayer, if used at all, are performed in isolated segments of performance, between clearly defined sets of music. In commercial establishments, dance receives the greatest attention. Song may remain a prominent part of performance, but it is clearly subsidiary to dance. Finally, in the electronic media, *amarg* dominates the short performance. The key element has been underlined in each diagram.

The selective emphasis on one aspect of performance or another in each situation can be traced directly to the physical ambiance, the nature of the audience and the *rwais'* relation to it. In the *ḥalqa*, the scale of performance, the proximity of performer to audience, and the means of collecting

Diagram 6
Form in Performance (Recapitulation)

1. The Rwais' Model of Performance

$$\#S + \underline{M} + TS + D + Q\#$$

2. The Ḥalqa

$$\#H + S + (Q) + T + TS + D + Q + (S) + \underline{M} + ((TS) + (\tilde{D}) + (Q)) + \underline{(C)} + F\#$$

3. Private Performance

$$\#(H) + S + T + TS + D_n^o + Q\#\quad (F)$$

$$\#S + \underline{M^1} + (((TS) + (D)) + ((Q) + (S))) + M^2 \ldots M^n + D_n^o + Q\#\quad (C)\quad (F)$$

4. Commercial Establishments

$$\#(S + T + TS + D + Q) + S + M + TS + \underline{D^1} + ((Q) + ((\emptyset) + (S))) \ldots D^n + Q\#$$

5. The Recorded Song

$$\#(S) + \underline{M} + (TS) + (D) + (Q)\quad \#_4^o$$

H	Ti-n-lhalqt
S	Astara
Q	Qta^c
T	Tbil
M	Amarg
TS	Tamsust
D	L-Adrub
C	Comedy
F	Fatha

payment lead to direct interaction between the *rwais* and individual spectators. Musicians and audience play a kind of cat and mouse game; the *rwais* try to wring the last centime out of the crowd, while the spectators try to hear as much *amarg* as they can for the smallest possible contribution. Competition between musicians and audience is further fostered by a kind of benign mutual disrespect.

At a private party there remains a kind of intimacy between the *rwais* and their audience. The *rwais*, however, behave in a manner appropriate to the more formal occasion, in hopes that their deference will appeal to the audience's sense of honor. The audience is assumed to include aficionados

Diagram 6 continued
The Rwais' Model of Performance[5]

#	Boundary of piece
( )	Optional segment
↓⌐	Option to repeat segment
$\underline{}_n^o$	Sequence of $\underline{n}$ different examples of same genre
[⁼]	Co-occurring segments
[_]$\underline{n}^o$	Simultaneous occurrence of $\underline{n}$ different realizations of same genre
∅	Silence
____	Featured element in performance situation
__/	May be accompanied by following segment

$$M = M_n^o$$

$$M_n^o = M^1 + (TS) + ((D) + ((Q) + (S))) + M^2 \ldots .M^n$$

$$D = D_n^o$$

$$D_n^o = D^1 + ((Q) + ((\emptyset) + (S))) + D^2 \ldots .D^n$$

$$H = \underline{} / \begin{bmatrix} \text{Tuning} \\ [S]_n^o \end{bmatrix}$$

$$F = \underline{} / \begin{bmatrix} [S]_n^o \\ M \\ D \end{bmatrix}$$

of *amarg*, and that inspires the *rwais* to put on their best, most complete performance. Song and dance are apportioned equally at parties, but the balance may shift towards one or the other depending on the context of the party (rural or urban) and the taste of the guests. Knowledge of the audience (expressed in *tashajiᶜt*), combined with tight performance and social deference are all meant to elicit greater contributions from the spectators.

In commercial establishments, the intimacy is broken; musicians and audience are separated physically, and often culturally. The audience frequents the establishments for a variety of reasons, but the *rwais* are generally at best a secondary attraction. The *rwais* therefore emphasize dance, the element of their act most easily accessible to a distant audience. Beyond that, the audience has little effect on the progress of performance. The *rwais* depend more on a regular salary from the management than on direct contributions from the spectators. The management in turn is concerned primarily with the punctuality and physical presence of performers, especially the *raisat*. The performance therefore becomes predictable and ofter, perfunctory.

Finally, in the media, the separation of *rwais* and audience is absolute. For that very reason, the media audience is assumed to include the *rwais'* most devoted fans, since they must listen to the *rwais* more from choice than circumstance, with no visual distractions. *Amarg* is the only element of the *rwais'* act that comes across intact in a recording. Other elements, which can be appreciated and inspired only by a live audience, must be cut.

NOTES

1. A brief pronunciation guide is in order. The phonetic system of *tashlḥit*, the dialect of *tamazight* (Berber) spoken in Southwestern Morocco, is subject to numerous regional variations. For example, the phoneme *gh* (roughly equivalent to an exaggerated Parisian *r*) in the western High Atlas, is pronounced *kh* in the central High Atlas, and *ḥ* in the Sus region. Thus *nigh* (I said) is pronounced *nikh* in the central High Atlas, and *niḥ* in the Sus. Similarly, in certain areas of the western High Atlas, in the Mtougga tribe, for example, *k* is often pronounced *sh*, so that *l-ḥakim* (judge or official) and ᶜAbdelKrim (a name) become *l-ḥashim* and ᶜAbdelShrim. Similarly, *t* sometimes becomes *s*. Most *tashlḥit*-speakers are aware of these differences, and are able to understand the different local pronunciations without difficulty. Nonetheless, misunderstandings sometimes arise. During the colonial period, for example, a tax collector is said to have asked a mountain farmer how many cows he owned. The farmer replied "she died" (*tmut*), which in his dialect was pronounced *smus*. The tax collector, however, confused *smus* with *semmus* (five) and duly taxed the farmer for five cows (Mohamed Najmi, Personal Communication).

In transcribing *tashlḥit* words, I have chosen to use the phonetic system found in most dialects of the western High Atlas. These are the dialects spoken by the majority of my informants, and the ones with which I am most familiar. Furthermore, the phonetic system of the western High Atlas is close to that of Moroccan Arabic, so the Arabic origin of many words remains clear in the transcription. I have tried to make the transliteration of words in *tashlḥit* and Moroccan Arabic sufficiently accurate to be of use to linguists and Moroccanists, without causing inordinate difficulties for other readers.

Transliteration	Description	Arabic Equivalent
a	low central vowel	‍ا
b	voiceless bilabial stop	ب
d	voiced dental stop	د ‍،‍ ذ
ḍ	emphatic, velarized voiced dental stop	ض

Transliteration	Description	Arabic Equivalent
e	schwa	
f	voiceless labio-dental fricative	ف
g	voiced velar stop	گ
gh	voiced uvular fricative; like Parisian r	غ
h	voiceless glottal fricative; like English h	ه
ḥ	voiceless pharyngeal fricative; like h in stage whisper	ح
i	high front vowel	(ي)
j	voiced alveo-palatal fricative; like French j in je	ج
k	voiceless velar stop	ك
kh	voiceless uvular fricative; like German ch in Bach	خ
l	dental lateral	ل
m	bilabial nasal	م
n	dental nasal	ن
o	mid-high back vowel	و
q	voiceless uvular stop; q in the back of the throat	ق
r	dental flap	ر
s	voiceless dental fricative	س

Transliteration	Description	Arabic Equivalent
s̩	emphatic, velarized voiceless dental fricative	ص
sh	voiceless alveo-palatal fricative	ش
t	voiceless dental stop	ت ، ث
t̩	emphatic, velarized voiceless dental stop	ط ، ظ
u	high back vowel	و
w	bilabial semivowel	و
y	palatal semivowel	(ي)
z	voiced dental fricative	ز
'	glottal stop	ء
--c	the Arabic letter ^cain; voiced pharyngeal fricative; rather like the sound of clearing the throat	ع

---

2. The bulk of research of which this study is based was carried out between 1975 and 1977 in Marrakech and a number of villages in the High Atlas and Sus regions of southwestern Morocco. The fieldwork was made possible by an International Doctoral Research Fellowship from the Social Science Research Council and the American Council of Learned Societies. Additional research was carried out in the summer of 1980, supported by a grant from the Council on Research in the Humanities of Columbia University. Earlier drafts of the paper have been read by Jere Bacharach, Carol Eastman, Robert Garfias, Fredric Lieberman, and Lorraine Sakata, all of the University of Washington. Their comments have been greatly appreciated; any flaws in the study, factual or theoretical, are my own responsibility.

3. The first union of *rribab and loṭar* may have taken place as recently as the late nineteenth century. Hajj Belaid, the most respected *rais* of this century, claimed to have been the first to implement the idea (Chottin 1933: 18). The staccato notes and trills of the *loṭar* provide the perfect complement to the sustained notes and *portamenti* of the *rribab*. Today, each instrument sounds naked without the other; the *rwais* maintain, however, that the instruments were initially so difficult to tune together that the first pair of musicians to try had to tune up for three days before they could play as an ensemble. The Berber *rribab* should not be confused with the *rebab andalusi*, a two-stringed boat fiddle used in Andalusian court music.

4. Migration is no longer entirely temporary. More and more *Ishlḥin* are bringing their wives and children to live with them in the city. The younger, urban-bred generation of *Ishlḥin* has little nostalgia for the mountains, and less taste for the music of the *rwais*.

5. The symbolic system chosen to represent the flow of segments in musical performance was inspired by Irvine (1974). The symbols resemble those used by linguists, but I do not mean to suggest any analogy between this analysis and transformational grammar. It has been shown repeatedly that musical analysis can be made to look like a transformational grammar in the Chomskian mould, but that is not my purpose here. Whereas linguistics deals with single words or relatively short utterances, the discussion here concerns the enchainment of larger elements, without considering their internal structure. Furthermore, transformational grammars do not deal with actual performance, which is, of course, the focus of this paper. However, I see no reason not to borrow such an economical symbology, whose meaning is well established, and can be easily explained or reinterpreted. After all, the linguists originally took their system from mathematics, logic, and the natural sciences. I am indebted to Carol Eastman for her help in producing this third generation (bar sinister) symbolic system.

6. Orthodox Muslim feasts and holidays are not tied to any particular season of the year. The Muslim calendar has 12 lunar months of 29 or 30 days, for a total of approximately 354 days. Events in the Muslim calendar therefore fall 10-12 days earlier each year in the solar calendar. When Ramadan coincides with the peak of the summer's heat, as happened in 1980, hunger, thirst, and the threat of sunstroke keep both performers and audiences off the square even in the late afternoon. As a result, virtually all afternoon activity ceases; many groups like the *rwais*, who would normally never play in the marketplace after dark, begin their performances only late at night, by the light of rented pressure lamps.

7. At one time or another, the city government has proposed various measures for regulating the number, type and location of musicians on the square. Various commercial interests have lobbied to turn all of Jamaᶜ l-Fna into a parking lot or developed real estate. A number of sources, including Eleanor Roosevelt and several musicians still active on the square, have claimed credit for interceding with the King or his late father to avert this tragedy. Nevertheless, Jamaᶜ l-Fna has changed along with the rest of the city. Wood-framed shops have replaced the tents shown in photographs from the 1920s, for example; and parked cars and motorbikes have taken over extensive areas once occupied by flea markets on the square itself and at its perimeter.

8. All unattributed quotations are taken from my own fieldnotes, 1975-77 and

1980. To protect the anonymity of informants, most musicians are identified only by two or three initials.

9. The *dirham* (Dh), the official unit of currency in Morocco, is divided into 100 centimes (formerly francs). In recent years, the exchange rate of the dirham has ranged, with the fluctuating value of the dollar, between 15¢ and 27¢. In most parts of the country, the standard, though unofficial, unit of currency is the *ryal*, worth five centimes.

10. The same device is frequently used by mystical brotherhoods and religious lodges to multiply their income from donations made by pilgrims and devotees (See Crapanzano 1973 and Gellner 1969).

11. Both tendencies have been noted in studies of Northern Morocco. Crapanzano (1973: 126) found the former phenomenon in the *bidonvilles* (shantytowns) around the city of Meknes. Rabinow (1975: 83) remarked on the opposite tendency in a soldier returned to his native village in the Middle Atlas.

12. The sexual segregation in *ahwash* is in direct contrast to the communal music of the Middle Atlas (*ahidus*), where male and female dancers frequently alternate in the same line.

13. For an analysis of the social implications of the distinctions between *ahwash* and the music of the *rwais*, see Schuyler (1979).

14. Until the early 1950s, when the mixing of *rwais* and *raisat* began to be common practice, there were at least a few ensembles consisting entirely of *raisat*, accompanying themselves on *rribab*, *lotar*, and *naqus*. Sometimes the women provided their own music and poetry, but more often they were under the tutelage of a *rais*.

15. Throughout most of the year, the average fee guaranteed to a group of *rwais* ranges from 100 to 500 Dh. One day a year, however, their price is inflated out of all proportion. On ʿAid el ʿArsh (the Feast of the Throne) shopkeepers and groups of businessmen are expected to express their satisfaction with the regime by sponsoring parties in their places of business. The more elaborate the party, the more favor the merchants gain with the local government. Practically every *rais* can expect to find employment on ʿAid el ʿArsh. Demand can push the fee for a mediocre group to 1500 Dh, and fees as high as 8,000-12,000 Dh have been reported for top stars.

16. The first drink with any customer is not watered, in case suspicion should lead him to take a taste. Thus, if a dancer moves around a good deal, she can end up consuming a considerable amount of alcohol.

17. I have witnessed similar acts of conspicuous generosity at private parties in both the city and the country. I mention them here, however, because, even in the country, they seem to be inspired not by *tashajiʿt* (praise singing), but by the presence of *raisat*.

18. The last few years have seen a considerable growth of interest in Berber, particularly *tashlhit*, culture among both Berbers and Arabs in Morocco. As a result, some groups of *rwais* have begun to receive top billing in concerts. In the spring of 1980, for example, Rais l-Hajj Mohamed ben Lahcen ed-Demsiri performed before sell-out crowds on several occasions at the Théâtre National Mohamed V in Rabat. I was unable to attend these concerts, but I presume that the reception was warmer than that described here. Nevertheless, the physical and economic separation of performers and audience, which determine the nature of the performance, remain the same as in other commercial situations.

19. Once a well-known record was played for ten seconds at double speed. Listeners who correctly identified the singer and song title were to be awarded a copy of the record.

20. Folk revival groups have received much the same treatment from programmers on the Arabic station. Indeed, both Arabic-speaking groups like Nass el Ghiwane and Jil Jilala, and Berber groups like Ousmane and Izenzarn, have gotten most of their airplay on the French network of RTM.

21. The problem of cassette piracy is not limited to Morocco. According to an article in *The New York Times* (April 5, 1981: 21), the International Federation of Producers of Phonograms and Videograms "estimates that about 18 percent of all prerecorded tapes sold in the United States are produced by pirates." Estimates range as high as 80 percent in a number of countries, including Portugal, India, Thailand, and South Korea.

22. As might be expected, television, offering images as well as sound, has a strong competitive advantage over radio. RTM's single channel broadcasts only in French and Arabic (both dialectical and standard). There is no *tashlḥit* program. Since 1977, *tashlḥit*-speaking groups have begun appearing more frequently than in the past, often in a series on Moroccan traditional music organized by Omar Amarir. But these performances are still explained and introduced in Arabic. So great is the fascination of television, however, that people will watch for hours without understanding a word, depending on educated youngsters for a translation, or debating hotly among themselves the possible interpretations of what they are witnessing. Some families solve their conflict of interests by turning off the sound of the television and listening to the radio as they watch.

23. Songs of praise for the King and other political figures constitute an obvious exception to this rule. Such songs might, however, be considered as history (or legend) as much as *tashajiᶜt*.

24. In examining the poetry of Sidi Hammu, it is often impossible to know which lines were actually composed by the poet, and which have simply been attributed to him. Any line in wide currency (with no overt reference to the twentieth century) may be credited to Sidi Hammu, particularly those which fall into his favorite metric scheme.

REFERENCES CITED

Amarir, Omar
    1975   *Ash-Shiᶜr al-maghribi al-'amazighi* (Moroccan Berber Poetry). Casablanca: Dar al-Kitab.
    1978   *Amalu: min al-funun ash-shaᶜbia al-maghribia* (Amalou: clartés sur les arts populaires marocains). Casablanca: Dar al-Kitab.

Amzal, Ahmed
    1968   *Amanar: Diwan Shiᶜri Shilhi* (The Lighthouse: Collection of Berber Poetry). Rabat: Al-Matbaᶜa al-Markazia.

Başgöz, Ilhan
    1975   The Tale-Singer and His Audience. In Dan Ben-Amos and Kenneth Goldstein, eds., *Folklore: Performance and Communication*. The Hague: Mouton. 143-203.

Bauman, Richard, and Joel Sherzer, eds.
  1974   *Explorations in the Ethnography of Speaking*. London: Cambridge University Press.
Berque, Jacques
  1955   *Structures Sociales du Haut-Atlas*. Paris: Presses Universitaires de France.
Blacking, John
  1981   The Ethnography of Musical Performance. In Heartz, Daniel and Bonnie C. Wade, eds., *Report of the Twelfth Congress* (International Musicological Society), *Berkeley, 1977*. Kassel-Basel-London: Bärenreiter.
Bouzid, Ahmed
  1973   "Shiᶜr Wahrush: Dirasa wa tarjama" (The poetry of Wahrouch: Study and Translation). University Mohamed V. Fes, Morocco.
Chottin, Alexis
  1933   *Corpus de Musique Marocaine, II: Musique et Danses Berbères du Pays Chleuh*. Paris: Heugel (Au Ménestrel).
  1939   *Tableau de la Musique Marocaine*. Paris: Paul Geuthner.
Crapanzano, Vincent
  1973   *The Hamadsha: A Study in Moroccan Ethnopsychiatry*. Berkeley: University of California Press.
Essyad, Ahmed
  1967   La Musique Berbère au Maroc. In Tolia Nikiprowetzky, ed., *La Musique dans la Vie: L'Afrique, ses prolongements, ses voisins*. Paris: Office de Coopération Radiophonique. 241-260.
Fogelson, Raymond
  1971   Cherokee Ballgame Cycle: An Ethnographer's View. *Ethnomusicology* 15 (3): 327-328.
Galand-Pernet, Paulette
  1972   *Recueil de Poèmes Chleuhs, I: Chants de Troveurs*. Paris: Editions Klincksieck.
Gellner, Ernest
  1969   *Saints of the Atlas*. Chicago: The University of Chicago Press.
Grame, Theodore C.
  1970   Music in the Jma el-Fna of Marrakech. *Musical Quarterly* 56: 74-87.
Harries, Jeannette, and Mohamed Raamouch
  1971   Berber popular Songs of the Middle Atlas. *African Language Studies*. London: School of Oriental and African Studies. University of London. 52-70.
Herndon, Marcia
  1971   Cherokee Ballgame Cycle: An Ethnomusicologist's View, *Ethnomusicology* 15 (3): 339-352.
Herndon, Marcia, and Roger Brunyate, eds.
  1975   *Form in Performance, Hard-Core Ethnography*. Austin: College of Fine Arts, University of Texas.
Irvine, Judith T.
  1974   Strategies of Status Manipulation in the Wolof Greeting. In Bauman,

Richard, and Joel Sherzer, eds., *Explorations in the Ethnography of Speaking*. London: Cambridge University Press. 167-191.

Johnston, R.L.N.
1907   *The Songs of Sidi Hammo*. London: Elkin Mathews.

Justinard, Commandant L.
1925   Notes d'Histoire et de Littérature Berbère. *Hespéris* 5(2): 227-239.
1928   Textes Chleuh de l'Oued Nfis. In *Mémorial Henri Basset*, vol. 1: Publications de l'Institut des Hautes Etudes Marocaines, XVII. Paris: Paul Geuthner. 331-337.
n.d.   *Le Tazeroualt: Un Petit Royaume Berbère, Un Saint Berbère Sidi*
(1953?) *Ahmed ou Moussa*. Institut des Hautes Etudes Marocaines. Notes et Documents XV. Paris: G.P. Maisonneuve Librairie Orientale et Américaine.

Lortat-Jacob, Bernard
1980   *Musique et fêtes au Haut-Atlas*. Paris: Mouton, "Les Cahiers de l'Homme."

Lortat-Jacob, Bernard, and Hassan Jouad
1978   *La saison des fêtes dans une vallée du Haut-Atlas*. Paris: Editions du Seuil.

Malinowski, Bronislaw
1948   Myth in Primitive Society. In *Magic, Science and Religion and Other Essays*, selected and with an introduction by Robert Redfield. Garden City: Doubleday Anchor.

McLeod, Norma and Marcia Herndon, eds.
1980   *The Ethnography of Musical Performance*. Norwood, Penn.: Norwood Editions.

Mustawi, Muhammad
1976   *Iskraf: diwan shiᶜr amazighi* (Iskraf: a collection of Amazigh poetry). Casablanca: Dar al-Kitab.
1979   *Tadsad imtawen: diwan shiᶜ r amazighi maghribi* (Laughter and tears: a collection of Moroccan Amazigh poetry). Casablanca: Dar al-Kitab.

Noin, Daniel
        La Population Rurale du Maroc. 2 vols. Paris: Presses Universitaires de France.

Rabinow, Paul
1975   *Symbolic Domination: Cultural Form and Historical Change*. Chicago: University of Chicago Press.

Roux, Arsène
1923   Les "Imdyazen" ou Aèdes Berbères. *Hespéris* 3: 231-251.
1928   Un Chant d'Amdyaz, L'Aède Berbère du Groupe Linguistique Beraber. In *Mémorial Henri Basset*, vol. 2: Publications de l'Institut des Hautes Etudes Marocaines, XVIII. Paris: Paul Geuthner. 237-242.

Schuyler, Philip D.
1978   *The Rwais: Moroccan Berber Musicians from the High Atlas*. New York: Lyrichord Discs, LLST 7316.
1979   The *Rwais* and *Ahwash*: Opposing Tendencies in Moroccan Music and Society. In *The World of Music* 21 (1): 65-80.

Waterbury, John
    1972   *North for the Trade: The Life and Times of a Berber Merchant.*
             Berkeley: University of California Press.
Westermarck, Edward
    1926   *Ritual and Belief in Morocco.* 2 vols. London: MacMillan and Co.

GLOSSARY

The linguistic origins of words are indicated as follows:
   (A) — Arabic
   (F) — French
   (S) — Sub-Saharan word, language unspecified
   (T) — *Tashlhit*, or, if specified, *tamazight*
   (A/T) — *Tashlhit* form derived from Arabic root

Abaraz (T) — Lit., battleground; poetic duel.

Abaraz in Ait Umarg (T) — Program on RTM devoted to *rwais* and *amarg*, produced and presented by Ahmed Amzal.

Agurram (pl. *igurramn*, T) — a saint; one who has acquired—by inheritance, devotion, or divine inspiration—large amounts of *baraka.*

Ahwash (pl. *ihwaishn*, T) — Lit., a dance; a line or circle dance from the High Atlas or Sus, generally with two antiphonal choruses and drum ensemble; an evening of dance; music in general.

Ait (T) — Lit., sons of, people of.

Ait Uhwash (T) — Lit., the people of *ahwash*; a group of young villagers who form the core of an *ahwash* performance.

ᶜAita (A) — Lit., call; a genre of rural, Arab music, generally performed by professionals; used here to refer generically to the professional music of the Atlantic plains.

Amarg (pl. *imurign*, T) — Lit., yearning (unrequited) love; poetry; used here to refer specifically to poetry of the *rwais*; may sometimes refer to music in general.

Amazigh (pl. *Imazighen*, f. *tamazight*, T) — Lit., free man; Berber from the Middle Atlas; sometimes used to refer to any Berber, regardless of dialect group.

Aqṣid (pl. *iqṣiden*, A/T, from the Arabic *qaṣida*) — poem or song text performed by the *rwais.*

Asarag (T) — Open space; threshing ground; any performance area.

Astara (A/T) — Lit., travel, wandering, stroll; free-rhythm introductory improvisation by *rwais* or *ᶜawwada.*

Baraka (A) — Blessings; goodness; wealth; spiritual power.

Baqshish (A/T) — In *tashlhit*, a comedian; in Arabic (from Turkish), tip, money, bribe.

Bengri (S) — a double-headed side drum used in *ahwash* of the central High Atlas; used originally by Gnawa.

Bendir (pl. *bnadr*, A) — Arabic term for a round, single-headed frame drum (cf. *allun, tallunt*).

Bu Naqus (A/T) — *Naqus* player.

Ḍḍerb (pl. *l-aḍrub*, A/T) — Measured, instrumental dance tune used by *rwais* and *ᶜawwada*, usually in compound duple.

Derbuga (A) — Single-headed, vase-shaped drum, used in Arabic folk, popular, and sometimes classical music.

Disk (pl. *dyask*, F) — A phonograph record; song text; complete performance by *rwais* from *astara to qtaᶜ*; first in a series of two enchained songs.

Fatha (A, from *al-fatiha*, the opening *sura* of the Qur'an) — A prayer; a plea for money or other donation.

Fraja (A) — Spectacle; dance performance by the *rwais*.

Funduq (pl. *fnadeq*, A) — Lit., a caravanserai, with lodgings, stables, and store-rooms for goods; an inn.

Ginbri (pl. *gnabr*, dim. *gnibri*, S/A) — 3- or 4-stringed fretless lute, generally with tear-drop shaped body covered with goatskin head; sometimes also known as *lotar*. Gnawa *ginbri* has rectangular wooden body, sliding leather tuning rings, and metal sound modifier.

Gedra (A) — Lit., cooking pot; drum made from clay pot; dance form from the northern Sahara.

Halqa (pl. *hlaqi*, A) — Lit., throat, circle; the circle of spectators around a public performer or preacher; performance in the marketplace.

Imdyazen (sing. *amdyaz*, T) — *Tamazight* term for small troupes of itinerant, male professional musicians in the Middle Atlas, specializing in songs of religious and moral commentary.

Ishlhin (A/T) — pl.. of *Ashlhi*; the *tashlhit*-speaking Berbers of the High Atlas and Sus regions of Southwestern Morocco.

Izlan (T) — Popular songs of the Middle Atlas (*tamazight*).

Kaman/Kamanja (A)—Arabo-Persian word for violin or viola.

L- — Definite article in Arabic, often assimilated into word when used in *tashlhit*.

L-adrub (A/T) — pl. of *dderb*.

L-ᶜasr (A) — Midafternoon prayer; one of the five daily prayers required in Islam.

L-fas (F/T) — Side, second side (of a record), from the French *face*; second of two enchained songs in performance.

Lhalqt (A/T) — *Tashlhit* version of *halqa*.

Lmherfin (A/T) — Lit., the professionals; *rwais'* slang term for themselves.

Lotar (A/T) — Lit., the string; fretless, 3- or 4-stringed lute with round body (enamel bowl) covered with goatskin head.

Maghreb (A) — Sunset; sunset prayer; the west; North Africa; Morocco.

Mashkhara (A) — Clowning; fooling around; masquerade.

Musem (pl. *mwasem*, A) — Annual festival for a saint.

Naqus (A/T) — Lit., bell; a piece of metal (usually a brake drum) beaten with metal rods, used to accompany *rwais* or village musicians.

Nuiqsat (A/T) — Lit., little bells; finger cymbals used by *raisat*.

Qa'id (a) — Tribal governor; rural administrative official.

Qtaᶜ (A/T) — Lit., cut; short cadential formula used to "cut" performance.

Rais (pl. *rwais*, f. *raisa*, A/T) — Lit., leader, president; leader of an *ahwash* or any musical performance; Berber professional musician from Southwestern Morocco.

Raisa (A/T) — Female professional singer or dancer in Southwestern Morocco.

Rkkza (A/T) — Lit., foot-stamping used in pounded earth construction; type of dance by the *rwais*, involving leaps and foot-stamping.

Rribab (A/T) — Monochord fiddle used by *rwais*.

Rwais (A/T) — pl. of *rais.*

Sheikh (pl. *shiakh*, A) — Lit., old man, leader; religious leader, master; village administrative official; professional musician (in Arabic and *tamazight*.)

Sirk (F) — Lit., circus, carnival; tent theater.

Suq (pl. *aswaq*, A/T) — A market.

Sura (pl. *-at*, A) — A chapter from the Qur'an.

Tacarija (pl. *tcarij*, A) — Small, hand-held pottery vase drum, with single head.

Tagʷmamt (pl. *tigʷmamin*, T) — Lit., reed, cane; a short, end-blown, flute, with six finger holes and thumb hole, played by *cawwada.*

Tallunt (pl. *tilluna*, T) — Lit., sieve; round, single-headed frame drum, with or without snares.

Tamazight (T) — The language of the Middle Atlas Berbers (Imazighen); sometimes used to refer to Berber language in general, irrespective of dialect.

Tamsust (T) — Lit., shaking, moving; short, accelerated section of drumming and handclapping in the *ahwash* of the Imi n Tanut region; among the *rwais*, an accelerated bridge between two songs, or between *amarg* or *tbil* and *l-adrub.*

Taqsim (pl. *taqasim*, A) — An unmeasured, instrumental solo, used as prelude or interlude, in Arabic classical or popular music.

Taqsitt (A/T) — Poem or song text performed by the *rwais.*

Tashajict (A/T, from the Arabic *shajic, courageous*, or *tashjic*, encouragement) — Praise singing.

Tashlhit (A/T) — Berber (*tamazight*) dialect spoken in the western High Atlas and Sus regions of Southwestern Morocco.

Tawriqt (pl. *tiwriqin*, A/T) — Lit., a sheet of paper or anything flat; a phonograph record.

Tbil (A/T) — Dance overture to a performance by the *rwais*; a composition in duple time made up of melodies from the *tbil* repertory.

Ti-n-lhalqt (A/T) — A rapid, undifferentiated pulse beat on the *naqus*, used to summon spectators to the *halqa*; sometimes used to accompany an *astara.*

Tiqarqawin (T) — Metal double castanets, used by Gnawa, and sometimes in *ahwash*; *tashlhit* term for *qaraqeb.*

Tolba (sing. *taleb*) — Lit., seeker (of knowledge); religious students, or low-level Qur'anic scholars; scribes.

cUd (A) — Lit., wood; the Arabic lute; in Morocco the instrument has 5 double courses and a single bass string, tuned DGAdgc.

4

American Traditional Fiddling: Performance Contexts and Techniques

Linda C. Burman-Hall

In the early years of the seventeenth century, the violin already played an important role in the dance music of English masques (Woodfil 1953: 192-193; Boyden 1964).[1] By mid-century during which the French violin performing idioms were finally regimented into a calculated national style by the dancer-violinist Jean-Baptiste Lully, we find this vigorous and disciplined dance music style established at the English Restoration Court of Charles II, whose preference for the French manner, acquired during his lengthy exile, may be held responsible for accelerating the importation and dissemination of the French playing style throughout the British Isles.

The simple dance music idiom, popular in France in all social ranks from the turn of the century, and even formally established in court from 1626 ("24 Violons du Roy" of Louis XIII) was presumably transmitted more frequently through oral tradition than through notation (Boyden 1964: 93-94). As a widespread and popular art, it encompassed a variety of interrelated assumptions about the function or context of the music, the habits and techniques of playing, the ideal form and adjustment of the instrument, and the appropriate musical repertory. Diffusing and flourishing among amateurs and folk players in England, Ireland, and Scotland alongside the newer, professional, virtuosic, Italian solo violin style and the genteel, expiring viol tradition, the French dance idiom rapidly absorbed compatible local elements to become a vital part of each British folk culture.

In view of the enormous popularity in seventeenth-century England of folk and cultivated violin players, and of performing techniques based on French dance music and on adaptations of division viol techniques (Burman-Hall 1974: 8-9; Boyden 1965: 230, 234, and passim), we may reasonably expect this portable social music to have been imported and diffused in the new North American colonial settlements from the earliest opportunities.[2] A known, and presumably typical, early figure in this long process was one John Utie of England, a professional "fidler" who brought his instrument and high hopes to Virginia in 1620, sailing in on the *Francis Bonaventure*. Unable to continue to support himself solely by music in the colonies, he consequently settled in as a planter.[3] The fiddlers he left behind in England might well have considered the advantages in colonizing new and open territories, since as early as 1586 Gasson remarked that London was "so full of unprofitable pipers and fiddlers that a man can no sooner enter a tavern, than two or three cast of them hang at his heels, to give him a dance before he departs" (cf. Chappell 1965: 108).

After a century and a half of concentration in the American southeastern seacoast regions, British settlers, along with their cultural baggage, began to move inland from the tidewater areas, and, by the time of the Revolution, appeared in the Appalachian chain and the hinterlands (Bolton and Marshall 1920: 309-328, 337; C. Eaton 1949: 9-10). Increasing numbers of European immigrants, channeled through the port of Philadelphia, followed this movement to the frontier, which, because of its harsh environment, formed a line of rapid and most effective Americanization (Jones 1960: 22-30, Turner 1920).

The overall pattern for southern migration in the early nineteenth century continued to move segments of the population in a generally southwesterly direction. Settlement of the public domain came in two distinct waves: first the herdsmen, who had the advantage of grazing cattle the year around in the warmer climate; and in close pursuit, since the better pasture lands are always best for farming, came agricultural immigrants who cleared, fenced and homesteaded (Owsley 1945: 149-151, 164-175). The migration of these farm folk followed isothermal lines, partially resulting from the practical standpoint of understanding the cultivation requirements of crops in the particular temperate zone and topography, but also for the psychological security of the familiar surrounding countryside. Since so many families, communities, and church groups migrated *en masse* to locations as similar as possible to those they had left, frontier settlements tended to be transplanted organisms rather than synthetic units. We may assume that the common musical tradition continued to follow this southwestern frontier, creating a wide diffusion of the traditional airs and folk performance styles of the early British settlers.

The existence of documentation and field collection for the southern diffusion of British-American instrumental music and the comparative paucity of similar data for the North, which we can assume originally shared the same ethnic, social, and cultural traditions, can be explained by two overall factors. On the one hand, the urbanization, economic prosperity, and eventual industrialization, as well as the greater influx of European immigrants bringing other musical traditions, all tended to alienate the more sophisticated, aspiring bourgeois northerner from the widespread British-based traditions; whereas, on the other hand, the agrarian economy and the resultant socio-economic hierarchy based on black slavery, as well as the increasing cultural isolation and defensiveness of the southerner over his much-criticized position, tended to conserve and insulate the traditional elements of the culture throughout the South (cf. Powell 1937), but especially in the piedmont and mountain areas (Cash 1941: 3; Jackson 1933: 396, 1964: 23; C. Eaton 1964: 238-239, 241-243; Odum 1964: 120-122). Although the traditional instrumental music was increasingly abandoned in the North, the old tunes and styles survived in the more rural areas, such as the Pennsylvania mountain regions and the farmlands and lumbercamp regions of New England, and in the Maritime Provinces of Canada. Because these northern survivals more often depend on transmission within occupational groups (Bayard 1953: 134; Cazden 1959: 327), and are subject to a wider variety of cultural influences,[4] modifications and dilutions of function, the present study is focused primarily upon British-American fiddling as manifested in southern traditions.

TRANSMISSION AND MUTATION BY TRADITIONAL MEANS

> *There is nothing in which the power of art*
> *is shown so much as in playing on the Fiddle.*
> *In all other things we can do something at first:*
> *any man will forge a bar of iron*
> *if you give him a hammer;*
> *not so well as a smith, but tolerably;*
> *and make a box, though a clumsy one;*
> *but give him a Fiddle and a Fiddle-stick,*
> *and he can do nothing.*
> —Dr. Samuel Johnson (1709-1794)

Since the seventeenth-century fiddler focused his efforts on accompanying popular and widespread dances, his repertory would normally have developed and expanded by contact with other dance musicians with whom he could exchange tunes by demonstration and imitation. Although popular collections of tunes appeared, the novice player, just as the novice dancer, would scarcely have been able to learn from notation alone, and without being able to observe more expert performers. For those who could read music and had some concept of the performance conventions associated with the idiom, dance collections of both the tune and the steps served as valuable sources of new material and ideas. Such collections, commonly intended for either the fiddler or piper, appeared from 1650, with the first of eighteen editions of John Playford's *The English Dancing Master*.[5] With new editions of this popular work appearing regularly through 1728, a second tutor-book series emphasizing Scottish and French tunes, called *Apollo's Banquet* (five editions, from 1669 to 1690), and the *Division-Violin* went through several printings from 1684. John Playford's heirs also brought out two editions of *A Collection of Original Scotch Tunes* in 1700 and 1701. That these volumes remained in great demand suggests a broadly based, vigorous practicing of the English, Scottish and French dances along with their tunes at a time when the fiddle had become more popular than the bagpipes (Spielman 1975: 196). The *Division-Violin*, a regular sampler of all playing styles currently popular in England, consisted mainly of the straightforward dance pieces and grounds in first position that any fiddler would have recognized.

In the same manner that the English traditional fiddler absorbed many elements of the Scottish and Irish dance music, and enjoyed the fashionable French and Italian styles, he and his descendants continued to coordinate or absorb materials from these and other European traditions in the colonies. As a result, numerous regional performance styles of fiddling have developed over the years throughout the British Isles and in North America, and one significant measure of the vigor of the British-American instrumental tradition is the degree to which these imported idioms have produced distinctive sub-styles by means of the folk communication process. The manner of acquisition, transmission, re-creation, and mutation in the instrumental tradition as it applies to these British-American fiddle styles generally reflects the normal characteristics of oral tradition in any culture,[6] and provides the beginnings of an explanation for this varied diffusion of the idiom (cf. Nettl 1953: 216-218, 220).

It seems likely that the acquisition of the idiom has always been an informal affair. At least the contemporary folk informant usually is quite vague about instructions gained from experienced performers (Bayard 1956: 17). Marion Unger Thede's survey on the background of traditionally-oriented fiddlers may provide some insight into the learning process followed in the past, even though her informants were not evenly distributed in all areas where the music flourished (1962: 21-23).[7] Thede's results, based on eighty-seven responses to a questionnaire, show that most of her informants learned to play early in life, between six and eighteen years of age, with about sixty-three percent (Ibid.: 21) stating that no one actually taught them.[8] Their first tune usually took less than a month to learn, with many taking less than a week. The estimates range from satisfaction on "the very first try" to "can't do it very good even now" (Ibid.: 22). Most of Samuel Bayard's informants said that it took years of more-or-less constant practice to obtain the appropriate facility, although their estimates of time, usually five, seven or nine years, resembled traditional folk formulae more than memories (1956: 17).

The fiddler learning by ear, and reworking the repertory in his personal style, also differs from the violinist in the method of acquiring technique (De Ryke 1964b: 183). Rather than repeating exercises or scales, the fiddler learns by absorbing the bowings and fingerings of each melody, mastering one tune at a time, in a sort of graded series (Bayard 1956: 16-17; 1966: 54).

At the end of this period, the novice player has generally reached a point

beyond which he will try to expand his repertory in preference to deliberately improving his technique (Bayard 1956: 17). The eventual gradient of
players, from the carefully refined on down to the "rough and tumble"
variety, produces marked, and sometimes highly personalized, individual
styles beyond the habitual regional tendencies.

The resulting method of tune re-creation according to the individual
player's proclivities, is equivalent to the foreground realization of a general
structure and therefore analogous to a reversed Schenkerian process (see
infra: 172-174; Burman-Hall 1978). According to Thede, the fiddler presumably retains the characteristic structure of the air, experimentally supplying
a set of notes by the dictates of his fancy until a somewhat fixed version
emerges, which comes to be preferred by the fiddler and perhaps his family
(Thede 1967: 26).

Of course, some traditional performers have always insisted upon the
identity of their rendition with that of their source. Statements of this sort
appear in the notes of field collectors and in the literature of folk scholars
from the early years of this century,[9] usually with an increasing degree of
pride on the part of the informant as the pressures on his heritage have
increased; but it must be borne in mind that the nature of re-creation in a
healthy oral tradition always mitigates this intention.[10]

Few folk musicians have ever bothered to learn or use music notation.
One exception to this is that Scottish fiddlers around the turn of the
eighteenth century, when the distinction between amateur violinists and
folk fiddlers was not so apparent, occasionally copied out favorite
traditional tunes for their own use (Collinson 1966: 205). Likewise, Charles
Seeger remembered hearing about similar manuscripts from American
tradition, sometimes in a personal tablature, although I have not been able
to examine any (private interview, April 15, 1969; cf. Thede 1967: 160). In
Thede's survey, about one-third of her informants responded positively to
some degree, and these had mostly acquired the skill later in life, long after
their repertories and habits were fixed (1962: 23-24; cf. Bayard 1956: 16).
Bayard found that even when the fiddler had reference to a printed version
of a tune, the playing resembled the local rendition; except in a few cases
where the tune had been freshly taken from print, the melodic formulae of
local oral tradition dictated the changes from the published form (1956: 16).
These regional variants and local idioms are so deeply implanted that the
traditional player usually feels strongly that unfamiliar variant forms are
simply "wrong" (Grainger 1915: 421). Of course, printed tune versions
congruent with particular regional sub-styles of the tradition eventually
may cause tunes to stabilize to some degree in these areas (Jabbour 1971: 8).

The sharing and transmission of the tunes has been as informal as the
means of attaining competence in the tradition. In communities which
worked together at providing the common necessities, tune swapping was
accomplished naturally. In more sparsely settled areas of the Southwest, the

trading post, where the settlers brought grist to be ground for meal, became an important center for the transmission and diffusion of the tunes over a wider geographic area. More recently, this function has been filled by the widespread fiddlers' contests.

In oral tradition, tunes and idioms shared by a culture appear, at least to some degree, in all vocal and instrumental forms. The research of Samuel Bayard illustrates the effects of long contact between the fiddler and the traditional fifer (1966: passim; see infra: 172). Many folk instrumentalists have been both, and the interchange of idioms and repertory has been extraordinary. Traditional fiddle tunes have become marches when adopted and adapted by fifers; and conversely, fife tunes have been played by fiddlers (Ibid.: 57). Familiar airs have in many cases become impossible to assign to one tradition or the other, with the diatonic properties of ancient fifing now thoroughly implanted in the fiddle performances of this shared repertory, and even in vocal style. Many rural communities took great pride in their volunteer fife-and-drum bands, which thrilled one and all with the old pipe and tabor tunes of the British and European heritage up through the Civil War period (Bayard 1967: 23-24). Although this ancient art has now almost totally disappeared, the stamp of its long familiarity remains in the intonation habits of the fiddler.

The changing times of the nineteenth century brought a gradual influx of the materials and styles of urban culture to be accepted or rejected, absorbed and reshaped in the crucible of tradition. As D. K. Wilgus has shown, whatever the prior conditions of oral tradition in the South, selected musical materials from the North and West penetrated even the southern highlands in the years following the Civil War. The much-celebrated isolation of the mountain folk, a recurrent theme of both in-group folk jests and ethnographic reports, was increasingly diminished by the effects of transportation and travel. The steam packet and railroad, the return of loggers who had rafted timber and of westward migrants, and the contact with traders and "jolt-wagon" drivers who visited the settlements all brought news and new cultural elements (Wilgus 1965: 197). That the development of the southern rural musical culture was never wholly free of commercial influences or the influx of urban ways is significant in regard to the later developments brought about by mass media.

Channels of culture change prior to 1920, such as the "tent repertoire," or travelling medicine show, brought the popular styles of Tin Pan Alley and vaudeville to the back-regions, as did also the travelling salesman and the country boy returning from urban employment. By the 1930s fiddlers and fiddle bands were in demand at fairs, barn dances, and ballroom dates, and often played at civic auditoriums, school houses and tents (Shelton 1966: 53).

And so, gradually the changes affecting the whole country brought urban styles and tastes to the rural South; and of these changes, scarcely one can be construed as anything but inimical to the continuation of the British-

American traditional music. The minstrel show and vaudeville, the sentimental composed song, the music of Tin Pan Alley, the blues and other song forms of the Afro-Americans, and in certain places, music of other ethnic minorities, such as the Cajuns of Louisiana and the Mexican-Americans in the southwest (see infra: 171-172), all had a lasting influence on our traditional instrumental and vocal styles, and had a part in the creation of the hybrid varieties preserved in early recorded country music in the 1920s.

This interdependence of folk, popular, and fine art idioms has been discussed as a norm in music history by Charles Seeger (1940: 118; 1957: passim; 1966: passim). In this case, the assimilation of urban style by folk style is dependent upon the natural selective processes of the folk aesthetic,[11] whereby individual urban melodies and idioms, regardless of origin, are either accepted or rejected (Malone 1968: 23). Norman Cohen, following Charles Seeger's theme, suggested that rural folk music of the South exists in a symbiotic relationship with urban popular music, with the basic resulting hybrid category of "hillbilly" often functioning as the agency of communication between the two (1965: 243); and similarly, D. K. Wilgus described this "bridge" between rural folk and urban mass cultures as made "solid" by World War II (1968: 269-270).

The traditional means of transmission and mutation of British-American instrumental idioms survived and functioned well until at least World War II, despite the increasingly massive injections of urban styles. This persistence of tradition was due to the relatively small amount of commercial pressures on the early recording artist. Since the survival of the once-widespread imported style was confined largely to the South, the folk performer and his audience still shared the same basic cultural combination of social, economic, and religious influences. The performer therefore had no reason to change for his audience, and promoters from the music industry, not yet realizing that a wider market was possible, also had not pressured the traditional performer to modify his style (Malone 1968: 362). For this reason, the decades before World War II were called the "Golden Age" of country music by collector John Edwards, a term perpetuated by those who feel, as he did, that the continuity of tradition was broken by such pressures (Edwards 1971: 178; Malone 1968: 45).

Although folklorist Guy B. Johnson has expressed the belief that an item ceases to be folk when put on the phonograph record, since the folk setting and normal mode of diffusion are lost (1929: 88; cf. Karpeles 1951: 13; cf. Rhodes 1966: 15), evidence linking the early assimilation of urban popular style by the folk performer with the analogous British broadside tradition exists in the early commercial history of country music. According to Jim Walsh, "the Broadway tunes learned from records sank back into the red-brush and emerged later, in altered form, as folk music" (1951). Thus, several commercial records of the 1920s, thought at the time to be from folk tradition, may be demonstrated to have previous urban roots as composed popular music. D. K. Wilgus showed that the entry of broadside material into British-American balladry provides a model for the effect of the early phonograph record upon a vigorous folk tradition in which transmission and mutation still function well (Wilgus 1965: 196; cf. 1969: 186), but the gradual undermining of oral folk tradition by the spread of mass media leaves little hope for the continued existence of this folk process. The vast quantity of extraneous material spread by efficient media is now far beyond what the traditional folk performer can assimilate, and has thus become more of a destructive influence than an inspiration (Karpeles 1951: 12).

We know very little about assimilation and mutation in the tradition-based fiddling of today, but the matter has been given brief consideration by fiddler Marion Unger Thede, who reports that she has been somewhat surprised to see that her informants have not taken to each other's tradition-based regional manners of playing as readily as she expected they might when brought together. Only she has changed her version (1967: 25). As an interesting related experiment, she composed a new fiddle tune, matching it as best she could to those in the local tradition. Thede then tried for a solid year to put it into local currency, playing it countless times on the radio and at gatherings of old-time performers, with no success whatsoever (Ibid.: 25-26). One can only speculate that this apparent reluctance of today's traditionally-oriented fiddler to absorb new aspects or items in his own tradition may be due to the decay of the old folk art and its traditional processes (Bayard 1967: passim), as well as to the results of a trend toward a negative view of mass media (cf. C. Seeger 1951: 16).

SOCIAL CONTEXT, FUNCTION AND MUSIC-MAKING

> *A poor fiddler is a man and fiddle*
> *out of case, and in worse case than his fiddle.*
> *One that rubs two sticks together*
> *(as the Indians strike fire),*
> *and rubs a poor living out of it;*
> *partly from this, and partly from your charity,*
> *which is more in the hearing than giving him,*
> *for he sells nothing dearer than to be gone.*
> *He is just so many strings above a beggar,*
> *though he have but two;*
> *and yet he begs too,*
> *. . . and his face is more pin'd than the blind man's.*
> —Microcosmography, or a Piece of the World
> *by Dr. John Earle, Bishop of Worcester (1628)*

Dr. Earle's timeless lines speak of the often thankless lot of the street musician and itinerant fiddler. To judge from his description, a musician could scarcely imagine a more pathetic plight; and yet evidence suggests that a sufficient number of these musical panhandlers became proficient enough to work steadily as dancing masters. Even much later in the seventeenth century, when the violin was emerging as the most popular dance instrument, the fiddler was still low on the social scale, even among musicians. But more and more fiddlers and amateur violinists could be found; and even during the Civil War and Commonwealth (1649-60) their numbers increased, "for many chose rather to fidle at home, than to goe out & be knockt in ye head abroad" (North 1925: 10). The establishment of a carefully chosen and well-rehearsed dance ensemble of "24 Violins" by Charles II brought French players to court and sent English ones to Paris to study the French dance style (Boyden 1965: 230). And what was popular in the Restoration court would soon have had a turn in the countryside; and what was done in the homeland was eventually sure to be fashionable throughout the colonies.

Although evidence is scarce regarding the dance fiddler in colonial America, we have an account of Captain Miles Standish and his soldiers halting a Massachusetts May Day celebration in 1628 at which he found settlers and Indians dancing together around the maypole, accompanied by a fiddle and Indian drums.[12] Fiddles were seemingly still in demand for dance music and not yet easily available in Massachusetts 32 years later when a young Harvard student, Josiah Flynt, apparently wrote to his uncle in London, requesting a fiddle. The uncle, Reverend Leonard Hoar, who in 1660 had not yet seen the French dance style sweep the country, spoke for the genteel classes of the older generation in his denial of young Josiah's request on the basis of such a diversion being unwise for a young, flighty student.[13] Yet dancing schools are known to have survived in the Boston area through the later years of the seventeenth century, with nine references from as early as 1672 for their presence in New England. By the early eighteenth century, even the Reverend John Cotton, spiritual leader of the conservative Boston flock, had specifically approved dancing (Damon 1952: 65). With instruments more numerous and dances more frequent, comparisons between players were sure to follow. The first documentation for an organized competition appeared in the Williamsburg newspaper in 1736 announcing a St. Andrews Day fiddlers' competition (November 30) among other festivities, with "a fine Cremona fiddle" as a prize.[14]

Thus it appears that the main features of the imported American fiddling tradition were already present long before the Revolution: coexisting and interrelated written and aural transmission of the tunes, playing the fiddle for formal and informal step-dances and country dances, and even the habit of competition in fiddlers' contests (cf. Blaustein 1975: 14-15).

However, transmission of dance music to be played on the fiddle was by no means limited to the British-American and other white settlers. Through the colonial era, in both New England and the southern settlements, slaves were encouraged to learn fiddling and other instruments, and were relied on

as musicians for formal balls and dancing classes, country dances and even
backwoods hoedowns (Southern 1971: 27-50). Whereas the white settler
could only decline in status by devoting all his energies to dance fiddling,
the black slave apparently could only increase in status and in value to his
owner, and could perhaps even buy his freedom with money he had earned
(Southern 1971: 123-124).[15]

Despite the continuing low status of the dance fiddler, he was very much
in demand at gatherings of many sorts and was quite an important person in
the life of his community in the years before the advent of mass media
entertainment. His music was popular and had a variety of functions. He
played for his own enjoyment, for the entertainment of his community
(Bennett 1940: 6-10), and for dances as often as three times a week (Ibid.:
20). In the western range area, where population was most scattered, dances
were held less frequently but sometimes lasted for three days. The traditional airs accompanied the steps of the dances, which often varied along
with their calls in different communities (see infra: 170; Bennett 1940: 31;
Burchenal 1951: 20-21; Holden 1951: passim; Grayson 1969: 30). The
majority of collected British-American tunes were intended for the dance,
usually the "running set" or square dance,[16] and therefore were characterized by strong and regular rhythms.

Besides the tradition of dance music, the fiddler usually will know one or
more British-American instrumental airs of the same form and meter as the
dance tunes. These tunes are not played at dance tempo ($\quad$ = 112-132)
however, but in a stately tempo of $\quad$ = 60-84, with a freer and more lyrical
manner of rendition, and often with a special story or tradition associated,
and programmatic effects.[17] Nevertheless, the overwhelming majority of
fiddle tunes are intended for the group dancing which follows communal
labors.

The frontier and farming communities gathered for many varieties of
work, after which there was usually a meal for the workers, eventually
followed by dancing accompanied on the fiddle, with singing and merry-
making frequently continuing until dawn (Bennett 1940: 19; see infra: 170).
Thus, the fiddler held a position of considerable prestige for such "frolics"
or work gatherings as log-rolling (Shelton 1966: 25), log-raising for barns
and cabins (De Ryke 1964: 181), husking bees (Ibid.: 181; Bennett 1940: 19),
bean stringing, apple cutting (Shelton 1966: 25), hog killing (Bennett 1940:
19), molasses making (Shelton 1966: 25), and quilting (Bennett 1940: 19).
Folk informants have also mentioned a number of other purely social
activities, for which the fiddler was always in demand, i.e., weddings,
shivarees, wakes (De Ryke 1964: 181), the end of the cattle-drive or round-
up (Sanders 1951b: 24), and even the community pie and ice cream suppers,
sometimes called "moonlights," which were invariably held out of doors,
with ice cream made on the spot (Coppage 1961: 8-9; Calhoun 1941: 22).
The normal procedure at such affairs logically grouped pieces by key

because retuning instruments was an involved project, so that all pieces in D were usually followed by those in A, and then most likely any in G (Calhoun 1941: 24-25; see infra: 163-164).

This close association of traditional music with the work habits of daily life strengthened the bond between the folk and folk tradition. Alan Lomax popularized the theory that the function of the British-American idiom is to provide security for the native of the culture, because it symbolizes the "emotional texture" of birth, religious experience, work and daily life of the folk (cf. Sanders 1951a; Lomax 1959: 929-930, 947, 950), and may be said to have a high nostalgic value like Southern gospel music, which is a descendant of shape-note hymnody (Anon. 1969b: 5).

For this reason, the audience for the commercial country music offshoots of the older traditions could be distinguished from Tin Pan Alley fans by their loyalty to the idiom (Shelton 1966: 18), which has kept many early commercial releases selling steadily "like sugar in a grocery store" over an extended period of time (Leamy 1969: 9, 11). This loyalty was expressed by former Tennessee Senator Estes Kefauver, who, like many other Southern politicians, habitually used the music to good advantage in campaigning through the years (Shelton 1966: 18), thus becoming aware of its powerful effect on his followers: "Country music has been the expression of the inner beings of our people. This is the only pure American music" (1966: 18). And so, as our life turns more and more to ferro-concrete, many Americans listen with increasing pleasure to the hillbilly as a channel of communication with their own folk heritage (Cohen 1965: 243; Barzun 1956: 90-91; Wilgus 1968: 269-270).

The old tunes and styles of playing have always been popular in rural areas of our country characterized by isolation and poverty; and similarly, the fiddler has been closely associated with the agricultural occupations. Of the hundreds of traditional and transitional fiddlers interviewed in the early 1960s by De Ryke, the great majority were found to be living or to have lived at one time in rural communities or on farms (1964: 182). Those who had moved to the cities were primarily blue-collar workers. It is significant that only a couple were even rumored to be wealthy, suggesting that traditional instrumental music has succumbed perhaps as automatically to the occasional upward economic mobility of the farmer in rural areas as it has to encroaching urbanization and general education.

All but one of the informants interviewed by De Ryke were found to be quite friendly and eager to talk about their art, provided such an interview was not conducted by another of these "cussed folklorists."[18] Similarly, Calhoun dramatically reported that previous researchers and enthusiasts in his isolated sector of south central Kentucky had been threatened with guns, and that it was only his credentials as a native and his prowess as a fiddler which ensured their tolerance and eventual cooperation (1941: 9).

Only very rarely nowadays, as in the past, does one encounter the traditionally-oriented fiddler who makes his living as a full-time or professional musician playing for square dances (P. Seeger 1959: 1). The heritage was always related closely to its social function and rural context, and now that many aspects of its traditional setting have fallen by the wayside in the name of progress, the true art is becoming increasingly limited to aging informants, who, from Maine, North Carolina and Texas respectively, lament the break in continuity of the once-thriving folk art of their youth:

"I have played more jigs and reels than any living man in Maine, I think. All the other fiddlers are dead."

"I know a bunch of old-time tunes that nobody else can play around here. I learned them from some old-time fiddlers back in the Blue Ridge Mountains around forty years ago, and they are dead now. There aren't many fiddlers that can play them like they ought to be played anymore."

"We don't have very many old-time fiddlers here anymore." (De Ryke 1964: 185-186).[19]

The effect of near commercialization of folk tunes by the recording industry starting in the 1920s, the profusion of radio broadcasts in the 1930s, and especially the work of the folklorists, the WPA and the Library of Congress in the 1940s eventually persuaded the urban-intellectual element to confer a measure of respectability upon our native folk music, and catalyzed a "citybilly" revival of the old rural idioms resulting in the present hegemony of hybrid folk-popular sub-styles (Seeger 1957: 290-291). Of course, many facets of the old style of melodizing have survived in a somewhat altered form in this commercial country music output, but the loss of much of the functional aspect has gradually and surely taken the art away from the common folk and placed it in a hybrid form in the hands of the modern professional. If one is to believe Bascomb, who wrote in 1909 from extensive North Carolina song collecting experiences, that "the mountaineer who cannot draw music from the violin, the banjo, or the 'French harp,' is probably non-existent" (1909: 238), it is necessary to conclude along with Samuel Bayard that the folk,[20] having lost the context of their musical tradition, and consequently now abandoning the once universally appreciated conventions and the familiar home-music of their British forebears, no longer have a music of their own (1967: 24).[21]

TRADITIONAL CHARACTERISTICS OF THE INSTRUMENT

Nothing made so great a denouement in musick
as the invention of horse-hair, with rosin,
and the guts of animals twisted and dryed.
            —The Memoires of Musick *by the*
        Hon. Roger North, *Attorney General*
                to King James II (1728)

The folk fiddle, while basically a violin, has been characterized by certain distinctive modifications affecting not only the tone, but the pitch content of the music as well. These practices, passed down through the generations, give us some insight into the aesthetic of the folk art of fiddling, and illustrate the interrelationship of instruments and tunes in folk tradition.

It is reported that the ever-resourceful southern highlander was able to actually make a wide variety of instruments for his own use when none were available or when factory-made instruments were beyond his means or did not suit his fancy.[22] The fiddle was one such instrument, made by his hand in all areas of the South, though not always of wood. A crude fiddle made from rosined corn stalks, perhaps adapted by the Apache and other tribes in the form of a mescal-stick fiddle (Densmore 1927: 98) or, more likely, inspired by widespread Indian use (McAllester 1956: 1-2), was used in both the southern and western areas (A. Eaton 1937: 198; De Ryke 1964: 184; Welsch 1964). The common long-necked garden gourd, made variously into the bugle or horn, or with a stretched and tanned animal skin top (Keasler 1962: 3) into the fiddle or mandolin, has also been popular on the frontier, although neither it nor the corn stalk lasted very well (A. Eaton 1937: 198, 205-206).

Popular woods for the making of the fiddle were curly maple, poplar (Ibid.: 207-208), apple (Calhoun 1941: 12-13), or pear tree stumps, although any handy piece lacking in knot holes would do. Marion Thede reports the appropriation of old boxes, wagons and furniture by her informants (1967: 142). Once chosen, the one and one-half or two inch thick block was hollowed out in a violin shape, leaving the sides intact, the surplus outer corners were whittled away, and a top was fitted. For reasons of resonance, another wood was chosen for the top, usually pine. All bridges, pegs, fingerboards and tail pieces were made painstakingly by hand. Gut strings were usual, though wire strings, which produce greater volume, seem to have been popular when available (Anon. 1969, see infra: 164). Sometimes elaborate carvings across the back and scrollwork of human or animal heads appeared. Other refinements were inlay and varnish, which became more popular as time went on. The bow was fashioned from hickory or birch, with horsehair or sometimes fine thread run together and rosined, although some examples of a more primitive bow consisting of only a rosined stick have been reported (Thede 1967: 142). Both Thede and De Ryke mention informants who still prefer to make their own fiddles, sometimes using discarded parts of factory-made instruments (Ibid.: 159; De Ryke 1964: 181).

The bridge is commonly whittled down, as on the *hardingfele* in the manner suggested by Mersenne (1957: 240, 263), for the early violin (Boyden 1965: 169-170, 1-9) until it is quite flat, not only facilitating double-stopped and drone styles of playing, but also causing a larger number of accidental contacts with other strings (Bennett 1940: 37). Bennett suggested that the greater ease with which string crossings are accomplished may be another factor (Ibid.: 11). The flatter, lower bridge may result in greater volume from the instrument, but often produces a percussive effect when strings vibrate against the fingerboard, because of the shallow action (Ibid.: 11, 37). James Talbot, writing between 1685 and 1701 of the Cremona type violins, noted a precise measurement for the bridge height of only an inch—about ¼ inch lower than the modern violin bridge—as well as a curvature which varied considerably. The degree to which the bridge contour varies with British-American regional traditions is still uncertain, although another perhaps related vibration-producing trait is documented from all parts of the South and seems to be connected with folk music as well as lore.

Folk informants explain the curious custom of keeping one or more rattle-snake rattles in a fiddle to give a "real vibration"[23] and a good tone to the instrument (Bennett 1940: 11). Art Satherly, talent scout for the early country music industry, reported that the fiddler was expected to kill the snake himself, and that the charm was believed useful for keeping moisture, dust and spiders away from the fiddle (Sanders 1951: 23; Zolotow 1969: 41). Similarly, Bennett's informant believed that his rattles would scare mice away (1940: 11). Most likely, the effectiveness of the rattle is limited to its dust-gathering abilities, keeping the interior clean as efficiently as the more prosaic grains of rice sometimes temporarily introduced by classical violinists (Robert Stern: private interview, Santa Cruz, California, April 16, 1973). Whatever the stated reason, the traditional player often will not play without his rattles and believes that their addition makes the instrument sound different from the violin (Sanders 1951: 23; Zolotow 1969: 41)—and he may be right, depending on their number and size, although it is difficult or impossible to discern the very slight muting and vibrating effect caused by a single rattle.

Fiddlers adjust their instruments in a variety of other ways in order to sound distinctly different from each other, although they play thereafter without concern for any special quality. Some prefer a softer, mellower tone, and others enjoy the more penetrating or even shrill sound. The height and shape of the bridge, its frequent placement nearer the tailpiece, which Boyden suggests may have been sixteenth-century practice (1965: 68-69), the position of the sound post and bass-bar, and the overall condition of the instrument as well as the use of the special tunings described below, all contribute to the individual styles of folk fiddlers (Bayard 1956: 18). Another widespread factor which narrows frequency response is the rosin deposit under the bridge, chronically left by traditional players who prefer a thinner, more metallic tone. In former days, according to Thede, rosin was scarce and players would often allow it to accumulate, passing the bow under the bridge to re-use it for economy (1967: 15). The tension, condition, type and width of bow hair and the amount of rosin applied affect the size and nature of the tone and the types of articulation (Boyden 1965: 70-71; Spielman 1975: 311-330).

The popularity among fiddlers of scordatura tunings, called variously "keying," "discording," "cross-tuning" or "cross-fingering," has been re-marked by all researchers of the tradition. Ira Ford found that many old-time players felt this mode of playing came about by accident (1965: 125). Self-teaching probably accounts for much of this convention, since many tunes can be played with only one or two fingers by beginners who have tuned the strings close together; moreover, the usual manner of holding the instrument makes it difficult to play many double-stops in standard tuning. Thede suggests that one of the origins of cross-tuning may also be the difficulty of tuning homemade instruments with whittled pegs (1967: 142).

Another possibility is that the scordatura as practiced widely in the viol, viola d'amore and violin music of the seventeenth century had entered folk tradition and was imported with the instruments and airs.[24] In England, the first recorded instance of the use of scordatura is seen in John Playford's *Division-Violin*, published in 1685 (Russell 1938: 88), although continental use precedes this by over a century.[25] According to Theodore Russell, Scottish reel players were using the a-e'-a'-a-e" tuning frequently "with rousing effect" (Ibid.: 94).

Perhaps the most widespread tuning of the instrument other than the standard 5ths tuning, called the "Natural Flat," is this "A-minor," a-e'-a'e" (5th-4th-5th) tuning of the "bass" and "counter" strings (Thede 1967: 17; Ford 1965: 125-128; Jabbour 1971: 18),[26] sometimes given a separate name by fiddlers.[27] Thede felt this tuning, once widely used among fiddlers in the lower Mississippi valley, had evolved to prevent stretching the third finger for c# *sul* g and g#' *sul* d' for the keys of D and A (1966). The combined reluctance of the fiddler to shift to higher positions or use his fourth finger and his fondness for the prime, or unison, produced by a stopped and an open string (Thede 1967: 17) has made another tuning widely popular. A number of researchers report the b-e'-b'-e" tuning (4th-5th-4th) (Thede 1967: 19; Bayard 1944a: xv; Bennett 1940: 12-13), which was said by Reverend Richard Henebry to have been used by traditional Irish fiddlers (1928: 67). In this tuning, the prime can be produced in two octaves by the open string and third finger. Thede felt that the combined use of standard tuning with primes formed by the open string and fourth finger indicates that the tune was originally played with the lower strings tuned up a whole step into this scordatura (1967: 15).[28]

Tunings which combine 5ths and 4ths in other ways are also traditional. Bennett and Thede both reported a 5th-5th-4th tuning (given respectively as a-e'-b'-e" and g-d'-a'-d") (Bennett 1940: 12; Thede 1967: 19), and a tuning of 4th-5th-5th (a-d'-a'-e") was given by Bayard and Thede (Bayard 1944a: xv; Thede 1967: 19). According to Thede, these are referred to as "cross-keys" (1967: 17).

The tuning of the lowest string to a drone an octave below the adjacent string is also quite common for certain of the tunes, especially those not intended for dancing. Antonio Lolli, an Italian violinist, dazzled Parisian audiences in 1764 with his technical brilliance and by rendering the lower register more sonorous with a scordatura of d-d'-a'-e", which apparently became popular enough that the custom of lowering the fourth string may have been brought to America by the European folk performer. Both Ford and Thede gave the widespread octave-5th-4th tuning (d-d'-a'-d"), now best known for "Bonaparte's Retreat" but also used in "Kingdom Coming" and other airs (Ford 1965: 129-130; Thede 1967: 19), and Thede also reported the use of an octave-4th-5th (e-e'-a'-e") scordatura (1967: 19). Other "cross-keys" remarked by Thede include the 5th-4th-major 3rd scordatura recommended by Playford in 1685, and a tuning of 5th-major 2nd-5th (a-e'-f#"-c#") (1967: 19). Calhoun reported that fiddlers in the south central Kentucky regions traditionally emphasized the supportive drone possibilities suggested by this low octave tuning of the g-string. His informants actually removed the frog from the bow in order to reassemble the bow with the stick between the top plate and the strings, and the hair upwards and stretched over the strings, producing thereby the continuous but presumably awkward open-stringed drone appropriate to "Bonaparte's Retreat" (1941: 37).

In addition to these traditional ways of tuning, fiddlers often deliberately tune their instruments one or more tones flat for a softer tone quality or because their instruments cannot be brought up to pitch. Evidence suggests that the more widespread preference of tuning low must survive from early English and continental violin practice. Muffat observed that French players, specifically the Lullists, habitually pitched their instruments a whole step or even a minor 3rd below the Germans (1895; Boyden 1965: 204, 247), while Mersenne spoke of the English preference for tuning their viols a tone lower than the French (1957; Boyden 1965: 185-186).[29] Although the standard of pitch in the seventeenth century varied enormously between nations, regions, even within towns (Mendel 1948), and probably also between players of art and folk music, such observations suggest a widely-established preference for lower pitch, at least among English viol players, which may in fact have been assimilated with other viol techniques (see infra: 173) by early violinists and eventually imported to America to survive now by oral tradition among folk fiddlers. It is therefore no surprise that this practice of tuning low and the less common practice of tuning high should persist even when standard pitch is made available to the fiddler for reference. Bennett's informant, quite aware of his relationship to the modern standard, said he preferred to tune "a little sharp," which, when checked, turned out to be a' = 445 (1940: 11), whereas Calhoun reported that all south-central Kentuckians who had migrated from the Blue Ridge through Cumberland Gap tuned one and one-half steps flat (1941: 14). Tuning flat, or more rarely, sharp, is thus another deliberate and archaic way of individualizing the traditional player's sound, and cannot be explained simply by the absence of a standard.

In scordatura, the lower strings most commonly provide a drone functioning as a "dancer's continuo" (Kennedy 1956) and quite possibly derived, along with the reel, from seventeenth-century contact with the Scottish bagpipe (Lindsay 1954: 350) and with the hurdy-gurdy tradition. Although Boyden reasoned from the use of gut strings that the lowest string with its poor response must have been virtually unused until the late seventeenth century (1965: 69-70; cf. van der Straeten 1911: 21), and believed it was not used as a drone by early dance violinists (private interview, Berkeley, California, January 30, 1973), its response was quite adequate for this use, as on the contemporary lira da braccio, and the Renaissance fiddle, and eighteenth-century French players actually referred to the string when bound with wire as a "bourdon."[30] It therefore may be that the later influence of the Scottish bagpipe was upon an already-established tradition making some use of open-stringed drones. Flood sweepingly claimed Ireland as the sole source of the entire "pedal point" tradition, and more to the point, traced its supposed origins back to the sixth century Irish *cronan*, perhaps an indication of an early and enduring preference for the drone (1906: 67). It is still common practice in Scotland for a dance fiddler to be joined by a 'cello continuo which reinforces the drone, according to Collinson (1966: 227), although this tradition, of course, cannot be isolated from the surrounding bagpipe idiom. Additional evidence suggesting that the drone may have been used by violinists of the sixteenth and seventeenth centuries is provided by Frank and Joan Harrison's study of the Zinacanteca violin of the Mayans in Chiapas, Mexico, which derives from the *violetta* of c. 1575-1650, and is invariably played with simple double-stopping including some drone effects (1958: 7). Drone strings tuned by the traditional fiddler also may vibrate sympathetically without being bowed, as on the viola d'amore, and on Norway's folk fiddle, the *hardingfele* (Burman-Hall 1975: 49; cf. Boyden 1965: 199; Bjørndal 1956: 13).[31] One informant says this practice "makes a good vibration."[32] Most likely, this practice, just as the many shapes and adjustments of bridge, soundpost, bass-bar and bow, and the predilection for the various traditional scordatura, is simply another means of producing the unique personal sound apparently much admired by the traditional fiddler.

While these adjustments are certainly widespread, some players still feel that the most significant and only sure distinction between the violin and fiddle is the musician and his attitude. Thus, violins are kept in violin cases, fiddles in pillow cases (Sanders 1951: 23).

CONVENTIONS OF PERFORMANCE:

Attitude, Position and Technique

> *A squeaking engine he apply'd*
> *Unto his neck, on north east side,*
> *Just where the hangman does dispose,*
> *To special friends, the knot or noose*

. . . .

His grisly beard was long and thick,
with which he strung his fiddle-stick;
For he to horse-tail scorn'd to owe,
For what on his own chin did grow.
          —Hudibras I:2 by Samuel Butler
                  (1662)

The traditional player relates to his instrument and to the situation of performance in certain ways that are passed along with the tunes from each generation to the next. Among folk fiddlers, the bow and fiddle grips, consequent patterns of bowing and fingering, use of vocal tune-versions and special effects, and the spontaneous variations caused by re-creation of the tune while playing are related on the one hand to the form of the instrument itself, and on the other, to the nature and variety of the repertory (cf. Burman-Hall 1975: 48). As with the resulting versions and variants of the airs themselves, these mannerisms of relating to the instrument may eventually be shown as regional variables.[33] Research is complicated by the various and common personal mannerisms, which are often difficult to distinguish from learned habits; similarly, the description of styles of variation used in the re-creation of a tune is sometimes confused by the effects of age and faulty memory, deafness, rheumatism and nervousness (Bayard 1956: 18; cf. Kidson 1891: xiv).

It has been said by the traditonal musician Clarence Tom Ashley that "country people play their feeling and feel their playing" (Shelton 1966: 23). Certainly the fiddler obviously may be said to enjoy his playing characteristically keeping time in dance tunes with his whole body and with his heel or toe (Bennett 1940: 11, 14), and usually playing steadily and with untiring vigor (Bayard 1956: 17-18).

Traditional fiddlers, like folk singers, normally sit to perform (Bayard 1944: xiv) with feet on the floor or the chair rungs, or with legs crossed or with one foot on another chair (Osborne 1952: 212; Anon. 1969: 29), although some prefer to stand, leaning against the wall or erect (Osborne 1952: 212). The left elbow or even the violin neck may commonly rest on the left knee when the cross-legged position is chosen (Bennett 1940: 10; Osborne 1952: 212). A number of ancient ways of holding the instrument have been recorded. One of the oldest, identical to that of sixteenth-century violinists playing in a string band for "la volta" at the Valois court of Henry III (Boyden 1965: 66), is generally thought to be the method of inclining the fiddle inward while holding it against the chest, although other common sixteenth- and seventeenth-century shoulder or upper arm positions have also been current among fiddlers (Thede 1967: 15; King 1969: 93; Bayard 1944: xiv; Osborne 1952: 212; P. Seeger 1959: 4). Bayard observed traditional players with the fiddle held between or on the knees, like a viol, or on the lap (1944: xiv).

Complete musicological documentation by David Boyden for the variety and currency of early violin playing positions, and their relationship to the early sixteenth-century techniques of the viol, rebec, lira da braccio, and Renaissance fiddle, provides many clues and possibilities for speculation on the origins and derivation of apparently identical techniques now found only among a dwindling number of American folk fiddlers. Although Boyden was unaware of the possible survival of these early practices in traditional fiddling of the South until his book was already in page-proof (Frank Harrison: private interview, Princeton, New Jersey, March 23, 1969; David Boyden: private interview, Berkeley, California, January 30, 1973), a case for establishing the continuity of these positions is readily apparent based on his accumulated evidence:

1. The early violin was, from its beginnings in the 1520s, the province of the lower classes, who held it against the chest, shoulder, or upper arm; it was thus restricted to dance music, and associated with tunes in oral tradition and with the profane (1965: 72, 94, passim).

2. These positions, originally taken over from older string playing techniques, survived especially among lower class, musically illiterate players of dance music in France, England and the British Isles (by influence from France), and to a lesser degree in Italy, throughout the seventeenth century, becoming less prevalent only after the French began to imitate the parallel and competing Italian virtuosic tradition's techniques and, by necessity, the bow grip and neck position (often with chin support) in the 1720s, but not virtually obsolete in western Europe until 1750, a time well after the settlement of the American colonies by a great number of emigrants of lower class British origin (Ibid.: 51, 133, 230, 234, 357, 360, passim).[34]

These archaic methods, current for approximately two hundred years in Europe and preserved in American folk tradition for approximately two hundred more, are less common nowadays. Folk players usually position the fiddle naturally under the chin, with the thumb or palm of the hand supporting the instrument, or the wrist clamping, and with the left arm still held low in front of or on the hip (Thede 1967: 15; Osborne 1952: 212; Bennett 1940: 11), in the manner of mid-eighteenth-century professional technique as pictured and described by Leopold Mozart (1756: frontispiece; Boyden 1965: Plate 39, 357-358, 368-369). Very recently, the old mannerisms have been observed to shift toward classical violin technique, and today the left-handed fiddler who fingers with his right hand is quite rare, no doubt due to the influence of television and "personal appearances" of professional artists on the few remaining tradition-oriented fiddlers (Thede 1967: 15).

These comfortable ancient ways of holding the fiddle result in a tendency to play only in first position (Boyden 1965: 66, 68-69; Bennett 1940: 11) and thus primarily in the fingering of the keys of G, D, and A, with some tunes in C and E (Thede 1962: 20),[35] although the fiddler does not think in terms of keys recognizable by pitch. Each fiddler is likely to have a special preference for one or two of these keys with their resultant characteristic intonational patterns, in which he will play most of his tunes (Bayard 1944a: xv; Jabbour 1971: 17). Although fiddlers do not learn by the standard hand positions, many have learned, as did violinists before Geminiani's reforms of 1751, to play "all over the fiddle" with accuracy and comfort (Bayard 1944a: xiv; Boyden 1965: 369-370, passim). Unorthodox fingerings, such as the use of the first finger on the e″-string to stop both f#″ and g″, were reported by Bayard to be a matter of habit not dictated by a desire to play higher without moving the hand. Some traditional players use the fourth finger constantly, but most prefer to avoid it (Ibid.: xiv; Thede 1967: 15) except perhaps on the e″-string (Calhoun 1941: 17-18). Thede and Boyden agree that the holding of the fiddle with the palm of the hand makes the use of the fourth finger especially difficult (Thede 1967: 15; Boyden 1965: 153), a circumstance which encouraged the development of traditional scordatura (Thede 1967: 15).

Another characteristic that relates to both folk and pre-Baroque ways of holding the fiddle is the near absence of vibrato in the traditional aesthetic (Bayard 1944a: xvi; 1956: 17-18; cf. Boyden 1965: 68-69, 177-178). Precise studies of violin vibrato, largely a consciously cultivated mechanical device, unlike the more organic and inevitable vocal vibrato, indicate that the pitch vibrato (average .25 step) is chronically heard by musicians as being of a much smaller extent than it actually is (H. Seashore 1932: 221-224, 229-235; Hollinshead 1932: 281-282; C. Seashore 1936: 47). Although competent auditors usually underestimate the pitch and intensity variance present in all but the shortest stopped notes and open-stringed modern violin playing by one-half to three-quarters, these pitch variations produce periodic intensity and timbre fluctuations (Reger 1932: 330-331; C. Seashore 1936: 80-83, 89), and the resulting string sonance is commonly and easily associated with the sincerity and involvement characterizing impassioned folk and primitive vocal performances (Metfessel 1928; Tiffin and H. Seashore 1932: 351-353; C. Seashore 1936: 53-59, 110). Since at least the initial string displacement which begins a bow stroke and the resonance of the instrument produce respective periodic intensity and periodic timbre variations that cannot be avoided, measurable vibrato is present in folk fiddling, even though the traditional fiddler has not cultivated the pitch vibrato. Extensive testing by the Seashore circle indicated that these various components of the sound cannot ordinarily be distinguished by musicians, who may nevertheless form strong opinions regarding whether they have heard pitch or amplitude fluctuations (C. Seashore 1936: 104-105). While it is thus difficult to say precisely how vibrato-like effects occasionally heard from the fiddler are actually produced, it is probably reasonable to assume that regular periodic vibrato is the result either of conscious pitch fluctuation or of tuning discrepancies causing beats. The rare use of visible or otherwise obvious pitch vibrato by the folk fiddler of today almost invariably suggests the encroachment of violin technique (P. Seeger 1959: 4).

The bow is also grasped in traditional ways connected with performance idioms. The most usual way, popular among sixteenth-century violinists (Boyden 1965: 75) and now perpetuated among fiddlers by oral tradition, was to grasp the stick about a third of the way out from the frog, with the thumb straight or bent backwards, rather than flexed as in modern violin playing. Marion Thede reasonably concludes that, for the fiddler, this compensates for the excess length of the modern bow (1967: 15), which is, according to Boyden, at least six and perhaps as much as ten inches longer than French bows of the sixteenth and seventeenth centuries (1965: 111-112, 206-210). This grasp facilitates short, vigorous strokes (Bayard 1944a: xv; Thede 1967: 15), more vertical than horizontal (P. Seeger 1959: 4), which are used by most fiddlers. Since length of stroke is not required, the straight thumb is comfortable (Thede 1967: 15). Although bow crossings are more comfortably done in the middle or upper part of the bow where the traversed arc is smaller (Ibid.: 14), traditionally-oriented Canadian fiddler Jean Carignan has expressed the opinion that the best players in any style of the art have held the bow for longer strokes.[36] That this is not simply an incursion of violin aesthetics, but a counter-tradition with its own history, may be borne out by accounts of folk fiddlers who have preferred to hold the bow near to or at the frog, sometimes in the manner of a German double-bass grip.[37] Generally, bowing style varies from the straight-wristed approach to a technique in which the wrist was arched over the bow with only the forearm moving (Bayard 1944a: xiv). These varied habits of grasping and moving the bow, the speed of the stroke, the sector used, and the resulting possibilities of phrasing all serve to distinguish personal styles within the art and add uniqueness to each performance.

Vocals and Special Effects

The performance of the fiddle and banjo dance airs has often been accompanied by vocal verses to the tune, or by square dance calling. The close association of vocal and instrumental versions of many of our older tunes has made it impossible to determine which form came first, words or music, or fiddle-song or banjo-song, since all may now be equally widespread, popular and meritorious. We know that in former days, when no fiddler could be found for a dance, the tunes were sung in simplified or abbreviated form, with traditional or improvised rhymed verses, called "fiddle-songs" or "dance-songs" (Bayard 1944a: xxiii; Gordon 1938: 71; McCulloh 1965: xiii). This convention was also followed when the fiddler was available, with the words serving to "add brightness and relieve monotony" during the events. According to Robert Gordon, the performance of the fiddle tune would typically inspire the fiddler, or a dancer or onlooker, to provide a single standard rhymed couplet for the tune, suggesting "another and another until a sequence of similar verses is built up" on this model largely by improvisation.[38]

These simple verses, writes folklorist Vance Randolph, whether humorous or obscene, have been set to nearly all of the old fiddle-tunes; in many cases the details of the vocal cadence and delivery of these presumed outgrowths of the tune have subsequently been imitated by the roguish fiddler. "Familiar with these [bawdy] words myself, I have been amazed at the distinctness with which the fiddle pronounces them" (1932: 71-72).

Conventions seem to govern the appearance of the fiddle song verses during the playing of the tune. In the early years of the century, apparently the verses were sung during a pause in the fiddler's playing (Coppage 1961: 10). Gordon remarked that the verses tended to appear in groups at irregular intervals (1938: 71-72), although Thede, familiar principally with western tradition, described the current practice as generally regular. She observed that when each strain was regularly repeated, the song entered after one strophe, with verses accompanying only the initial playing of the first strain in each strophe, until all verses were sung (1967: 26). Some tunes, such as "Old Joe Clark," have given rise to words for both strains and follow individual patterns (Ibid.: 28).

Sometimes the fiddler himself called the figures for the dance, but more often this was done by another in the local style, which varied from simple prompting of the dancers, through continuous rhymed pattern of equal parts dance jargon and cliché, to the singing calls which fit the instructions to the simplified melody of the tune (Burchenal 1951: 21; Sanders 1951: 26), allowing the fiddler to concentrate on his playing (P. Seeger 1959: 4; Bennett 1940: 8).[39]

The rapid-fire tense style of singing appropriate to the fiddle tune and to square dance calling is often indistinguishable from southern vocal style as described through the years by ballad scholars. Louise Rand Bascomb characterized the style in 1909 as:

an indescribably high, piercing nasal head tone, which carries remarkably well, and which gathers to itself a weirdness that compels the blood to jump in the veins (1909: 240).

Strangely enough, no matter how sad the words may be, they are always rendered as rapidly as is compatible with the skill of the musician, and without inflection (Ibid.: 238).

In addition to singing, square dance calling, shouts, laughs and other vocal effects, the traditional performer may employ "straw-beating" or other related rhythmic effects. Making sounds like Spanish castanets, "the fellers that han'l the bones [straws or sticks]" (Bascomb 1909: 239) hammer rhythmically on the fiddler's unused open drone strings over the fingerboard.[40] A similarly curious custom is current among French Basque *txistulari* musicians in the pipe and tabor (or "whittle and dub") tradition of accompanying forms of the Morris Dance. The performer plays a primitive three-holed whistle held with the left hand, while clamping a small coffin-shaped box across which strings are stretched using the same arm which holds the whistle. This instrument, called the *tchun-tchun* or *tun-tun*, is beaten with a flexible stick held in the other hand to produce a rhythmic drone along with the piping (Kennedy 1964: 98; McCall 1969; Alford 1935). It is a definite possibility that this easily-portable Basque one-man band may have confronted and impressed the American folk fiddler during the Basque migration to the western triangle roughly outlined by the states of Nevada, Oregon, and Montana (Sharp 1954: 397), but more likely the fiddler has inherited the effect from the *col legno* of the violin, introduced in the early seventeenth century as an imitative device first given for the viol by Tobias Hume (1605), and later for the violin in an unpublished manuscript of Carlo Farina's *Capriccio Stravagante* (1627) (Harnoncourt 1970; Boyden 1965: 132 and 1980: 561; van der Straeten 1911: 20-23). Pizzicato with the left hand, introduced as a special effect in classical violin technique by Paganini (Apel 1965: 586), survives also in the fiddler's repertory of technical devices.[41] The story of these conventions remains to be discovered, but one certainly may suspect influence from the closely-associated fife tradition in these stylized programmatic imitations of battle-sounds and drums.

THE FIDDLE TUNE

One of the most prominent characteristics of British-American folk music is the rather high degree of formal organization exhibited by the melodies. The instrumental tradition differs from the well-known and thoroughly-researched folk balladry primarily in the greater amount of influence exerted by non-British idioms.[42] Tunes and styles of old-world instrumental folk musics have been so well preserved in parts of the United States that it is now impossible to determine which melodies in this tradition evolved in America, or even to know with certainty whether any of the variants of well-known tunes may have arisen in the New World (Bayard 1967: 22). The many difficulties of establishing reasonable criteria for determining the boundaries of a tune family, which have generated a great deal of debate among ballad-tune scholars (e.g., Gerould 1932: 76-77; Bayard: 1944b, 1951; Poladian 1942, 1951; Bronson 1951; cf. Burman-Hall 1978), also demonstrate the high degree of cross-influence exerted from within the tradition (Bayard 1953: 126-130). This cross-influence has caused convergence as well as divergence in the repertory. Thus, American renditions of tunes, being in general easier to finger and to bow, and less complex in figuration, correspond more closely to the relatively straightforward and direct English manner of playing than to the ornate Gaelic tradition.[43]

Tunes preserved in American tradition may be either pentatonic or diatonic in genus (Cazden 1971), with the 4th and 7th degrees as the least stable structural elements when present.[44] Although the pentatonic is widespread as a genus alternate to the diatonic, it would seem that the great majority of traditional fiddle airs and fiddle players are distinguished by diatonicism in their respective variants and performance versions (Bayard 1966: 53). In traditional tunes of the diatonic genus, chromatic ornaments, directionally inflected pitch for one or more scalar degrees, and even microtonal variants occasionally appear, but do not affect the underlying genus. Consequently, as Cecil Sharp first remarked, folk singers, "not having any settled notions with regard to the pitch of the third note of the scale," vary their intonation according to the nature of each phrase, producing two or even three shades of intonation within a single tune, "not arbitrarily, but systematically, i.e., consistently, in every verse" (1907: 71). The same effect in the intonation patterns of folk fiddlers prompted Bayard to credit the influence of flutes, fifes, flageolets and whistles of the large family of pipers' instruments, which retain the fixed spacing of holes, and thus produce slightly low major 3rds and 6ths as well as neutral 7ths when played without the use of cross-fingerings. These intervals, established and transmitted in the diatonic idiom as a function of the ancient fife airs, created what Bayard termed "a crystallized tradition of melodizing" (1966: 53) which has influenced the performance of both traditional fiddling and folk song wherever piping has been common.[45]

As tunes generally associated with square dancing, the "reels," "hornpipes," "jigs," or "quadrilles" of the British-American tradition ordinarily consist of two symmetrical strains in a moderate duple meter ($\quad$ = 112-132), although there is evidence that the tempo of former days may have been somewhat more deliberate (Bayard 1956: 17). In performance, phrases occasionally lose a beat, or acquire an additional beat, even in tunes from the dance repertory (cf. Burman-Hall 1975: 53). The two strains, which often may share a common cadence, normally differ in melodic compass. The "Coarse" is characteristically played on the lower (coarser) strings, and has a more restricted compass. In recent times the "Fine," usually the more distinctive of the two, has been played first more often than not, reversing what in some areas is an older ordering of the strains so that now the most striking part is heard first. The length of a particular performance, and the repetition patterns of the strains, each of which may be heard two or more times consecutively, depend on the length of the dance and the preferences of the performer in the context of regional tradition, as discussed in Burman-Hall 1975.

MELODIC REALIZATION

We may suppose the ancient folk convention of perpetually varying a tune realization was established even before the sixteenth-century beginnings of violin performance. Although studied elaboration and improvisation is not specifically mentioned before Mersenne's treatise of 1636, David Boyden has wisely suggested that early performers must have imitated improvised viol divisions (1965: 89-90, 94-95), described in the literature from the fifteenth century onwards (Tinctoris 1950; Ganassi 1924). Comparing the problems of scholarship generated by his attempt to reconstruct this early stage of violin technique to the more recent difficulties encountered by historians of early jazz development and improvisation, Boyden said:

The dance violinist of the sixteenth century may have occupied a social and musical position not much different from the saxophonist today; and similarly, not only was the music of both infrequently written down, but the manner of performing may well have been practically impossible to notate with any accuracy (1965: 94).

In view of Boyden's opinions, it seems reasonable to assume that these unwritten early violin variation techniques, about which we know so little, may have been sharpened and sophisticated by the more musically literate under the influence of current instrumental idioms into the stylized virtuosic variation devices surviving from the seventeenth century, and still have simultaneously persisted with comparatively little change, passing through the hands of the illiterate European amateur and of the British folk musician to the traditional fiddler of the American South (Burman 1968: 60-61). Bayard also attached much importance to this phenomenon being a clear indicator of the archaic nature of the tradition and its tunes (1953: 125). As the convention comes down to us, the folk fiddler may freely employ alternate realizations of the basic tune outline each time it is played. Even slight, perhaps inadvertent changes in bowings and phrasings result in differences in the droned accompaniment and may affect the apparent melodic shape of the tune. More obviously, deliberate alterations in rhythm and melodic decoration are also traditional (Burman 1968: 55). The simultaneous retention of basic melodic design, internal form and harmonic outline mark variations on this foundation as "clear examples of the melodico-harmonic variation technique" (Ibid.: 60), as described for fine art music by Robert Nelson in his excellent study of variation techniques (1948: 16). These often slight and elusive variations of detail, introduced into the successive repetitions of the air, have the cumulative effect within the performance of the tune of producing a curious and hypnotic freshness (Bennett 1940: 32, 43; Mellers 1964: 266). It was perhaps a similar but more self-conscious melodico-harmonic variation technique current among Polish musicians which caused Telemann to remark in his *Autobiography* of 1739 (Mattheson 1740):

one would hardly believe what wonderfully bright ideas such pipers and fiddlers are apt to get when they improvise, ideas that would suffice for an entire lifetime (cf. Boyden 1965: 353).

While we now cannot establish what it was that inspired Telemann, we may probably assume the variation to have been relatively constant in the performance, for, as Béla Bartók saw it, the best folk musicians not only can vary tunes constantly, but also strongly prefer to do so (1931: 2), as verified by most collectors of traditional British-American music.[46]

The semi-sophisticated written tune versions from seventeenth-century violin tutors which interacted with this aural tradition, show a range of contrapuntal expansion devices from the simple, such as we might expect to find in almost any aural traditional tune family, to rather studied techniques, reminiscent of the more virtuosic violin literature of the German and Italian traditions.[47]

Although this conventional variation practice does not involve a studied, elaborated development of a basic melody, as in other British fiddling and piping traditions, it is clear that the long-term effect of such experimental re-creation on items in a traditional repertory is potentially enormous. With several equally acceptable versions of particular passages in tunes of similar tempo, form, rhythm and mode,[48] the interchange and migration of common melodic patterns results in the patchwork creation of many substantially new tunes in this and in other genres of folk music (Poladian 1931: 32; Bayard 1951: 45).[49]

This process can be observed in detail for Southern American examples of the ancient and well-diffused "Soldier's Joy" tune complex.[50] Study of this "Soldier's Joy" complex and of the slow air tune complex involving "Bonaparte's Retreat" eventually suggested a geographically based division into four distinct southern regional styles.'[51]

The Blue Ridge Style, with all examples following a line parallel to and east of the Appalachian mountains; the Southern Appalachian style, with examples from West Virginia to Mississippi along the line of the mountain range and west; the Ozark Mountain style; and Western style, being principally the style of Texas and Oklahoma, sometimes appearing in states farther to the West.

(Burman-Hall 1975: 56)

Tables 1 and 2 show the most representative strains from 22 recorded performance versions of the "Soldier's Joy" tune, with Tables 3 and 4 indicating what seem to be the uniform underlying structures which provide the basis for performance variation.[52] The existence of widely variant forms of this and many other of our traditional tunes shows the long-term effects of much diffusion and improvisational re-creation by players in the past (Ibid.: xvi-xvii).[53] It is therefore to be expected that analysis of the use and currency of this most interesting performance technique will reveal it to be a major variable in the definition of distinct sub-styles in southern British-American fiddling, and for other traditional instrumental music.

A COMPARISON OF BOWING AND
RELATED RHYTHMIC FACTORS

Aspects of bowing form perhaps the most important complex of stylistic determinants for the analysis of regional styles of fiddling. Samuel Bayard has observed three traditional styles of bowing:

1) the Plain, involving only the single melodic string in a variety of bowing patterns; 2) the Harmonic, having frequent or intermittent double-stopping intended to produce harmony at some or most points in the tune, often with the supporting note fingered and typically with shorter strokes; and 3) the Drone, using virtually constant double-stopping with open strings tuned to the key and generally long bow strokes producing a bagpipe-like effect (Burman-Hall 1975: 63; cf. Bayard 1944a: xv-xvi; 1956: 18).

These may be combined in some cases, but usually the style chosen by a particular fiddler remains constant for tunes of the same function in his repertory. Although such factors as the increasing popularity of accompanying instruments and the desire for greater volume have tended to change regional preferences for particular combinations of these bowing styles, the recorded performances chosen for this study seem typical of traditional practices. Of even greater importance than the degree to which double-stopping is employed are the rhythmic types, locations, and the degree of uniformity of the numerous bowing patterns. Other significant related factors include the tendency to accent certain strokes, the occasional use of pizzicato in a bowing pattern, and the habitual fingering of certain melodic rhythms within the bow-stroke.

The bowing style of the Blue Ridge fiddlers showed a distinction between Virginia players and those of North Carolina and Georgia. Informants from Virginia played with a fuller sound, and generally adopted the Harmonic style of bowing for "Soldier's Joy," with only a very small amount of Plain bowing in the third measure of a single informant's Fine strain (Table 5A, Example 6-F). Fiddlers from North Carolina and Georgia, while also fond of Drone and Harmonic styles, are apparently more likely to include the Plain style of bowing in their performances, since all versions of the tune from these two states contained Plain bowing style in some, most, or all of the Fine strain in all but one case, in which the Plain style was instead used in the Coarse ("Soldier's Joy," Table 5E, Example 1-C). In Blue Ridge examples, as elsewhere, the performance of dance music proved to be closely associated with the Harmonic style of bowing, with the shorter strokes of the harmonic notes providing rhythmic emphasis, while the longer-bowed Drone style was reserved for the slower genre of fiddle tunes which are not intended for the dance.[54] The typical Blue Ridge bowing patterns seem to be rhythmically more complex than those of the non-dance

Table 1 "Soldier's Joy" Variants — Fine Strain

177

Table 1 (*continued*)

Table 1 (*continued*)

style, but remain almost totally free of ties between beats, with the exception of ties between measures, which occur commonly. Although duple divisions and sub-divisions of the beat predominated in the transcribed sample, trochaic triplet sub-divisions also tended to appear (cf. Table 5A, Examples 3-F, 4-F and 5-F, and Table 5E, Example 5-C). Performances occasionally included repeated instances of an iambic bowing rhythm (e.g. ♫. in Table 5A, the Fine of Example 5-F) related to the "Scotch snap" as preserved in American traditional music by fifers as well as by fiddlers (cf. Bayard 1944a: xvi; Jabbour 1971: 5-6), and which sometimes also appeared as a fingering rhythm (cf. infra: 59). Although this rhythm was used only very infrequently in the Blue Ridge examples from Virginia, it did not ever occur in transcribed performances from the Southern Appalachian region. In the sample studied, distinctive Blue Ridge dance music bowing patterns governed the selection of the ♫♫ or equivalent ♫♫ bowing rhythm for the third beats of measures in the Coarse of "Soldier's Joy" in all but one instance (Table 5E, Example 1-C). Although most variants of the tune in other areas presented the melodic line with this rhythm, only one informant from outside the Blue Ridge and Ozark regions actually bowed this same pattern to emphasize the melody of the Coarse (Western Style, Table 5H, Example 4-C). Versions from Georgia (Table 5A, Examples 1-F and 2-F and Table 5E, Examples 1-C and 2-C) were unique in their consistent use of short, even "saw strokes" (cf. Schwarz 1965:3) usually of sixteenth-note value in both strains, but especially in the Fine, and thus were closest to the general patterns of bowing found in the non-dance style. Otherwise, all other examples of "Soldier's Joy" by Blue Ridge fiddlers featured a distinctive one-measure bowing pattern (or less often, a two-measure pattern) for each strain acting as an ostinato rhythmic pattern sometimes known among traditional players as a "swing" (Thede 1967: 20).[55] While the connection between the presumed currency of this device among dance violinists of the early seventeenth century and its appearance among traditional fiddlers of the Blue Ridge may be direct and historical, since the Blue Ridge and points east were settled well before the other style regions, with the use of "swings" apparently less common in each area farther to the West, it may also be indirect and functional, due to the simple and obviously idiomatic nature of this approach to bowing.[56]

Southern Appalachian performance conventions are markedly different from those of the Blue Ridge in both style and patterns of bowing. In this tune, as in the slow playing style, most fiddlers mixed their Drone or Harmonic bowings with Plain playing of the tune, whereas only a few Blue Ridge informants, from Georgia or North Carolina exclusively, used the Plain style at all. As in Blue Ridge style, the ratio of Plain to double-stopped playing seemed about the same in slow air playing as in the dance tune style. Thus, only two out of the eight fiddlers for "Soldier's Joy" used no Plain style playing in their performances.[57] The remaining fiddlers used

Table 2 "Soldier's Joy" Variants — Coarse Strain

Table 2 (*continued*)

Table 2 (*continued*)

Table 3   Graph of Fine Strain from "Soldier's Joy"

Table 4   Graph of Coarse Strain from ''Soldier's Joy''

both styles in both strains, either equally or with more Plain playing or even exclusively with Plain bowings in the Coarse, or with both strains relying heavily on Plain style playing, or infrequently, with Plain bowings only in the Fine.[58] In Blue Ridge examples, occurrences of Plain bowings were generally confined to the Fine strain, whereas in the Southern Appalachian style, the majority of fiddlers utilizing greater amounts of Plain playing in one strain showed it in the Coarse. Unlike the Blue Ridge sample which included at least two sub-styles of bowings throughout its range, the Southern Appalachian group showed no clear sub-styles in its comparable area. The largest group, informants from Kentucky, presented all of the bowing style combinations previously described as characteristic of the overall style; one fiddler (Example 2—Ending) even used pizzicato briefly as an alternative to bowing, although this is traditionally acceptable in this region primarily in music not intended for the dance.[59]

The bowing patterns characteristic of Southern Appalachian style in general are quite different from those of the Blue Ridge region, although individual performances from each style may sometimes be very similar. The bowing patterns used at dance tempo in the Southern Appalachian region seem to be distinguished from those of the Blue Ridge area by the frequent use of ties between beats within the measure. Evidence suggests that these common bowing patterns, "the very soul of this widespread fiddling style," survive from late eighteenth and early nineteenth century British (presumably Irish) practice (Jabbour 1971: 12). Almost no ties between the internal beats of measures occurred in the transcribed examples of "Soldier's Joy" from the Blue Ridge area, whereas seven out of the eight Southern Appalachian performers made extensive use of well-established ties between beats,[60] five of these doing so in both strains, while two featured tying in only one strain (Table 5B, Example 6-F, and Table 5F, Example 8-C). Bow strokes tied over the measure were used generally in one or both strains by both Blue Ridge and Southern Appalachian players (cf. Bayard 1944a: xvi). Considered without the complication of ties between beats, the beat subdivisions bowed by the Southern Appalachian performers matched those of the Blue Ridge fiddlers, with variously mixed duple and triple patterns and with frequent use of the bowed iambic triplet rhythm. One important difference between Southern Appalachian and Blue Ridge bowing patterns seems to be the less frequent use of an ostinato or "swing" bowing pattern throughout one or both strains by Southern Appalachian informants. Over half of the Southern Appalachian players in this sample developed a true ostinato bowing pattern of one or two measures, but even among those who did, the technique was limited to only one of the strains.[61] The majority of examples approached a true "swing" pattern in at least the Coarse strain by using identical or similar bowings in two of the measures, usually the first and third, by association with the melodic repetition, though in one case the second and third (Table 5B, Example 2-F), but in general varied the bowing

Table 5   "Soldier's Joy" — Fine Strain

A.   Blue Ridge Style

1-F
(Ga.)

2-F
(Ga.)

3-F
(Va.)

4-F
(Va.)

5-F
(Va.)

6-F
(Va.)

7-F
(Va.)

B.   Southern Appalachian Style

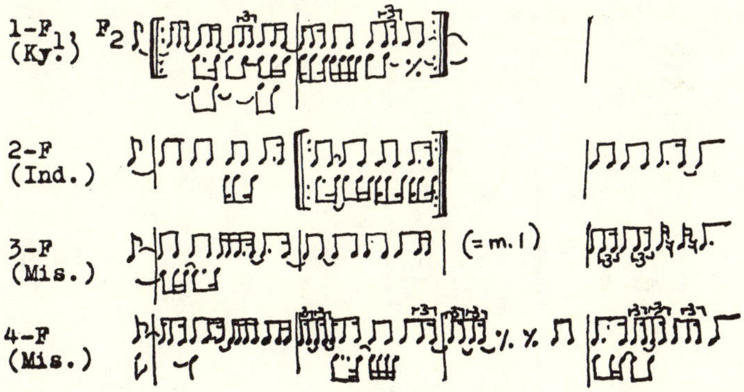

1-F
(Ky.)

2-F
(Ind.)

3-F
(Mis.)

4-F
(Mis.)

Table 5 (*continued*)

C. **Ozark Style**

D. **Western Style**

E. Blue Ridge Style

1-C.
(Ga.)

2-C₁} C₂
(Ga.)

3-C
(Va.)

4-C
(Va.)

5-C
(Va.)

6-C
(Va.)

7-C
(Va.)

F. Southern Appalachian Style

1-C₁
(Ky.)
C₂

2-C₂
(Ind.)
C₁

3-C
(Mis.)

4-C₁
(Mis.)
C₂

Table 5 (*continued*)

5-C$_1$, C$_2$
(Miss.)

6-C
(Ky.)

7-C
(W. Va.)

8-C
(Ala.)   (= m. 2)

G. Ozark Style

1-C
(Ark.)

2-C
(Mo.)

3-C
(Mo.)

H. Western Style

1-C
(Tex.)

2-C
(Tex.)

3-C
(Ariz.)

4-C
(Ok.)

patterns in a unit that truly stabilized at only the four-measure level, if at all. Just as the variation style typical of Southern Appalachian fiddling involves the greatest amount of alteration between strain re-creations within a performance, so the freer presentation of the basic bowing vocabulary also creates variation, within rather than between strains.

The tendency to accent certain strokes of the bow or, in cadential situations, a specific part of the stroke, is more pronounced in Southern Appalachian style than elsewhere (cf. Bennett 1940: 32), and as in the case of Blue Ridge bow accents, often serves to exaggerate the characteristic subdivision of the beat chosen for bowing changes. Two performers in the "Soldier's Joy" sample accentuated the off-beat bowings, with three additional "Soldier's Joy" renditions including a comparable usage on the fourth beat of the cadential measure of the Fine, an equally weak structural rhythmic point.[62] One of the earliest recordings of "Soldier's Joy" from this region (Example 1) documented a fiddler who accented all his bow changes slightly, emphasizing the beginnings of beats as in the Blue Ridge style.

As in the sample of Blue Ridge playing, examples of bowing from the Ozark region seemed typically to be in Drone or Harmonic style with only a little Plain playing. Two of the three Ozark performances of "Soldier's Joy" were virtually double-stopped throughout in Harmonic style (Tables 5C and 5G, Examples 1 and 2).

Examples of the dance-music bowing patterns used by Ozark fiddlers in "Soldier's Joy" showed a great similarity to Blue Ridge style. Nearly all features of Blue Ridge dance music bowing patterns appeared in these Ozark examples, and most of the Ozark patterns closely resembled the ostinati patterns of the Blue Ridge examples. Although the strict use of a distinctive ostinato rhythm was limited in these performances, two players used sixteenth-note patterns much as were found in the playing of Georgia fiddlers, and all tended toward a "swing" in the Southern Appalachian manner, but with a greater number of identical or similar measures.[63] One distinction between the two regional bowing styles is that triplet bowings seem to be less common in Ozark performances, whereas many appear in Blue Ridge bowing patterns (e.g., Table 5A, Example 3-F). In examples from the Ozarks, the distinctive ♫♫ rhythm was taken up on the third beat of Coarse strain measures (Table 5G, Examples 1-C and 3-C), as in the Blue Ridge sample, as was the occasional choice of an iambic rhythm (e.g., ♪♩• in Example 2-F Fine).

The Western style area is characterized by the greatest use of the Plain performance style, a development perhaps caused or exaggerated by the traditional association of the Spanish guitar with the fiddle through contact with Mexican culture throughout the Southwest. Thus, the Fine strain was at least partially Plain in execution, and usually totally or almost totally without double-stops, whereas the Coarse strain was likely to contain some Harmonic or Drone style execution.[64] One version was almost completely Plain throughout (Tables 5D and 5H, Examples 3-F and 3-C).

Traditional bowing patterns shown by Western performances were extremely simple and straightforward, as were the uncomplicated typical patterns of Blue Ridge examples. One difference in Western performances was the much less frequent occurrence of ties over bar lines: this bowing habit, universally found in Blue Ridge examples, appears to have a more limited currency in the Western style. Such ties seem to appear more often at the beginning of the strain than between internal measures, and were used extensively in single strains by only two performers (Table 5D, Example 3-F, and Table 5H, Example 2-C). Characterizing the performance of both strains of "Soldier's Joy" and also examples of the slow air style of playing, this lack of bowing strokes tied over the measure combined with the use of very simple bowing rhythms similar to those of the Blue Ridge style area produced the most uniformly straight-forward bowing effects found in any of the four traditional styles studied. Both of the Texas fiddlers for "Soldier's Joy" bowed one-measure ostinato patterns in both strains (Tables 5D and 5H, Examples 1-F and 2-F, 1-C, 2-C), and the performance from Oklahoma also relied on similarly simple repetitious rhythm in the Fine strain, while the Coarse strain was bowed with a two-measure "swing" (Table 5H, Example 4-C).[65] The Arizona version was thus unique in its use of a flexible bowing scheme, but otherwise matched the Texas and Oklahoma performances in bowing style. Triplet bowings in trochaic mode appeared frequently in half of the versions of "Soldier's Joy" (Examples 1-C and 3-F and 3-C), and the bowed iambic rhythm occasionally found in Blue Ridge and Ozark examples of dance-style fiddling was used as a variation in the Arizona performance only (Example 3-F).

The characteristic third-beat Coarse bowing rhythm (𝄽) of Blue Ridge and Ozark examples of "Soldier's Joy" appeared also in the Oklahoma version from Western tradition (Example 4-C), suggesting perhaps that the total absence of this usage in the examples of Southern Appalachian style reflects a preference therein for bowing patterns which contradict rhythms naturally arising from the widespread melodic variants of tunes, just as the straightforward accentuation of the binary dance-meter is countered by the typical Southern Appalachian tied bowing patterns.

One bowing idiomatic to traditional fiddling from all southern style areas was the tied post-cadential stroke. As previously described, this pattern often was associated with an accent in Southern Appalachian tradition, where its use, preceded by numerous tied off-beats in about half of the "Soldier's Joy" examples, was less obvious than in the other regions.[66] Somewhat more remarkable was its appearance in several examples of Blue Ridge cadences (Examples 1-F and 1-C, 3-F, 5-F, 6-F, 7-F and 5-C, 6-C and 7-C), with the greatest number of appearances in performances from Virginia, which also employed more frequent ties between the internal beats of the measure. The prominence of this bowing habit was much greater in performances from the Ozark and Western styles, both of which averaged fewer ties between beats in most cases. Two out of three players of the tune from Ozark sources used the post-cadential tie, and similarly, three out of four Western informants included the stroke in both strains of "Soldier's Joy." (Table 5C, Examples 1-F, 2-F, and Table 5D, Examples 2-F, 3-F and 4-F). Therefore it would seem that the use of the tied stroke post-cadentially is a widespread traditional idiom, acceptable or popular in regions where other ties between internal beats of a measure are not, and perhaps even most popular precisely in these regions which lack other tied bowings.

The rhythms of the melodic fingerings within individual bow strokes showed a close relationship to the overall bowing patterns in each of the style regions studied. Most sub-divisions of the bow stroke created the same familiar duplet and trochaic triplet rhythms of the bowing patterns. Southern Appalachian performances also exaggerated the trochaic mode in a dotted fingering rhythm (e.g., ♫♩ from Table 5B, Example 3-F).

Another stylistic factor resulting from the regional concept of rhythm is the degree to which structurally significant pitches of the particular variant are reiterated by the fiddler. The tendency for important tones to be repeated and thus reinforced in some styles of folk music was stressed as a unifying factor by Bruno Nettl (1956: 198), but the importance of reiteration as a determinant of regional style has been generally overlooked. Excluding the repetition of drone or harmonically supportive tones, half or more of the informants in the Southern Appalachian and Ozark areas incorporated a significant amount of pitch repetition in their versions of the tune.[67] This probably indicates general regional tendencies toward the treatment of traditional tunes. The infrequent occurrence of this distinctive pitch repetition in Blue Ridge and Western performances was limited to one informant from each area (Blue Ridge Style, Example 4, and Western Style, Example 2).

Although the stylistic profile for each region depends on the interaction of many musical variables,[68] the complex involving the styles and patterns of bowing and related rhythmic habits proved to be a particularly reliable guide.

CONCLUSION

The story of traditional fiddling, like other folk idioms, cannot be told without constant reference to the cultural setting and to the various performance habits, conventions and attitudes which frame the actual playing of the tunes. Each aspect of the time-honored traditions for making and adjusting the instrument, for holding and bowing, and for spontaneously realizing the tune, thoroughly distinguishes the fiddler from the modern violinist, and thoroughly demonstrates the living survival of the complex of performing techniques associated with the instrument from its earliest appearance. Since the art of fiddling depends on the capacity of the folk performer to repeat these basic cultural messages over and over in subtly varied ways, it is inevitable that this detailed idiomatic language should be changed and nearly lost as a direct result of the urbanized life patterns and authoritative mass media of the twentieth century. Yet many aspects of the venerable traditions may be seen to have survived in altered forms in the thriving commercial descendants of folk fiddling, such as the string band, Western Swing and Bluegrass, and by deliberate cultivation of increasing numbers of traditional music enthusiasts, though that story must wait to be told.[69]

NOTES

1. For Thomas Campion's account of the masque celebrating the marriage of Lord Hayes (1607), see Boyden (1964): 139.

2. Regarding the similarity of ethnic and social backgrounds for the majority of pre-revolutionary settlers, from Maine to Georgia, see Beard (1944): 17-27, 47; cf., Malone (1968): 3; and Greene and Harrington (1966): 3-10.

Since, as Charles Seeger pointed out, it is unreasonable to assume that the first soldiers, churchmen and immigrant settlers did not bring with them a representative sampling of the music current in their countries of origin, it at first seems remarkable that scarcely a trace survives of the contemporaneous fine and popular arts of music, while the folk idiom has flourished. One reason is that the decline of English minstrelsy due to the rise of a smaller number of salaried professional musicians or *waits* who enjoyed increasing status, protection and patronage in the seventeenth century must have caused the more widespread fiddling, piping, and singing traditions of the humble folk to predominate among those in search of a better life across the seas (Woodfill 1953: 56-59, 201-203, passim; Bridenbaugh 1968: iii, 157-158; Hart 1881: 445-446). A taste for the more highly cultivated court music of Europe was also unlikely among American immigrants characterized primarily by Protestant opposition to the established Church of England and by middle-class (agricultural, mercantile, and artisan) origin (Beard 1944: 17-18, 22-23, 33, 47). Moreover, the conditions of North American frontier life eliminated the salon and the necessary leisure for pursuit of cultivated music, and made fine instruments, their makers and repairers, and especially audiences, unavailable outside a few cities. Throughout the New World, European folk musics prospered under these adverse conditions, while other idioms, even when heroic colonialist efforts were made, eventually were exhausted (Seeger 1957: 282-283; 1961: 368-370, 372). In this light, both the ambitious, tenacious Mexican "schools" of Spanish Renaissance choral composition and performance and the determined efforts of the American colonial bourgeoisie to transplant the European salon, and later, to upgrade congregational singing by importation of British hymns, shared, despite their manifest differences, a common antagonism to surrounding folk idioms and an ultimate decline, presumably due to the high expenditures, irrelevance of content, low return, and consequent disinterest of the populace. It would thus seem that automatic, unconscious cultivation, rather than this deliberate, melioristic transplantation has been responsible for the preservation of British-American folk idioms; although the loss of repertory in the process has been considerable, surviving tunes and styles have been more tenacious in the New World than in the various countries of origin (1957: 282-283; 1961: 369).

3. Minutes of the Council and General Court in *Virginia Magazine of History and Biography* 19 (1911: 374-76), cited in Maurer (1950): 511 and Spielman (1975): 191.

4. According to Bayard, Irish printed versions of dance tunes have been in limited circulation throughout the New England area from the eighteenth century, so that this tradition, unlike that in the South, has never been completely without printed music (private interview, State College, Penn., November, 1971).

5. The book appeared in 1650, although it was actually dated 1651.

6. The working of "oral tradition," the process of culture communication in folk or non-literate society, is clearly described for the hypothetical Kentucky mountaineer by Bruno Nettl (1965: 3-4), and applied to fiddling and instrumental traditions by Charles Seeger (1972: 825, passim).

7. About two-thirds of her informants lived in the western states at the time they absorbed the idiom.

8. Fifty-five of the eighty-seven had no coaching.

9. Bascomb, for example, reports a ninety-four-year-old fiddler claiming prior to 1909 to be playing his great-grandfather's "pieces," who would presumably have been born prior to the American Revolution (1909: 239).

10. Bayard reported that versions and variants of a tune sometimes may seem to coexist unnoticed or as equally acceptable even within a family, while slight variations of these versions and variants performed by outsiders provoke scorn and are often treated condescendingly, a situation which he feels marks the decline of the tradition and typifies the attendant crystallization of tunes and tune-versions (private interview, State College, Penn., November, 1971).

11. According to Seeger's formal description of selection as a conceptual operative technique for discussing music as communication, the individual carrier cultivates new operative materials and techniques according to his perception of the potential variance of the tradition and his ability to incorporate these into an individualized communication. Only when new materials and ways are repeatedly manipulated with success according to a consensus of the more competent carriers of the tradition, are they to be considered "incorporated in the funded aggregate of operative materials" and stylistic norms (1962: 159-160).

12. Moody (1968): 3, as cited in Spielman (1975): 203.

13. Howard (1965): 21-22; Lowens (1964): 20.

14. Reprinted in Hulan (1969): 15-18; see also Spielman (1975): 207-208. Apparently it was a success, with twenty competitors and a repeat of the event the following year (cf. Morgan 1952: 88).

15. Since the repertory was largely determined by the white patronage, we may suspect the playing was not intended to differ extensively from the British-American models. Tantalizing occasional references to "Negro tunes" suggest numerous other hybrids may have also thrived alongside this repertory (cf. Spielman 1975: 227).

16. For scholarly and popular speculations on the relation of the square dance to European models, see Sharp (1909) Part V: 7; Burchenal (1951): 21; Grayson (1969): 30.

17. An example of a slow air widely diffused in American tradition is "Bonaparte's Retreat." Cf. Burman-Hall (1974): 92-93 and 1978: passim.

18. Miss De Ryke is herself a tradition-oriented fiddler.

19. Identified only as G.M., Maine; J.M., North Carolina; and A.C., Texas, interviewed prior to 1964.

20. I.e., rural and urban descendants of the typically impoverished and isolated carriers of British-American oral tradition (cf. supra: 158-159).

21. Despite the popularity of hybrid commercial outgrowths of British-American traditional music, based on the cultural associations described by Lomax, Kefauver, Cohen and Barzun (supra: 159), the ability to perform is now lost to all but a small minority of professinal musicians. "Folk music is home music . . . Their music now comes to them in its entirety from the outside, along with standards of virtuosity in performance which few of them can meet, but devoid of other standards in particular" (Bayard 1967: 24, 28-29 n.5). Seeger estimated American folk musical impotence (i.e., inability to create and re-create the tunes and styles characterizing the oral transmission of the idiom) at now well over ninety-nine percent (1957: 292).

22. Banjos, flutes, fifes, piccolos, pipes, zithers, horns, bugles and at least one piano and one organ are reported in addition to the widespread and common fiddle and dulcimer making (A. Eaton 1937: 198).

23. Art Satherly quoting the traditional fiddler in Zolotow (1969): 41.

24. A Norwegian analogue derived from these continental instruments is the Hardanger Fiddle, which used twenty-four tunings as early as the middle of the eighteenth century (Bjørndal 1956: 13).

25. The first recorded use known to Russell was the 1587 Venetian edition of Concerti di Andrea e Giovanni Gabrieli—per voci e stromenti musicale (1938: 86).

26. According to Maud Karpeles, Cecil Sharp often found this tuning among fiddlers of the southern Appalachians (1949: 74-75).

27. Bennett's informant called this the "Shelton Laurel Key" for unknown reasons (1940: 13). The more usual designation "A-minor" or "playing in the minors" for this tuning and the associated class of tunes results from the habitual low seventh degree (second finger on the e' and e" strings), and the frequent low third degree (second finger on the a- and a'-strings) (Jabbour 1971: 18, 20).

28. Although this may often be the case, especially in the western region with which Thede is most familiar, some southern fiddlers play the prime in standard tuning as a matter of habit.

29. It seems that there is no clear way of establishing when the two centuries of continuous advice in viol and lute, and later, in violin treatises from Agricola in 1528 to Playford (1650-1728) to tune the top string "as high as it will bear" (Boyden 1965: 70, 186) referred in fact to an opposite and desirable practice of tuning higher than standard modern pitch, and when such advice was simply intended to counteract the fearful exaggerations among amateur readers of the already prevalent convention of tuning low.

30. Georg Simon Lohlein in Anweisung zum Violinspielen mit pracktischen Beyspielen . . . (Leipzig, 1774), quoted in van der Straeten (1911): 244.

31. Both conventions may descend from a common ancestor: Bjørndal suggests the device of sympathetic strings on the Hardanger fiddle actually was taken from the viola d'amore, popular in countries bordering northern England and Scotland from the sixteenth century, the very area from which many early settlers came to this country (see Burman-Hall 1974: 21).

32. Informant Ed Hicks, on "Paddy Won't You Drink Some Good Old Cider" (Thede 1967: 53); cf. "Finger Ring," 67. This is technically sound, as overtones of the tonic are reinforced by scordatura using the principal notes of a key (Boyden 1965: 130).

33. Cf. Spielman (1975): 311-330 and passim, for preliminary results.

34. Cf. Burman-Hall (1974): 57; cf. also Blaustein (1975): 10-11.

35. A very few traditional players have used F and B-flat (Bayard 1966: 53, 60), in which the position of the left hand must readjust to produce semitones between the open e"- and a'-strings and the first finger, and between the third and fourth fingers, which in itself may eventually cause the adoption of new intonational patterns for these tunes (Jabbour 1971: 11).

36. Interview with Peter Seeger, included in Seeger (1959): 14-15.

37. This grip, as described for one of Thede's informants, involves one finger atop the stick, one between stick and hair, and a third finger below the frog with the thumb on the side of the frog (1967: 110; cf. Bennett 1940: 11; Bayard 1956: 18).

38. Gordon plausibly suggested that these verses, excepting the few which derive from the black-face minstrel, represent a primitive literary or "blossom" stage in the development of the ballad and epic. Traits established at this point of literary growth persist later when true narrative elements develop, and when words become more important than music. Since only the tune and one or two verses remain fixed in performance, the average fiddler, who may say he has heard hundreds, will probably only recall a few (1938: 71-72, 76-77).

39. Directions given by the caller may serve as a cueing device for the fiddler as well as for the dancers, signalling strain repetition patterns and the end of the dance.

40. Beef rib-bones, slightly-curved sticks of locust, maple or other hardwood (6" × 1" × ¼"), straws or steel knitting needles are all traditional (Calhoun 1941: 13; Thede 1967: 16, 122; Ford 1965: 129-130; Wolf 1965: 319; Meade 1969: 27), though the fiddler may sometimes simply drum upon the strings with the wood of his own bow (Ford 1965: 129).

41. For examples, see Burman-Hall (1974) vol. 2: Appendix III: "Bonaparte's Retreat," Blue Ridge Style Example 2, Southern Appalachian Style Example 3. Left-hand pizzicato is also common to set- and show-pieces, as in the imitation of hiccups in "Rye Whiskey" or "Drunken Hiccups" (Jabbour 1971: 15).

42. Although the complete story of this influence, corresponding to the distribution of ethnic and national groups which preserved their language and customs, will probably never be known, Samuel Bayard's research on the problem of origin and mutation in instrumental tradition documents many Pennsylvania fife and fiddle airs of Germanic origins, brought with the early influx of German settlers, as well as a number that were international on the European continent, known in Romance as well as Germanic countries (1967: 22; 1944a: xx-xxi, No. 78; cf. Korson 1949). Various Northern European traditions were also imported with early immigration to America. In southern Louisiana, as in Quebec and the Maritime Provinces, the French idiom was most prominent, and in isolated settlements, Scandinavian and eastern European styles were heard (cf. Sharp 1954: 397; P. Seeger 1959: 1). Nevertheless, Irish and Anglo-Scottish idioms dominated the traditional music of the majority of the population. Thus, almost all of the airs Bayard was able to trace were British (Anglo-Scottish or Irish) in origin, with most of the others exhibiting similar characteristics (1944a: xx).

43. Bayard speculated on performance style, as did Cecil Sharp regarding the attendant complex of dances, that this simplicity may be the result of an older tradition surviving in America, or it may indicate simply a diminishing of technical skill necessitated from the beginnings of settlement by the rigors of pioneer life (Bayard 1944a: xxii; Sharp 1909, Part V: 7).

44. The relationship of genus to deep strain structure in American folk fiddling as a regional variable, and regional intonation patterns are discussed separately in Burman-Hall (1978) and (1974): 76-85.

45. Further data on the persistence of folk fife intonations in the fiddling idiom is given in Burman-Hall (1974): 88-90; (1975): 52; and Bayard (1944a): xxv, and (1966). For discussion of each particular alteration generally and regionally found in the American South, see Burman-Hall (1974).

46. According to Bruno Nettl, this characteristic repetition with changes may result historically from a need to limit "an otherwise unbridled tendency" toward improvisation (1956: 199).

47. For example, in Christopher Simpson's *Division Viol* (1659) and its imitation John Playford's *The Division Violin* (1684).

48. A similar conceptualization is expected of Persian art-music performers, who determine the degree of ornamentation and rhythmic nuance within the individual short piece called *gousheh*, which prescribed only tetrachord genre, stressed notes and cadential patterns, leaving the elaborated realization to the player (Zonis 1965: 642), a technique also commonly found in folk and popular music, particularly from the Khorosan region (Nettl 1970).

49. Wilfred Mellers correctly compared the connection and change of common melodic formulae to produce "new" British-American tunes (as described by Bayard) to the process of grouping *maqams* appropriate to each mode (*echos*) of Byzantine chant, and to the structural force of characteristic progressions and stressed tones in the *ragas* of Indian music (1946: 22-23).

50. For notes on the history and diffusion of this large complex, see Burman-Hall (1974): Part Two, Chapter 1; (1975): 55.

51. Research procedures and methodology for the comparative study are described in Burman-Hall (1975): 54-55. The performances were analyzed comparatively for approximately fifteen stylistic variables. Consideration of the location, nature and extent of variations, and the detailed analysis of bowing styles and patterns were the most significant indicators of regional style.

52. Explanation of graph technique, etc.: cf. Burman-Hall (1974): Part Two, Chapter 1; (1978): passim.

53. A much smaller, but complementary force results from the efforts of folk-based musicians who have been able to move in wider musical circles as semi-professionals, playing carefully worked-out uniform renditions with a resultant minimum of incidental variation (Jabbour 1971: 3).

54. Evidence suggests that bowing style and patterns may associate with function and tempo rather than with specific tunes. The performance of one informant from Virginia of "Bonaparte's Retreat," normally a slow air, began as such, and included a transition to "double quick time" (Burman-Hall 1974: 188). Patterns of bowing tend toward simplicity in Blue Ridge style. Here, as in some of the other dimensions of performance style, differences of practice seem to exist within the style. As the informant's tempo reached a square-dancing pace, bowing patterns typical of Blue Ridge examples of "Soldier's Joy" dominated the performance.

55. Cf. Table 5: Bowing Patterns—Blue Ridge Style performances of "Soldier's Joy." Only the Fine strain of Example 6-F lacked the short ostinato bowing rhythms.

The Fine of Example 5-F and the Coarse of Example 7-C included typical usage of two-measure bowing ostinati.

56. The role of such modified isorhythmic structures in unifying the performance of folk music has been perceptively analyzed by Bruno Nettl (1956: 197).

57. Tables 5A, 5B, 5E and 5F, Examples 6 and 7, were harmonic throughout.

58. Examples 1, 4, 5 and 8 had Plain playing exclusively in the Coarse; Examples 2 and 3 used the Plain style only in the Fine strain.

59. Documentation on another traditional use of pizzicato by a Southern Appalachian informant may be found in Bennett (1940): 34. Cf. two further examples from Southern Appalachian slow air style playing, in Burman-Hall (1974): 192. In all cases, the pizzicato was executed with the left hand.

60. Example 7-C, Table 5F lacked such ties in the Coarse strain, and had only a few in the Fine strain (7-F, Table 5B).

61. Example 1-C (Table 5F) included a pattern of one measure in the Coarse only, Example 3-C (Table 5F) a pattern of two measures in the Coarse only, and Examples 6-C and 7-C showed stable bowings only in the Coarse strain (Table 5F).

62. Informants for Examples 2 and 5 accentuated their off-beat bowings. The post-cadential beat usage, further weakened by the circumstance of being tied over from the preceding beat, was another instance of accenting the weak part of a beat (Examples 1 and 3—Coarse strain). An identical usage lacking the tie occurred in Example 4—Coarse. The fiddler playing Example 5 applied similar stress to the off-beat with a crescendo on the tied cadential bowing.

63. Example 3 included both Coarse and Fine strain rhythmic ostinati similar to that of Blue Ridge Style Example 4—Coarse strain. The Coarse strain of Example 1 was similar to that of Blue Ridge Style Example 2, while the Fine had "saw stroke" sixteenth notes, as found in Examples 1 and 2 of Blue Ridge Style. The Coarse variation of Example 2 made use of this same "saw stroke," but neither the principal Coarse nor the Fine had clear analogies in Blue Ridge Style, although the Coarse resembled that of Examples 3 and 6 from the Blue Ridge.

64. An exception was Example 3-C (Table 5H), which employed no double-stops before the cadence.

65. The determination of bowing patterns was complicated by the almost total absence of double-stopped playing. Some more recent examples of Western fiddling exhibit off-beat bowing idioms related to those of the Southern Appalachian region (Thede 1967: 20, 111).

66. Southern Appalachian Style performances with the tied post-cadential bowing included "Soldier's Joy," Examples 1, 2, 5, and 6 (both strains).

67. Southern Appalachian examples which stressed important tones by repetition included Examples 4, 5, 6, 7 and 8 of "Soldier's Joy." Ozark fiddlers using reiteration provided all examples of "Soldier's Joy."

68. Preliminary stylistic profiles (based on fifteen variables) for Blue Ridge, Southern Appalachian, Ozark and Western fiddling can be found in Burman-Hall (1975): 55-63.

69. The author wishes to thank noted Baroque scholar James Anthony of the University of Arizona, Baroque violinist Jaap Schröder of Amsterdam and Lawrence Libin, Curator of Instruments for the Metropolitan Museum in New York for reviewing the manuscript in 1982 in preparation for this publication.

DISCOGRAPHY

"Soldier's Joy" Complex: Transcriptions

Blue Ridge Style

1. Fiddlin' John Carson and the Virginia Reelers; string band. Fannin County, Georgia, 1925 (recorded)—1926 (released). Commercial release: Okeh 45011. Indiana University Archives of Traditional Music, 66 (77), Side II, No. 18.

2. Clayton McMichen, fiddle with banjo accompaniment. Allatoona, Georgia, June, 1939. Commercial release: Decca 2638-B (master 65711) Album 66 (6 sides—4). Included in medley: 1) "Soldier's Joy"; 2) "Arkansas Traveler"; 3) "Mississippi Sawyer." Courtesy of John Edwards Memorial Foundation.

3. Wade Ward, unaccompanied fiddle. Galax, Virginia, 1939. Collected by Peter Seeger and Alan Lomax. Library of Congress Item AFS 8764 B2.

4. Glen Smith, unaccompanied fiddle. Hillsville, Virginia, 1958-61. Commercial release: Folkways FS 3811, Side A, Band 2. "Traditional Music from Grayson and Carroll Counties."

5. Norman Edmunds, unaccompanied fiddle. Hillsville, Virginia, 1959. Collected by Peter Hoover. Indiana University Archives of Traditional Music, 65 (140), EC 854 (Tape 8, Side 1, No. 1).

6. William Marshall, unaccompanied fiddle. Hillsville, Virginia, 1961. Collected by Peter Hoover. Indiana University Archives of Traditional Music, 65 (140), EC 882 (Tape 38, Side 1, No. 11).

7. Hobart Smith, unaccompanied fiddle. Saltville, Virginia, 1963. Commercial release: Folk Legacy FSA 17, Side A, Band 7. "Hobart Smith of Saltville, Virginia."

Southern Appalachian Style

1. Luther Strong, unaccompanied fiddle. Hazard, Kentucky, 1937. Collected by Alan and Elizabeth Lomax. Library of Congress Item AFS 1535 B2.

2. Thomas M. Bryant, unaccompanied fiddle. Evansville, Indiana, 1938. Collected by Alan Lomax and Brewster. Indiana University Archives of Traditional Music, pre '54 (155), ATL 425.9.

3. John Hatcher, unaccompanied fiddle. Near Burnsville, Mississippi. Recorded in Iuka, Mississippi, 1939. Collected by Herbert Halpert. Library of Congress Item AFS 2998 B1.

4. W. E. Claunch, fiddle with guitar accompaniment (Mrs. Christeen Haygood). Near Guntown, Mississippi, 1939. Collected by Herbert Halpert. Library of Congress Item AFS 2971 A3.

5. Stephen B. Tucker, unaccompanied fiddle. Marion, Lauderdale County, Mississippi. Recorded in Meridian, Mississippi, 1939. Collected by Herbert Halpert. Library of Congress Item AFS 3045 B4.

6. Floyd Burchett, unaccompanied fiddle. Brushy Fork, Pike County, Kentucky. Recorded near Ironton, Ohio, 1954. Collected by Wyatt Insko. Indiana University Archives of Traditional Music, pre '54 (61), ATL 388.3.

7. Harvey Jeffreys, fiddle with guitar accompaniment (Peter Hoover). Kingwood, West Virginia. Recorded in Reedsville, West Virginia, 1960. Collected by Peter Hoover. Indiana University Archives of Traditional Music, 65 (140), EC 868 (Tape 28, Side 2, No. 14).

8. Emma Crabtree, fiddle with anonymous guitar accompaniment. Huntsville, Alabama. Recorded in Athens, Alabama, 1969. Collected by Doug Crosswhite. Indiana University Archives of Traditional Music, 70-90-F, EC 3230 (Vol. 2, Side 1).

Ozark Style

1. Lon Jordan, unaccompanied fiddle. Farmington, Arkansas, 1941. Collected by Vance Randolph. Library of Congress Item AFS 5379 A2.

2. Fred Painter, fiddle with string band; guitars (Cecil Stephens and Carl Tilden) and mandolin (Ralph Eutsler). Galena, Missouri, 1941. Collected by Vance Randolph. Library of Congress Item AFS 5280 A3.

3. Delbert McGrath, unaccompanied fiddle. Day, Missouri, 1942. Collected by Vance Randolph. Library of Congress Item AFS 5421 A2.

Western Style

1. E. K. Bowman, unaccompanied fiddle, with caller (Tobe Hilburn). Abilene, Texas, 1937. Collected by John Lomax. Library of Congress Item AFS 930 A2.

2. Mrs. F. E. Goodwyn, fiddle with guitar accompaniment (Frank Goodwyn). Hebbronville, Texas, 1941. Collected by Alan Lomax. Library of Congress Item AFS 5623 A2.

3. Bill Bradley, fiddle with anonymous guitar accompaniment. Recorded in Tucson, Arizona at Old Time Fiddlers' Contest by Wiley, 1948. Library of Congress Item AFS 9338 A2.

4. Tony Thomas, unaccompanied fiddle. Hugo, Oklahoma, 1966. Commercial release: Takoma A 1013, Side A, Band 12. "Tony Thomas." (Called "Bacon Rind").

"Soldier's Joy" Complex: Manuscript and Printed Sources

Manuscript Sources

Bayard, Samuel P.
    n.d.   MS collection of fiddle tunes and songs, mainly from southwest and
[c. 1928- central Pennsylvania, c. 400 items. Nos. 22, 62, 106, and 300.
    1938]

Beck, Henry
    1786   *Henry Beck's Flute Book.* MS, Music Division, Library of Congress, 35.

Osborn, Lettie
    1930s   Transcriptions of 59 Orange County, New York, fiddle tunes. Author's
              MS. Location unknown.

Shattuck, Abel
    c. 1801 *A. Shattuck's Book.* MS, Music Division, Library of Congress.

Wilkinson, Winston
    1930s   Transcriptions of over 100 fiddle tunes, songs, and ballads from James

H. (Uncle Jim) Chisholm of Greenwood, Albemarle County, Virginia. Author's MS. Location unknown.

Printed Sources

Adam, E. F.
  1928   *Old Time Fiddlers' Favorite Barn Dance Tunes.* St. Louis: E. F. Adam. No. 2, ". . . as played by Blind John."
Anonymous
  1908   *Jigs and Reels, Part II.* New York: The Academic Music Co. 22.
Anonymous
  1937   *Jigs and Reels.* Chicago: Belmont Music Co. 21, "The Soldier's Joy Hornpipe."
Artley, Malvin
  1955   *The West Virginia Country Fiddler: An Aspect in the Development of Folk Music in America.* PhD dissertation: Chicago, Roosevelt University. 55, Ex. 21. Anonymous fiddler, central West Virginia, early 1950s.
Bayard, Samuel P.
  1944   Hill Country Tunes: Instrumental Folk Music of Southwestern Pennsylvania. Philadelphia: *Memoirs of the American Folklore Society,* Vol. 39, No. 21, "The King's Head." Mrs. Sarah Armstrong, fiddle, near Derry, Pennsylvania, 1943.
Bennett, David Parker
  1940   "A Study in Fiddle Tunes from Western North Carolina." University of North Carolina. 76. Bill Hensley, fiddle, near Asheville, North Carolina, 1940.
Blake, G. E.
  c. 1815 *Blake's Evening Companion.* Philadelphia: Blake. N.p.a.
Bowman, S. A.
  1908a   *The J. W. Pepper Collection of 500 Reels, Jigs . . . for Violin.* Philadelphia: J. W. Pepper, No. 156, "Wild Bill Reel."
  1908b   *The J. W. Pepper Collection of 500 Reels, Jigs . . . for Violin.* Philadelphia: J. W. Pepper. No. 323, "Yellow Peaches Reel." This and the preceding are in all likelihood nonce titles.
Burchenal, Elizabeth
  1915a   *Folk-Dances of Finland.* New York: G. Schirmer. 36—"Ten Persons' British-American versions.
  1915b   *Folk-Dances of Finland.* New York: G. Schirmer. 36—"Ten Persons' Polka"; 78-79 include the entire British-American tune as the second part of a "Kontra."
  1918   *American Country-Dances, Volume I: Twenty-Eight Contra-Dances Largely from the New England States.* New York: G. Schirmer. 6, including old dance-figures.
Campbell, Joshua
  1778   *A Collection of the Newest and Best Reels and Minuets, Adapted for the Violin or German Flute.* Glasgow: Joshua Campbell. N.p.a. (Cf. Glen 1891 vol. I: xvii; Collinson 1966).
Cazden, Norman
  1955   *Dances from Woodland.* Second Edition. Bridgeport, Connecticut: N. Cazden. 35.

n.d.   *Reels, Jigs, and Squares.* Bridgeport, Connecticut: N. Cazden. 52.

Crampton, C. Ward

1930   *The Second Folk Dance Book.* New York: A. S. Barnes & Co. 57, "Sailor's Hornpipe."

Davis, Arthur K., Jr.

n.d.   *Folksongs of Virginia: A Descriptive Index and Classification.*

De Ville, Paul

1905   *Reels, Hornpipes, Jigs, Etc.: The Universal Favorite Contra Dance Album.* New York and Boston: Carl Fischer. No. 76.

Dunham, Mellie

1926   *"Mellie" Dunham's Fiddlin' Dance Tunes.* New York: Carl Fischer. No. 31.

Fillmore, Henry

1927   *The American Veteran Fifer.* Revised edition. Cincinnati: The Fillmore Bros. No. 93. Donated by W. A. Hopkins, Greenville, Ohio.

Ford, Ira

1965   *Traditional Music in America, 1940.* Reprint edition. Foreword by Judith McCulloh. Hatboro, Pennsylvania: Folklore Associates. 49; 95, second strain of "Coonie in the Creek" is Fine.

Greenleaf, E. B., and G. Y. Mansfield

1933   *Ballads and Sea Songs of Newfoundland.* Cambridge, Mass.: Harvard University Press. 377—a quadrille with a second strain equivalent to Fine strain of British-American version.

Harding

1932   *Harding's Original Collection of Jigs and Reels.* New York: Paull-Pioneer Music Corp. No. 20.

Heikel, Yngvar

1936   "Finlands Svenska Folkdiktning," VI, B, Folkdans (Helsingfors: Utgivna av Svenska Litteratursällskapet i Finland), no. 268. 69, "Gammalmodig Åtta"; 73, no. 1b, "Stampantakt"; 264, "Fein Engelska"; 283, "Kökar Engelska"; 310, "Sex Man Engelska." The names of the dances connected with these Swedish-Finnish versions suggest an introduction of both tunes and steps from British tradition.

Holden, Rickey

1951   *The Square Dance Caller.* San Antonio, Tex.: R. Holden. 34.

Howe, Elias

1851   *Howe's School for the Violin.* Boston: Oliver Ditson. 37.

Levey, R. M.

c. 1835 *A Collection of the Dance Music of Ireland.* London. No. 90.

Linscott, Eloise Hubbard

1939   *Folk Songs of Old New England.* Revised edition. Hamden, Connecticut: Archon Books, 1962: 110-111. Played by Willie Woodward, Bristol, New Hampshire.

McGlashan, Alexander

1781   *A Collection of Scots Measures.* Edinburgh: Neil Stewart. 32. "The Soldier's Joy."

O'Malley, J. and F. Atwood, eds.

1919   *Seventy Good Old Dances.* Boston: Oliver Ditson 14, No. 9.

O'Neill, Francis
    1903   *O'Neill's Music of Ireland: Eighteen Hundred and Fifty Melodies.* Chicago: Lyon and Healy. Reprint edition, New York: Daniel Collins [1964?]. No. 1642. Reproduced in *The Dance Music of Ireland: 1001 Gems.* Chicago: Lyon and Healy, 1907. No. 868.

Perrow, E. C.
    1915   Songs and Rhymes from the South. *Journal of American Folklore* 28 (108) (Apr.-June, 1915): 129-190. 185, "I Love Somebody." [East Tennessee, whites, vocal, 1905].

Roche, F.
    1912   *Collection of Irish Airs, Marches, and Dance Tunes.* 2 vols. Dublin: Pigott & Co.; London: Leonard & Co. Revised and enlarged edition, 3 vols., Dublin: Pigott & Co., 1928. Vol. II: 12, no. 216, "The Soldier's Joy."

Ruth, Viola H.
    1948   *Pioneer Western Folk Tunes.* Phoenix, Arizona: V. H. Ruth. 4, "Soldier's Joy No. 1, or King's Head"; 5, "Soldier's Joy No. 2, Best for Quadrille" (6/8).

Ryan, William Bradbury
    1883   *Ryan's Mammoth Collection.* Boston: Elias Howe. 264. Reprinted as *One Thousand Fiddle Tunes.* Chicago: M. M. Cole, 1940.

Saar, R. W.
    1932   *Fifty Country Dances.* London: W. Paxton. No. 14.

Sandburg, Carl
    1927   *The American Songbag.* New York: Harcourt Brace. 140-141, "Love Somebody, Yes I Do."

Seeger, Peter
    1959   *The Country Fiddle.* Pamphlet for film. New York: Beacon Films. 4, Oklahoma version; 7, Illinois version.

Smith, Frank H., and Rolf E. Hovey
    1955   *The Appalachian Square Dance.* Berea, Kentucky: Berea College. N.p.a.

Stewart-Robertson, James
    1884   *The Athole Collection of the Dance Music of Scotland.* Reprint edition, Edinburgh and London: Oliver and Boyd, 1961. Part I: 150.

Sym
    1930   *Sym's Old Time Dances.* New York: G. T. Worth. 13.

Thede, Marion Unger
    1967   *The Fiddle Book.* New York: Oak Publications. 118.

Tiersot, Julien
    1903   *Chansons Populaires Recueillies dans les Alpes Francaises.* Grenoble. 532, tune no. 3 [air (one of the "monférines") with a second part closely resembling the Fine strain of "Soldier's Joy"].

White, Charles
    1896   *White's Unique Collection of Jigs, Reels, and Hornpipes.* Boston: White-Smith Music. 69.
    1907   *White's Excelsior Collection of Jigs, Reels, and Hornpipes.* Boston: White-Smith Music. 72.

Winner, Septimus
　　1894　　*Music and Steps of the Round and Square Dances for the Violin.*
　　　　　　Boston: Oliver Ditson. 78.

Chronology of Manuscript and Printed Sources

1778　　Campbell, Joshua. *A Collection of the Newest and Best Reels and Minuets, adapted for the Violin or German Flute.* Glasgow: Joshua Campbell.

1781　　McGlashan, Alexander. *A Collection of Scots Measures.* Edinburgh: Neil Stewart. 32, "The Soldier's Joy."

1786　　Beck, Henry. *Henry Beck's Flute Book.* MS, Music Division, Library of Congress. 35.

1801　　Shattuck, Abel. *A. Shattuck's Book.* MS, Music Division, Library of Congress.

c.1815　　Blake, G. E. *Blake's Evening Companion.* Philadelphia: Blake. N.p.a.

c.1835　　Levey, R. M. *A Collection of the Dance Music of Ireland.* London. No. 90.

1851　　Howe, Elias. *Howe's School for the Violin.* Boston: Oliver Ditson. 37.

1883　　Ryan, William Bradbury. *Ryan's Mammoth Collection.* Boston: Elias Howe. 264. Reprinted as *One Thousand Fiddle Tunes.* Chicago: M. M. Cole, 1940.

1884　　Stewart-Robertson, James. *The Athole Collection of the Dance Music of Scotland.* Reprint edition, Edinburgh and London: Oliver and Boyd, 1961. Part I: 150.

1894　　Winner, Septimus. *Music and Steps of the Round and Square Dances for the Violin.* Boston: Oliver Ditson. 78.

1896　　White, Charles. *White's Unique Collection of Jigs, Reels, and Hornpipes.* Boston: White-Smith Music. 69.

1903　　O'Neill, Francis. *O'Neill's Music of Ireland: Eighteen Hundred and Fifty Melodies.* Chicago: Lyon and Healy. Reprint edition, New York: Daniel Collins [1964?]. No. 1642. Reproduced in *The Dance Music of Ireland: 1001 Gems.* Chicago: Lyon and Healy, 1907.

　　　　　Tiersot, Julien. *Chansons Populaires Recueillies dans les Alpes Françaises.* Grenoble. 532, tune no. 3 [air (one of the "monférines") with a second part closely resembling the Fine strain of "Soldier's Joy"].

1905　　De Ville, Paul. *Reels, Hornpipes, Jigs, Etc.: The Universal Favorite Contra Dance Album.* New York and Boston: Carl Fischer. No. 76.

1907　　White, Charles. *White's Excelsior Collection of Jigs, Reels, and Hornpipes.* Boston: White-Smith Music. 72.

1908　　Anonymous. *Jigs and Reels, Part II.* New York: The Academic Music Co. 22.

　　　　　Bowman, S. A. *The J. W. Pepper Collection of 500 Reels, Jigs . . . for Violin.* Philadelphia: J. W. Pepper. No. 156, "Wild Bill Reel."

　　　　　Ibid., No. 323, "Yellow Peaches Reel." This and the preceding are in all likelihood nonce titles.

1912　　Roche, F. *Collection of Irish Airs, Marches, and Dance Tunes.* 2 vols. Dublin: Pigott & Co.; London: Leonard & Co. Revised and enlarged edition, 3 vols., Dublin: Pigott & Co., 1928. Vol. II: 12, no. 216, "The Soldier's Joy."

1915 Perrow, E. C. Songs and Rhymes from the South. *Journal of American Folklore* 28 (108) (Apr.-June, 1915: 129-190. 185, "I Love Somebody" [East Tennessee, whites, vocal, 1905].

Burchenal, Elizabeth. *Folk-Dances of Denmark*. New York: G. Schirmer. 42-43. Identical to British-American versions.

Burchenal, Elizabeth. *Folk-Dances of Finland*. New York: G. Schirmer. 36—"Ten Persons' Polka"; 78-79 include the entire British-American tune as the second part of a "Kontra."

1918 Burchenal, Elizabeth. *American Country-Dances, Volume I: Twenty-Eight Contra-Dances Largely from the New England States*. New York: G. Schirmer. 6; including old dance figures.

1919 O'Malley, J., and F. Atwood, eds. *Seventy Good Old Dances*. Boston: Oliver Ditson. 14, no. 9.

1926 Dunham, Mellie. *"Mellie" Dunham's Fiddlin' Dance Tunes*. New York: Carl Fischer. No. 31.

1927 Fillmore, Henry. *The American Veteran Fifer*. Revised edition. Cincinnati: Fillmore Bros. No. 93. Donated by W. A. Hopkins, Greenville, Ohio.

Sandburg, Carl. *The American Songbag*. New York: Harcourt, Brace & Co. 140-141, "I Love Somebody, Yes I Do."

1928 Adam, E. F. *Old Time Fiddlers' Favorite Barn Dance Tunes*. St. Louis, E. F. Adam, 1928. No. 2, ". . . as played by Blind John."

c.1928- Bayard, Samuel P. MS collection of fiddle tunes and songs, mainly
1938 from southwest and central Pennsylvania, c. 400 items. Nos. 22, 62, 106, and 300.

1930 Crampton, C. Ward. *The Second Folk Dance Book*. New York: A. S. Barnes & Co. 57, "Sailor's Hornpipe."

Sym. *Sym's Old Time Dances*. New York: G. T. Worth. 13.

1930s Osborn, Lettie. Transcriptions of 59 Orange County, New York, fiddle tunes. Author's MS. Location unknown.

Wilkinson, Winston. Transcriptions of over 100 fiddle tunes, songs, and ballads from James H. (Uncle Jim) Chisholm of Greenwood, Albemarle County, Virginia. Author's MS. Location unknown.

1932 Saar, R. W. *Fifty Country Dances*. London: W. Paxton. No. 14.

Harding. *Harding's Original Collection of Jigs and Reels*. New York: Paull-Pioneer Music Corp. No. 20.

1933 Greenleaf, E. B., and G. Y. Mansfield. *Ballads and Sea Songs of Newfoundland*. Cambridge, Mass.: Harvard University Press. 377—a quadrille with a second strain equivalent to Fine strain of British-American version.

1936 Heikel, Yngvar. Finlands Svenska Folkdiktning, VI, B, Folkdans (Helsingfors: Utgivna av Svenska Litteratursällskapet i Finland), no. 268, 69, "Gammalmodig Åtta"; 73, no. 1b, "Stampantakt"; 264, "Fein Engelska"; 283, "Kökar Engelska"; 310, "Sex Man Engelska." The names of the dances connected with these Swedish-Finnish versions suggest an introduction of both tunes and steps from British tradition.

1937   Anonymous. *Jigs and Reels*. Chicago: Belmont Music Co. 21, "The
        Soldier's Joy Hornpipe."

1939   Linscott, Eloise Hubbard. *Folk Songs of Old New England*. Revised
        edition, Hamden, Conn.: Archon Books, 1962: 110-111. Played by
        Willie Woodward, Bristol, New Hampshire.

1940   Bennett, David Parker. "A Study in Fiddle Tunes from Western North
        Carolina." University of North Carolina. 76. Bill Hensley, fiddle, near
        Asheville, North Carolina, 1940.

1944   Bayard, Samuel P. Hill Country Tunes: Instrumental Folk Music of
        Southwestern Pennsylvania. *Memoirs of the American Folklore
        Society* 39, Philadelphia. No. 21, "The King's Head." Mrs. Sarah
        Armstrong, fiddle, near Derry, Pennsylvania, 1943.

1948   Ruth, Viola H. *Pioneer Western Folk Tunes*. Phoenix, Ariz.: V. H.
        Ruth. 4, "Soldier's Joy No. 1, or King's Head"; 5, "Soldier's Joy No.
        2, Best for Quadrille" (in 6/8).

1951   Holden, Rickey. *The Square Dance Caller*. San Antonio, Tex.:
        R. Holden. 34.

1955   Artley, Malvin. *The West Virginia Country Fiddler: An Aspect in the
        Development of Folk Music in America*. PhD dissertation: Chicago
        Roosevelt University. 55, Ex. 21. Anonymous fiddler, central West
        Virginia, early 1950s.

        Cazden, Norman. *Dances from Woodland*. Second edition. Bridge-
        port, Conn.: N. Cazden. 35.

        Smith, Frank H., and Rolf E. Hovey. *The Appalachian Square
        Dance*. Berea, Ky.: Berea College. N.p.a.

1959   Seeger, Peter. *The Country Fiddle*. Pamphlet for film. New York:
        Beacon Films, 1959. 4, Oklahoma version; 7, Illinois version.

1965   Ford, Ira. *Traditional Music in America*. 1940. Reprint edition. Fore-
        word by Judith McCulloh. Hatboro, Penn.: Folklore Associates. 49;
        95, second strain of "Coonie in the Creek" is Fine.

1967   Thede, Marion Unger. *The Fiddle Book*. New York: Oak Publications.
        118.

n.d.   Cazden, Norman. *Reels, Jigs, and Squares*. Bridgeport, Conn.:
        N. Cazden. 52.

        Davis, Arthur K., Jr. *Folksongs of Virginia: A Descriptive Index and
        Classification*.

Selected Historical and Folkloristic References

Bennett, David Parker
    1940   "A Study in Fiddle Tunes from Western North Carolina." University
            of North Carolina. Commentary, 55 (erroneous).
Cazden, Norman
    1971   A Simple Mode Classification for Traditional Anglo-American Song
            Titles. *Yearbook of the International Folk Music Council* 3: 45-78.
            Commentary and theoretical observations regarding "Soldier's Joy" as
            given in 1955: 35.

Malone, Bill C.
>1968   *Country Music, U.S.A.* American Folklore Society Memoir Series,
>   vol. 54. Austin, Tex., and London: The University of Texas Press.
>   Commentary, 26.

Osborne, Lettie
>1952   Fiddle Tunes from Orange County, New York. *New York Folklore*
>   *Quarterly* 8 (3): 211-215. Brief mention, 212.

Seeger, Peter
>1959   *The Country Fiddle.* Pamphlet for film. New York: Beacon Films.
>   Commentary, 4.

Shelton, Robert
>1966   *The Country Music Story.* With photography by Burt Goldblatt. New
>   York, Kansas City, Indianapolis: The Bobbs-Merrill Co. Picture of
>   6-piece twin-fiddle hillbilly band from Cove, Georgia, playing
>   "Soldier's Joy" for President Roosevelt, 1933.

Wilkinson, Winston
>1942   Virginia Dance Tunes. *Southern Folklore Quarterly* 6 (1): 1-10. Brief
>   commentary, 3.

Wolf, John Q.
>1965   A Country Dance in the Ozarks in 1874. *Southern Folklore Quarterly*
>   29 (4): 319-321. Brief mention, 319.

REFERENCES CITED

Alfrod, Violet
>1935   Some Notes on the Pyrenean Stringed Drum, with Five Musical
>   Examples. *Revista Internacional de los Estudios Vascos* (Paris: Society
>   of Basque Studies "Eusko-Ikaskuntza") 26: 567-577.

Anon.
>1969a   Georgia's Unwritten Airs Played by Old "Fiddlers" for Atlanta Prizes.
>   *Musical America.* March 21, 1914. Reprinted in Guthrie T. Meade,
>   From the Archives: 1914 Atlanta Fiddle Contest, *John Edwards Me-*
>   *morial Foundation Quarterly* 5, part 1 (13): 29.
>1969b   Gospel Hymns for 80,000,000. *The Nation* (New York: Nation Asso-
>   ciates) 87 (2251), 1908. Reprinted in Gentry, *A History and Encyclo-*
>   *pedia of Country, Western, and Gospel Music.* 3-5.

Apel, Willi
>1965   *Harvard Dictionary of Music.* Cambridge, Mass.: Harvard University
>   Press (sixteenth printing).

Bartók, Béla
>1931   *Hungarian Folk Music.* Translated by M. D. Calvocoressi. London:
>   Humphrey Milford.

Barzun, Jacques
>1956   *Music in American Life.* New York: Doubleday.

Bascomb, Louise Rand
>1909   Ballads and Songs of Western North America. *Journal of American*
>   *Folklore* 22 (74): 238-250.

Bayard, Samuel P.
  c.1928- MS collection of fiddle tunes and songs, mainly from southwest and
    1938   central Pennsylvania. c. 400 items.
  1944a   Hill Country Tunes: Instrumental Folk Music of Southwestern Penn-
           sylvania. *Memoirs of the American Folklore Society* 39, Philadelphia.
  1944b   "Aspects of Melodic Kinship and Variation in British-American Fiddle
           Tunes," papers read at the International Congress of Musicology: New
           York, 1939. 122-129.
  1951   Principal Versions of an International Folk Tune. *Journal of the
           International Folk Music Council* 3: 44-50.
  1953   American Folksongs and Their Music. *Southern Folklore Quarterly*
           17 (2): 122-139.
  1956   Some Folk Fiddlers' Habits and Styles in Western Pennsylvania.
           Journal of the International Folk Music Council 8: 15-18.
  1957   A Miscellany of Tune Notes. In W. Edson Richmond, ed., *Studies in
           Folklore: in Honor of Distinguished Service Professor Stith
           Thompson.* Bloomington, Indiana: The University Press. 151-176.
  1966   Scales and Ranges in Anglo-American Fiddle Tunes: Report on a
           Desultory Experiment. In Kenneth Goldstein and Robert Byington,
           eds., *Two Penny Ballads and Four Dollar Whiskey: A Pennsylvania
           Folklore Miscellany.* Hatboro, Pennsylvania: Folklore Associates.
           51-60.
  1967   Decline and "Revival" of Anglo-American Folk Music. In Horace P.
           Beck, ed., *Folklore in Action: Essays for Discussion in Honor of
           MacEdward Leach* (Philadelphia: American Folklore Society) 14 (2):
           21-29.
Beard, Charles A. and Mary R.
  1944   *A Basic History of the United States.* Philadelphia: Blakiston.
Bennett, David Parker
  1940   "A Study in Fiddle Tunes from Western North Carolina." University
           of North Carolina.
Bjørndal, Arne
  1956   The Hardanger Fiddle: The Tradition, Music Forms, and Styles.
           Journal of the International Folk Music Council 8: 13-15.
Blaustein, Richard
  1975   "Traditional Music and Social Change: The Old Time Fiddlers Asso-
           ciation Movement in the United States." Indiana University.
Bolton, Herbert E. and Thomas Maitland Marshall
  1920   *The Colonization of North America 1492-1783.* New York: Macmillan.
Boyden, David
  1965   *The History of Violin Playing from its Origins to 1761 and its Relation-
           ship to the Violin and Violin Music.* London: Oxford University Press.
  1980   Col legno. In Stanley Sadie, ed., *The New Grove Dictionary of Music
           and Musicians* 14: 561.
Bridenbaugh, Carl
  1968   *Vexed and Troubled Englishmen 1590-1642.* New York: Oxford
           University Press.

Bronson, Bertrand H.
    1951   Melodic Stability in Oral Transmission. *Journal of the International
              Folk Music Council* 3: 50-55.
Burchenal, Elizabeth
    1951   Folk Dances of the United States: Regional Types and Origins. *Journal
              of the International Folk Music Council* 3: 18-21.
Burman, Linda C.
    1968   The Technique of Variation in an American Fiddle Tune: A Study of
              "Sail Away Lady" as Performed in 1926 by Uncle Bunt Stephens.
              Ethnomusicology 12(1): 49-71.
Burman-Hall, Linda C.
    1974   "Southern American Folk Fiddling: Context and Style." 3 vols. Prince-
              ton University.
    1975   Southern American Folk Fiddle Styles. *Ethnomusicology* 19(1): 47-65.
    1978   Tune Identity and Performance Style: The Case of "Bonaparte's
              Retreat." Selected Reports in *Ethnomusicology* III(1): 77-98.
Calhoun, Cecil Warner
    1941   "Selected Instrumental Folk Music of South Central Kentucky." Uni-
              versity of Iowa. 88 pp.
Cash, Wilber J.
    1941   *The Mind of the South*. New York: Alfred A. Knopf.
Cazden, Norman
    1959   Regional and Occupational Orientations of American Traditional
              Song. *Journal of American Folklore* 72(286): 310-344.
    1971   A Simple Mode Classification for Traditional Anglo-American Song
              Titles. *Yearbook of the International Folk Music Council* 3: 45-78.
Chappell, William
    1965   *The Ballad Literature and Popular Music of the Olden Time*. London:
              Chappell and Co., 1859. Reprinted in 2 vols., New York: Dover.
Cohen, John
    1965   The Folk Music Interchange: Negro and White. *Sing Out!* 14(6): 42-49.
Collinson, Francis
    1966   *The Traditional and National Music of Scotland*. London: Routledge
              and Kegan Paul.
Coppage, Noel
    1961   Fights, Fiddles, and Foxhunts. *Kentucky Folklore Record* 7(1): 1-14.
Damon, S. Foster
    1952   The History of Square Dancing. *Proceedings of the American Anti-
              quarian Society* 62(1): 63-98.
De Ryke, Delores
    1964a   Old Time Fiddlers—Then and Now. *Country Music Who's Who 1965*.
              Denver: Heather. Part 7: 26-28.
    1964b   So Hell is Full of Fiddlers—Bet it Won't Be Crowded! *Western Folklore*
              23(3): 181-186.
Densmore, Francis
    1927   *Handbook of the Collection of Musical Instruments in the United*

States National Museum. Washington: Bulletin 136 of the United States National Museum.

Eaton, Allen
1937   *Handicrafts of the Southern Highlands*. New York: Russell Sage Foundation.

Eaton, Clement
1964   *The Mind of the Old South*. Baton Rouge: Louisiana State University Press.

Edwards, John
1971   Last Will and Testament. In Eugene W. Earle, "The John Edwards Memorial Foundation," *Western Folklore* 30(3): 177-178.

Flood, William H. Grattan
1906   *A History of Irish Music*. 2nd ed. Dublin: Browne and Nolan.

Ford, Ira
1965   *Traditional Music in America*. 1940. Introduction by Judith McCulloh. Hatboro, Pennsylvania: Folklore Associates. Reprint edition.

Ganassi, Silvestro de
1924   *Regola Rubertina*. Venice, 1542, 1543. Facsimile reproduction with preface by Max Schneider, 1924.

Gordon, Robert W.
1938   Fiddle Songs. *New York Times*, November 27, 1927, Sunday Magazine. Reprinted in *Folk-Songs of America*. National Service Bureau Publication No. 73-8. New York. 71-77.

Grainger, Percy
1915   The Impress of Personality in Unwritten Music. *Musical Quarterly* 1(3): 416-435.

Grayson, Esther
1969   The Country Dance Goes to Town. *New York Times*, March 31, 1940, Sunday Magazine. Reprinted in *A History and Encyclopedia of Country, Western, and Gospel Music*.

Greene, Evarts B. and Virginia D. Harrington
1966   *American Population Before the Federal Census of 1790*. Gloucester, Mass.: P. Smith.

Harnoncourt, Nikolas
1970   *Program Music of the Baroque Era*. Descriptive notes, Telefunken SAWT 9549-B Ex.

Harris, Clement A.
1933   Music in the World's Proverbs. *Musical Quarterly* 19(4): 382-392.

Harrison, Frank and Joan Rimmer
1968   Spanish Elements in Two Maya Groups in Chiapas. *Selected Reports* (University of California at Los Angeles: Institute of Ethnomusicology) 1(2): 2-44.

Hart, George
1881   *The Violin and its Music*. London: Dulay and Novello.

Henebry, Rev. Richard
1928   *A Handbook of Irish Music*. London: Longmans Green.

Holden, Rickey
    1951   *The Square Dance Caller*. San Antonio, Texas: R. Holden.
Hollinshead, Merrill T.
    1932   A Study of the Vibrato in Artistic Violin Playing. *Studies in the Psychology of Music* 1: 281-288.
Hopkins, Pandora
    1965   *Our American Music: A Comprehensive History from 1620 to the Present*. 4th ed. New York: Thomas Y. Crowell.
Hulan, Richard
    1969   The First Annual Country Fiddlers' Contest. *The Devil's Box*, Tennessee Valley Old Time Fiddlers Association newsletter, 8(1): 15-18.
Hume, Tobias
    1969   *The First Part of Ayres, French Pollish and others together . . . with Pavines, Galliards and Almaines*. London, 1605. Reprint edition.
Jabbour, Alan
    1971   *American Fiddle Tunes from the Archive of Folk Song*. Washington, D.C. Library of Congress descriptive pamphlet for 33⅓ rpm. record L62. 36 pages.
Jackson, George Pullen
    1933   Buckwheat Notes. *Musical Quarterly* 19(4): 393-400.
    1964   *White Spirituals of the Southern Uplands: The Story of the Fasola Folk, Their Songs, Singings, and "Buckwheat Notes."* Chapel Hill: University of North Carolina Press, 1933. Reprint edition, Hatboro, Pennsylvania: Folklore Associates.
Johnson, Guy B.
    1929   *John Henry: Tracking Down a Negro Legend*. Chapel Hill: University of North Carolina Press.
Jones, Maldwyn A.
    1960   *American Immigration*. Chicago: University of Chicago Press.
Karpeles, Maud
    1951   Some Reflections on Authenticity in Folk Music. *Journal of the International Folk Music Council* 3: 10-16.
Keasler, Michael
    1962   *An Interview with Eck Robertson*. Amarillo, Texas; December 30. Tape and TS deposited at John Edwards Memorial Foundation, University of California at Los Angeles.
Kennedy, Douglas
    1956   Some Folk Fiddlers' Habits and Styles in Western Pennsylvania. Comment on Samuel P. Bayard. *Journal of the International Folk Music Council* 8:18.
    1964   *English Folk Dancing: Today and Yesterday*. London: G. Bell.
Kidson, Frank, ed. and collector
    1891   *Traditional Tunes: A Collection of Ballad Airs, Chiefly Obtained in Yorkshire and the South of Scotland; Together With Their Appropriate Words From Broadsides and From Oral Tradition*. Oxford: Chas. Taphouse.
King, Nelson
    1969   Hillbilly Music Leaves the Hills. *Good Housekeeping* 138(6), 1954.

Reprinted in *A History and Encyclopedia of Country, Western, and Gospel Music*. 92-94.

Korson, George
1949   *Pennsylvania Songs and Legends*. Philadelphia: University of Pennsylvania Press.

Leamy, Hugh
1969   Now Come All You Good People. *Collier's Magazine* 84(18) (1929): 20, 58-59. Reprinted in *A History and Encyclopedia of Country, Western, and Gospel Music*. 7-13.

Lindsay, Maurice
1954   Folk Music: Scottish. In Eric Blom, ed., *Grove's Dictionary of Music and Musicians*. New York: St. Martin's Press. Vol. 3: 346-355.

Lomax, Alan
1968   *Folk Song Style and Culture*. Washington, D.C.: American Association for the Advancement of Science.

Lowens, Irving
1964   *Music and Musicians in Early America*. New York: W. W. Norton.

Malone, Bill C.
1968   *Country Music, U.S.A.* Publication of the American Folklore Society, Memoir Series. Austin: The University of Texas Press. Vol. 54.

Mattheson, J.
1969   *Grundlage einer Ehren-Pforte*. Hamburg, 1740. 2nd ed. edited by M. Schneider, Berlin, 1910. Reprint edition.

Maurer, Maurer
1950   The "Professor of Musick" in Colonial America. *Musical Quarterly* 36(3): 511-514.

McAllester, David P.
1956   An Apache Fiddle. *Ethnomusicology Newsletter* No. 8: 1-5.

McCall, Grant
1969   Txistulari. *Viltis: A Folklore Magazine* 27(5): 4-7.

McCulloh, Judith
1965   Introduction. In Ford, Ira. *Traditional Music in America*. Reprint of 1940 edition, ed. by Judith McCulloh. Hatboro, Pennsylvania: Folklore Associates.

Meade, Guthrie T., Jr.
1969   From the Archives: 1914 Atlanta Fiddle Convention. *John Edwards Memorial Foundation Quarterly* 5 part 1(13): 27-30.

Mellers, Wilfrid
1946   *Music and Society: England and the European Tradition*. London: Dennis Dobson.

1964   *Music in a New Found Land: Themes and Developments in the History of American Music*. London: Barrie and Rockliff.

Mendel, Arthur
1948   Pitch in the 16th and Early 17th Centuries. *Musical Quarterly* 34(1): 28-45 (Part I) *Musical Quarterly* 34(2): 199-221 (Part II) *Musical Quarterly* 34(3): 336-357 (Part III) *Musical Quarterly* 34(4): 575-593 (Part IV).

Mersenne, Marin
    1957   *Harmonie Universelle: The Books on Instruments*. Paris, 1636. Trans-
            lated by Roger E. Chapman. The Hague: M. Nijhoff.
Metfessel, M.
    1928   *Phonophotography in Folk Music*. Chapel Hill: University of North
            Carolina Press.
Moody, Ed
    1968   The Itinerant Fiddlers of New Hampshire. *Northern Junket* 9(2): 2-13.
Morgan, Edmund S.
    1952   *Virginians at Home*. Charlottesville: University Press of Virginia.
Mozart, Leopold
    1951   *Versuch einer gründlichen Violinschule*. Augsburg, 1756. Translated
            by Editha Knocker. London, 1948. 2nd (corrected) ed.
Muffat, Georg.
    1895   Florilegium Secundum, 1698. In *Denkmäler der Tonkunst in Oster-
            reich*. Vienna: Academic Press.
Nelson, Robert U.
    1948   *The Technique of Variation—The Study of Instrumental Variation
            from Antonio de Cabezón to Max Reger*. Berkeley and Los Angeles:
            University of California Press.
Nettl, Bruno
    1953   Stylistic Change in Folk Music. *Southern Folklore Quarterly* 17(3):
            216-220.
    1956   Unifying Factors in Folk and Primitive Music. *Journal of the Ameri-
            can Musicological Society* 9(3): 196-201.
    1965   *Folk and Traditional Music of the Western Continents*. Englewood
            Cliffs, N.J.: Prentice Hall.
    1970   Examples of Popular and Folk Music from Khorosan. *Musikals gestalt
            und Erlebnis Festschrift Walter Graf zum 65. geburtstag*. Vienna: H.
            Bohlau. 138-146.
Odum, Howard W.
    1964   A Southern Promise. In Katherine Jocher, Guy B. Johnson, George L.
            Simpson and Rupert B. Vance, arrs. and eds., *Selected Papers:
            Howard W. Odum*. Chapel Hill: University of North Carolina Press.
            113-127. Reprinted from Howard Odum, ed., *Southern Frontiers in
            Social Interpretation*. Chapel Hill: University of North Carolina Press,
            1925: 3-27.
Osborne, Lettie
    1952   Fiddle Tunes from Orange County, New York. *New York Folklore
            Quarterly* 8(3): 211-215.
Owsley, Frank
    1945   The Pattern of Migration and Settlement of the Southern Frontier.
            Journal of Southern History (Nashville, Tennessee: Southern
            Historical Association, Vanderbilt University) 11(2): 147-176.
Playford, John
    1685   *The Division Violin: Containing a Choice Collection of Division to a
            Ground for the Treble-Violin. Being the First Musick of this Kind Ever
            Published*. London: John Playford.

1728   *The Dancing Master.* 4th ed. London: Printed by W. Pearson and sold by John Young. 1st ed. published by John Playford in 1650.

1933   *The English Dancing Master.* Hugh Mellor and Leslie Bridgewater, eds. London: H. Mellor. Reprint of 1650 edition.

Poladian, Sirvart
1942   The Problem of Melodic Variation in Folk Song. *Journal of American Folklore* 55(220): 204-211.

1951   Melodic Contour in Traditional Music. *Journal of the International Folk Music Council* 3: 30-35.

Powell, John
1937   In the Lowlands Low. *Southern Folklore Quarterly* 1(1): 1-12.

Randolph, Vance
1932   *Ozark Mountain Folks.* New York: Vanguard Press.

Reger, Scott N.
1932   The String Instrument Vibrato. *Studies in the Psychology of Music* 1: 305-340.

Rhodes, Willard
1966   Folk Music, Old and New. In Bruce Jackson, ed., *Folklore and Society: Essays in Honor of Benjamin A. Botkin.* Hatboro, Pennsylvania: Folklore Associates. 153-168.

Ritsen, Joseph
1968   *Ancient Songs and Ballads.* London, 1790. Third ed. revised by W. Carew Hazlitt, London: Reeves and Turner, 1877. Reprinted Detroit: Singing Tree Press.

Russell, Theodore
1938   The Violin "Scordatura." *Musical Quarterly* 24(1): 84-96.

Sanders, J. Olcutt
1951a   Some Reflections on Authenticity in Folk Music. Comment on Maud Karpeles. (*Journal of the International Folk Music Council* 3: 10-16).

1951b   The Texas Cattle Country and Cowboy Square Dance. *Journal of the International Folk Music Council* 3: 22-26.

Schenker, Heinrich
1979   *Free Composition* (Neue Musikalische Theorien und Phantasien, III: Der Freie Satz). 3rd (translated) ed., edited by Ernst Oster. New York: Longman.

Seashore, Carl E.
1936   Psychology of the Vibrato in Voice and Instrument. *Studies in the Psychology of Music* 3.

Seashore, Harold G.
1932   The Hearing of Pitch and Intensity in Vibrato. *Studies in the Psychology of Music* 1: 213-235.

Seashore, Harold G. and Joseph Tiffin
1932   Summary of Established Facts in Experimental Studies on the Vibrato up to 1932. *Studies in the Psychology of Music* 1: 344-376.

Seeger, Charles
1940   Music and Culture. *Proceedings of the Music Teachers National Association* 64: 112-122.

1951   Some Reflections on Authenticity in Folk Music, comment on Maud
        Karpeles. (*Journal of the International Folk Music Council* 3: 10-16).
1957   Music and Class Structure in the United States. *American Quarterly*
        (Philadelphia, Pa.: University of Pennsylvania for the American
        Studies Association) 9(3): 281-294.
1961   The Cultivation of Various European Traditions in Music of the
        Americas. Report of the 8th Congress of the International Musicologi-
        cal Society; Kassel, 1961: 364-375.
1962   Music as a Tradition of Communication, Discipline, and Play. *Ethno-
        musicology* 6(3): 156-163.
1972   Oral Tradition in Music. In Maria Leach and Jerome Fried, eds.,
        Standard Dictionary of Folklore, Mythology and Legend. New York:
        Funk & Wagnalls: 825-829.

Seeger, Peter
1959   *The Country Fiddle*. Pamphlet for film. New York: Beacon Films.

Sharp, Cecil
1909   *The Country Dance Book*. London: Novello. Vol. I: Description of
        eighteen traditional dances collected in country villages. Vol. II:
        Thirty country dances from The English Dancing Master (1650-1680).
1954   Folk Music U.S.A. In Eric Blom, ed., *Grove's Dictionary of Music and
        Musicians*. 5th ed. New York: St. Martin's Press. Vol. 3: 387-398.

Sharp, Cecil and Maud Karpeles
1907   *English Folk Song: Some Conclusions*. London: Simpkin, 1 vol.
1909   *The Country Dance Book 2nd ed*. London: Novello, and New York:
        H. W. Gray. Vol. V: The running set, collected in Kentucky, U.S.A.

Shelton, Robert and B. Goldblatt
1966   *The Country Music Story: a Picture History of Country and Western
        Music*. Indianapolis: Bobbs-Merrill.

Simpson, Christopher
1659   *The Division-violist, or An Introduction to the Playing upon a
        Ground*. London, 1659.

Southern, Eileen
1971   *The Music of Black Americans: A History*. New York: Norton.

Spielman, Earl
1975   Traditional North American Fiddling: A Methodology for the Histori-
        cal and Comparative Analytical Style Study of Instrumental Musical
        Traditions. University of Wisconsin at Madison Ph.D. Dissertation,
        Music.

Spiro, Melford E.
1955   The Acculturation of American Ethnic Groups. *American Anthro-
        pologist* 57(6, pt. 1): 1240-1252.

Straeten, E. van der
1911   *The Romance of the Fiddle: The Origin of the Modern Virtuoso and
        the Adventures of His Ancestors*. London: Rebman.

Telemann, Georg Phillip
1739   [Autobiography] see Mattheson 1969.

Thede, Marion Unger
1962   Traditional Fiddling. *Ethnomusicology* 6(1): 19-24.

1966   Scales and Ranges in Anglo-American Fiddle Tunes: Report on a Desultory Experiment. Review of Samuel P. Bayard. In Kenneth Goldstein and Robert Byington, eds., *Two Penny Ballads and Four Dollar Whiskey: A Pennsylvania Folklore Miscellany* (Hatboro, Pennsylvania: Folklore Associates: 51-60) *Journal of the International Folk Music Council* 17: 161.

1967   *The Fiddle Book*. New York: Oak.

Tinctoris, Johannes

1950   De Inventione et Usu Musicae (c. 1487). In *The Galpin Society Journal*. London: The Galpin Society. Vol. 3.

Turner, Frederick Jackson

1920   *The Frontier in American History*. New York: H. Holt.

1932   *The Significance of Sections in American History*. Gloucester, Mass.: P. Smith.

Walsh, Jim

1951   Everyone's Writing P. D. Melodies as Tin Pan Alley Digs Hills for Hits. *Variety* (New York: Variety) 182(10): 41.

Welsch, Roger L.

1964   The Cornstalk Fiddle. *Journal of American Folklore* 77(305): 262-263.

Wilgus, D. K.

1965   Fiddler's Farewell: The Legend of the Hanged Fiddler. *Studia Musicologica* 7(1-4): 195-209 (*Journal of the International Folk Music Council* 17, part 2).

1968   The Hillbilly Movement. In Tristram P. Coffin, ed., *Our Living Traditions*. New York: Basic Books, Chap. 23.

Wolf, John Q.

1965   A Country Dance in the Ozarks in 1874. *Southern Folklore Quarterly* 29(4): 319-321.

Woodfil, Walter A.

1953   *Musicians in English Society from Elizabeth to Charles I*. Princeton: The University Press.

Zolotow, Maurice

1969   Hillbilly Boom. *Saturday Evening Post* 216(33), 1944. Reprinted in *A History and Encyclopedia of Country, Western, and Gospel Music*. 36-42.

Zonis, Ella

1965   Contemporary Art music in Persia. *Musical Quarterly* 51(4): 636-648.

Patterns of *Candomblé* Music Performance: An Afro-Brazilian Religious Setting

Gerard Béhague

Candomblé[1] is the term used specifically in the Brazilian northeastern region of Bahia to designate the various religious groups which exhibit varying degrees of West African religious beliefs and practices. The more traditional African-related groups are the Ketu, Ijexá (Yoruba), and Gêge (Fon), and Congo-Angola cults. The Ketu and Ijexá groups originating in Yorubaland in Southwestern Nigeria and South-Central Dahomey (today Bénin) are known generically in Brazil as Nagô. Other groups whose acculturation has been stronger and which, therefore, present more cultural traits of a local tradition include the *candomblé de caboclo* and the *Umbanda* cult groups (Carneiro 1954; Béhague 1975). In popular Bahian language, the term *candomblé* also refers to the locale of the cult center and to a specific public ceremony otherwise known as *xirê*[2], an important musical event described below.

While *candomblé* dogmas in general follow those of the Yoruba and Fon religions of Nigeria and Dahomey, the various myths of the many deities or *orixás* (also referred to as *santos*, *voduns* for the Gêge, *inquices* for the Congo-Angola) vary considerably on both sides of the Atlantic (Verger 1957). Moreover, as a result of the contact in Brazil of several prevailing African cultures, *candomblé* became a sort of cultural synthesis of the West African mythological world. Indeed, most *candomblé* houses in Bahia worship the major Yoruba and Fon deities, as opposed to the West African practice in which a religious center, and sometimes a whole village, is dedicated primarily to the worship of one particular *orixá* or *vodun* (Bastide 1958).

Ample historical evidence has been gathered (Viana Filho 1976; Verger 1968) to explain the Yoruba and Fon (i.e., Nagô) cultural religious predominance in Bahia. During the sixteenth and seventeenth centuries most Africans came from various tribal groups inhabiting the Portuguese colony of Angola, and the Congo basin, but from the eighteenth century up until

1817 (the official beginning of prohibition of the slave trade north of the Equator) the Brazilian traders obtained their supply primarily from the Guinea or Benin Gulf Coast. The need for more slaves coincided exactly with the discovery of gold and precious stones in Minas Gerais, which was reached through Bahia. But only a small number of Benin-Gulf-Coast Africans actually reached Minas Gerais, as they were traded in Bahia to tobacco plantation owners. This explains the heavier concentration of Nagôs in Bahia. The fact that they were the last to take root in Brazil partially explains their cultural prevalence in Bahia in modern times.

The earliest establishment of the Nagô slaves' religious organization in Bahia cannot be determined accurately. According to local oral sources it was around 1830 that the first cult center was founded in Salvador (the present capital of the state of Bahia, also referred to as Bahia) by three African priestesses. This center was known as Ilê Iyá Nassô (House of the Priestess Nassô), the African title of one of them. From this center, of Ketu affiliation, originated the largest and best-known *candomblé* houses in Salvador during the twentieth century, particularly the Engenho Velho (also known as Casa Branca), the Gantois, the Axé Opô Afonjá and the Alaketo (Ilê Maroialaje). Yoruba or Nagô liturgy exerted a lasting influence on *candomblés* of other affiliations, for instance the Congo-Angola people who use that liturgy rather freely, and the Caboclos who tend to simplify it in their attempt to nationalize the African and Amerindian beliefs. The Fon or Gêge (Ewe) initially maintained their vodun belief system (quite similar to the Yoruba religion in Africa (cf. Paul Falcon 1970), but subsequently integrated it, so that nowadays virtually all Ketu cult houses are recognized as Gêge-Nagô. In Salvador, only one cult center, the Bogum, still follows the vodun liturgy strictly. Although relatively small in number, the Gêge-Nagô cult centers continue to enjoy power and prestige among the Bahian population, about 70 percent people of African ancestry.

I. "CANDOMBLE" SOCIAL ORGANIZATION AND MUSIC

It is well known that music and religion are closely related in all cultures. But, while music may appear simply as an ornamental, complementary yet essentially reinforcing element of certain religious practices, it has an organic functionality in most traditional cultures. In certain religious rituals, such as the Afro-Bahian *candomblé*, music and dance become the main vehicle of religious fulfillment and, therefore, are fully integrated within the social organization of those religions. Although no one could rightly maintain that ritual and music operate at analogous cultural levels, the Radcliffe-Brownian functionalist notion of ritual (Radcliffe-Brown 1922) properly expanded by Clifford Geertz (Geertz 1958; 1966) can at least further our understanding of the ways music, and especially musical performance, contributes to the expression of the sociocultural meanings of ritual. If indeed, following Geertz's insights, religion is a system of symbols which operates so as "to establish powerful, long-lasting and pervasive moods and motivations" (1966) in the members of a given culture, music as a natural expressive means would seem essential in order to bring forth the expression of that culture's ethos. Moreover, music partakes of that system of symbols with its own referential network, notably in sacred ritual contexts.

Although the term "liturgy" is generally applied to Christian religions and churches, it seems perfectly suitable for certain traditional, non-Christian religions when religious behavior and all elements of religious practices are sanctioned by prescribed sets of rules which should be understood as much as possible in terms of native cognitive categories. These rules affect, of course, the whole range of musical behavior of initiates into a given religious group, as well as that of the musicians themselves or any other person with an active role in the musico-ritual performance. It is the responsibility of the ethnomusicologist to attempt to identify such rules, and, above all, to determine the degree of variation, or tolerance, allowed within the rules, since such a study would be related directly to the question of cultural change. In addition, these rules generally provide important clues to certain patterns affecting musical performance practices, as defined in the Introduction to this volume.

There are a number of *dramatis personae* involved in the various contexts of music-making in Afro-Bahian *candomblé*. Vivaldo da Costa Lima, particularly, has studied what he called the "religious family" ("*família-de-santo*") from a socio-anthropological viewpoint (Lima 1977). For our purposes, we will limit our comments here to the various musical functions or attributes of the most essential members of the religious family.

1. The Cult Leader

Variously called *babalorixá, pai de santo* (both designations for men), *ialorixá, mãe de santo* (for women), the cult leader appears to be the major repository of musical repertories. Besides his functions of consulting the deities through the divination game related to Ifá (see Bascom 1969) and transmitting their messages, of organizing and supervising the various ceremonies, especially initiation rites, the *pai* or *mãe de santo* leads the singing on most occasions. Thus, the observation of the proper sequence of songs in a given ceremony, which determines the proper religious dénouement of that ceremony, depends on the cult leader. His/her knowledge of musical repertories and of ritual dancing is most important for the initiation ceremonies during which the novices will learn these repertories and the mythical choreography. The cult leader will gain recognition among the members of the center if the initiates can show a good knowledge of music and dance, since good schooling is the responsibility of the *babalorixá*. The profound power of music is recognized in *candomblé* language through the expression *ser de fundamento* (to be of fundamental principle, i.e., to have a basic power) applied to a cult leader with esoteric knowledge (to know things of *fundamento*) of divination techniques and secrets, sacred plants, sacred rites, and, of course, music. The latter is therefore equated with some of the most important elements of the religious dogmas and practices. This quality of *fundamento* is also extended to specific songs which are believed to hold particular power in connection with a given god or a given ritual situation, or which refer to some of the quintessential myths associated with a given deity. Thus, value is not placed as much on the extensiveness of the song repertories of a given cult leader as on the knowledge of specific songs of *fundamento* to bring about the desired and necessary ritual effect.

The extensiveness of music repertories in Gêge-Nagô *candomblés* is quite considerable. Although the cult leader is himself an initiate to a given *orixá* or *vodun*, and continues to be dedicated to that god throughout his life, he must also know the song repertories for all *orixás* since he bears the responsibility of teaching all new initiates in his center, and of presiding, at least in theory, over all private or public ceremonies. In such occasions, he is expected to lead the singing. In practice, however, he relies on numerous helpers, such as his master drummer, his *ogans* (civil protectors of the house, honorific title), or his *mãe pequena* (or *iakekerê*). Yet, as with any aspect of *candomblé* life, the cult leader appears as the supreme authority on musical matters, although not all leaders are performers themselves.

2. The Master Drummer

Melville Herskovits (1944) has revealed the important position held by the master drummer or *alabê* in *candomblé* social hierarchy. His major function, Herskovits emphasized, is to bring about spirit possession of the initiates. It should be pointed out, however, that while he contributes substantially to the appearance of the trance phenomenon by means of his drumming, numerous other factors are necessary for dissociation to occur. For example, the cult leader who celebrates his or her *orixá* once a year is more likely to "fall" into trance (Portuguese *cair no santo*) on that occasion than on any other during the year. In other words, the degree of expectation of the community quite often influences the predisposition and overall religious behavior of members of that community. Moreover, since most of the religious choreography involves varying degrees of reenactment of Yoruba myths, as known in Bahia, the potential presence of certain gods on a given occasion may have a definite influence on certain initiates' predisposition to become gods. The initiates' knowledge of certain myths may also impel them to become active protagonists in the mythical performance for which spirit possession is necessary. Nevertheless, it is true that in most ritual contexts the immediate call to possession comes from the music itself, which helps to explain in part the occurrence of this phenomenon.

As with any other important positions in the social hierarchy of *candomblé*, seniority of initiation into the cult determines the social status of *alabês*. Thus, the master drummer is, as a rule, the oldest initiate among drummers and, in practice, plays any drum he wishes on a particular occasion. The actual organization of the musical performance is the responsibility of the master drummer who not only commands the drumming but frequently leads the singing as well. His wide knowledge of song repertories and sequences is necessary as the drumming is inseparable from the canticles. Drumming is done by three drummers in the Ketu or Gêge cult houses. The smallest drum (*lê*) and the middle-sized drum (*rumpi*) reiterate regular rhythmic patterns. The *agogô* (bell) also repeats its own patterns throughout a song. The largest drum (*rum*), played by the master drummer, provides improvisations or simply rhythmic variants. The dancers pay attention primarily to the *rum*, which musically organizes the choreography. This is achieved by means of repetitions of improvised rhythmic patterns at shorter time-intervals, often twice as short, hence the terms *dobrar* (to double, to split) and *virar* (to turn to another rhythmic pattern) used by drummers. This generally calls for a faster execution of dance figures in the dancing round. In effect, the master drummer exercises pressure on the mental state of the dancers by forcing them to dance at a faster pace, thus stimulating deeper concentration on their dancing. Specific dances (*satô*, for example) are organized according to various sequences of rhythmic patterns. The proper performance of such sequences is also the responsibility of the master drummer. Our field observations have shown that the master drummer often also acts as the lead singer. In that capacity, he may also exert influence and authority on the course of the ceremony. He may, for example, single out certain initiates by singing more songs (and some of more *fundamento*) to their particular gods, without deviating from the established order of song sequences. This inevitably serves as a cue to the degree of behavioral expectation of those initiates. In theory, the Gêge-Nagôs sing three to seven songs for each god in the first part of the *xirê* (a ceremony described below), but in practice the number of songs for each god can vary considerably. The leader's motivation for singling out some of the initiates may depend on the specific occasion of a particular ceremony.

Further responsibilities of the master drummer in certain performance contexts are mentioned below.

3. The "Iakekerê" or "Babakekerê"

The *iakekerê* or *mãe pequena* (little mother) is the immediate substitute of the *ialorixá*. If a given cult center has a *babalorixá*, then the second in command is a man known as the *babakekerê*, or *pai pequeno*. In practice, numerous *babalorixás* have *iakekerês*, thus the great majority fulfilling this role are women. She is generally the member closest to the cult leader, and almost always the *iaô* who has been initiated by that cult leader for the longest period of time. Very rarely is the *iakekerê* simply a very close friend or a blood relative of the cult leader. The *iakekerê* exhibits as much knowledge of the rites as any cult leader, and, in principle, becomes the *ialorixá* upon the death of the cult leader, upon consultation of the gods through divination. This rule is not always observed, however, since the succession of a cult leader involves as much politics as in any other social organization where positions of power are involved.

The *iakekerê* fulfills many functions, but none as important in the liturgy and from a musical viewpoint as those discharged during the initiatory rites. She directs the daily activities of the initiates in reclusion and supervises their development into the sacred world, including their learning progress. Many activities—the awakening at dawn, the morning bath, the meals, the various prayers, the ritual dancing lessons—are accompanied by singing. The *mãe pequena* also has the responsibility of leading and teaching the special canticles of each daily activity. She is also present at all of the more important phases of initiation, such as the preparation of the *abô* (a sacred liquid), of the *kelê* (a thin collar), the *contregun* (a braided thread made of straw and cowry shells worn around the arms as protection from the spirits of the dead), and other fetishes, the performance of the *bori* (an offering to the novice's head to reinforce her spiritual strength, or *axé*), various rites of scarification, the *saida* (exit) of the *iaôs*, and others. While the cult leader presides over such ceremonies, his or her *iakekerê* most often executes the appropriate ritual gestures and frequently acts as the organizer of the choral response to the singing.

4. The "Iaôs/Adoxus"

Within *candomblé* social and religious hierarchy, the *iaôs/adoxus* (i.e., initiates) could be said to represent the raison d'être of the religious group. Religious practices involve the initiates almost constantly, since they not only serve the African gods and thus assure the continuity of the cult, but become gods themselves, or the "horses of the *orixás*" (*exin orixá*, in Nagô language). The "horse" is the initiate who is possessed by the deity through the thought-image of that deity coming down and "mounting" his or her devotee, who finally assumes the personality of the god. Initiation represents the highest level of participation in *candomblé*, and is also determined by the gods. The will of the gods is believed to manifest itself through certain signs. Constant physical pains, sickness without apparent cure, or a sudden, uncontrollable crisis of spirit possession, called *santo bruto* (wild god) are signs whose interpretation by the cult leader, who also acts as diviner (*babalaô*) through the divination game (*eluwô*), determines whether initiation is indicated and, if so, the particular *orixá* to whom each *iaô* will devote herself or himself. To refuse to go through initiation when the gods demand it is considered extremely dangerous since physical harm and even death could occur in a state of *santo bruto*. Thus, initiation accomplishes the relative control of trance behavior, by properly "placing the *orixá* in the head" of the *iaôs*, and by teaching them how to respond to the various stimuli to their condition as gods. Music is one such stimulus. The *iaôs'* music-learning process is consequently of paramount importance. While they are being prepared during initiation to serve their gods according to the particular traditions of their groups, the various stages of initiation constitute true musical occasions not only because of the occurrence of their musical education at that time, but also because music functions as a sanctifying and sacralyzing element.

There is no doubt that the initiates represent the chief protagonists in most performance contexts of Bahian *candomblé*.

II. PERFORMANCE CONTEXTS

1. Types of Contexts

The description and interpretation of the performance contexts presented here are not intended to be comprehensive but simply illustrative of *candomblé* musical life. Basically, two types of performance contexts are recognized, the public and the private rituals which take place during the various *obrigações* (obligations) observed by the worshippers. *Obrigações* are ritual offerings to the deities, required by them (as the name implies), to propitiate them and to receive their assistance in various spiritual or material matters. All members of a cult center must carry out their "obligations" regularly, but the initiates, by definition the closest members to the *orixás*, must fulfill a weekly, monthly and yearly offering to their individual gods. In addition, to commemorate their first, third and seventh anniversaries of initiation, they must perform a special ritual offering. Initiation itself is conceived as an "obligation," specifically as *obrigação de cabeça* (obligation of the head), because initiation amounts to "placing or fixing the deity in one's head," as mentioned above. From a strictly liturgical viewpoint, private ceremonies generally display a more meaningful significance than public ceremonies. The social importance of the latter, however, is paramount. Private rituals include numerous ceremonies which involve animal sacrifices (*orô de matança, sacudimento*, etc.), the use and manipulation of sacred plants (preparation of *abô, amaci*, sacred liquids) and almost all phases of initiation. The privacy of such events (limited to the essential members of the cult house—all initiates) is necessary because the most vital principle of *candomblé* life—the *axé*—is invoked. *Axé* (from the Yoruba meaning order, command, power) is conceived as the dynamic force of the deities, their power of fulfillment, symbolized in the animal, vegetal and mineral worlds through certain objects or matter, such as animal blood, sacred plants and trees, and stones which appear as the fixing and revitalizing elements of this spiritual force. These symbols are kept secret to assure the spiritual security of the cult center, hence the need for privacy in those rites in which symbolic activity is at work. Music of *fundamento*, it will be seen, is an integral part of that activity.

Public ceremonies are essentially social, religious affairs, which take place in the main dancing room (known as *barracāo* or *salāo*) and during which the relative richness of performance of a given cult center is exhibited. Careful attention is given to the decoration of the *barracāo* with pennants hung from the ceiling, of the specific colors of the main deity of the house, with the large branches of palms or other plants attached around the entrance door and placed at the corners, and proper lighting with electric bulbs (when electricity is available) or kerosene lamps. Drums are "dressed" for the occasion, with an *ojá* (*odjá*), a long, wide scarf tied in a bow around the drum's body. The initiates appear as *orixás* in their most sumptuous attire, considered a basic source of pride of the whole cult center. For such public occasions, members of a particular *candomblé* house are expected to be present but friends and members of other cult centers are welcome and are often sent written invitations. Outsiders, including tourists, may observe public ceremonies. Their behavior within the *barracāo* is strictly monitored by *ogans* who indicate to them where they should sit and call their attention to the smoking, photographic and other restrictions. Such policing reinforces the desire of the cult members to communicate to outsiders their expectation of respect for their own worldviews as reflected in the specific performances.

In most cases, public ceremonies represent the culmination of a series of religious acts. For example, any *obrigação* which includes several private rituals generally ends with a *candomblé*, *xirê*, or *festa* (i.e., an obligatory ceremony closing the cycle of ritual observance). Confirmation ceremonies for *ogans* or for *alabês* (drummers) occur at the end of another ritual cycle and are true consecrations. Concurrently, public ceremonies give rise to communal social interaction of essential significance for an understanding of the ethnography of musical performance, and through it an appreciation of the cultural focal point that music exhibits for the Afro-Brazilians.

2. The "Baptism" of Drums

In the article "Música de culto afrobahiana," co-authored by Melville Herskovits and Richard Waterman, Herskovits pointed out the difficulty of assessing the wealth of ritual songs in Afro-Bahian *candomblé*:

The important place occupied by ritual songs in the African cults of Bahia has been recognized in the many studies on that subject, since the times of Nina Rodrigues and Manoel Querino to the recent investigations of Arthur Ramos and others. Nevertheless, the assessment of the wealth of these musics is really difficult until technical advances allow a systematic and extensive program of recordings and musicological analyses capable of completing the ethnographic background [Spanish *fondo*] of these songs. With such resources, the range of song types used in these cults and the rules which guide their interpretation (performance) will be better explored (Herskovits and Waterman 1949: 65).

Herskovits's own collection, gathered in Salvador, Bahia, in 1941 and 1942, and analyzed by Alan P. Merriam in his doctoral thesis (1951), supposedly numbers 671 songs. In reality, this collection includes many items which are not religious, such as the songs accompanying the so-called *samba-batuque* and *samba de roda*. But, more importantly, Herskovits himself revealed that many of the songs recorded were not collected in the context of the ceremonies, but in a laboratory installed in the State Museum (Museu do Estado). In addition, neither he nor anyone else after him ever paid attention to that "ethnographic background" of the songs, or stated differently, the liturgical contextual practices that govern the musical repertories and therefore dictate their internal structure and justify the performance order.

Herskovits (1944) also reported the religious significance of drums and drummers in the Bahian cults. Since he worked among many cultsmen of both the most traditional and African-related religious groups, specifically the Ketu, Gêge (or Gêge-Nagô), Congo-Angola cults, and the Candomblé de Caboclo, his description and interpretations of the ceremonies involving drums seem to be the result of a generalization from the various groups. But the terminology itself used by Herskovits tends to indicate that he paid greater attention to the Gêge-Nagô cult group in which sacred language is derived from the Yoruba language. Yet, some elements of his description of ceremonies affecting drums are not characteristic of the Gêge-Nagô group, but of the Caboclo group. Thus, it is impossible to determine whether any particular group served as his basic reference. Moreover, his previously mentioned collection does not include any items specifically associated with drum ceremonies.

Since the functional aspects of *candomblé* music have never been studied by anyone and the song repertories have not been codified, the first step in reaching an understanding of the structure of the performance should be the documentation of the specific ritual or liturgical order in which songs should theoretically be performed in this ceremony, and the determination of the reasons for such sequences according to prevailing religious belief systems and practices. The assumption of a "theoretical" sequence of songs comes from opinions expressed by cult leaders of some of the oldest centers of Salvador, Bahia. What seems to be "theoretical" is dictated by tradition in the minds of these leaders. The actual uses of repertories reveal frequent departure from the theoretical orthodoxy and have received close attention in my own studies.

My factual data concerning drum "baptism" are based on about fifteen such ceremonies observed between 1967 and 1979 among the Gêge-Nagô and the other cult groups. A comparison of Herskovits's description of that ceremony and present-day practices among the various religious groups could have been helpful to illustrate the process of change in the study of musical functions in a traditional repertory. But, for the reason previously mentioned, a generalization among the various cult groups would be premature.

Despite syncretism with Christian elements, Afro-Brazilian *candomblé* continues to be essentially animistic in nature. Since drums (known as *atabaques, tabaques, ilus*) have the primary religious function of calling the gods, and thus of bringing on spirit possession which is the ultimate purpose of most Afro-Bahian rituals, they are believed to have a "voice" of their own, irresistible to the gods, and their *axé* or spiritual force needs to be reinforced through "nourishment." Thus, because of this quasi-personification of the instruments, a proper spiritual treatment is essential. This treatment not only includes the initial rite of "baptism," but occasionally the actual naming of the drums and annual "feeding" to prolong and assure the power received at the baptismal ritual. Although religious syncretism with Catholicism is well known, the term "baptism" is not used by cultsmen or cult leaders. Rather, the native expression is *dar de comer ao couro* (to feed the hide or leather). Herskovits used the word "baptism" in its symbolic meaning of ablution, as part of the rite of passage from the secular to the sacred world. Yet, he saw in it

an example of the striking quality possessed by such African cults as have survived in New World Catholic countries, a quality by means of which African and Catholic elements are harmoniously combined (Herskovits 1944: 484).

Syncretistic elements have been overemphasized. I subscribe to the interpretation that the apparent existence of features of Christian belief systems was the result of sociohistorical accommodation in the slave quarters of the plantations. Today, however, a recognized awareness of the value of traditional popular culture tends to minimize this "harmonious combination."A concrete example would be the use of water in the "baptism" of drums. According to Herskovits,

the priest or priestess takes holy water, obtained from a Catholic church, and speaking entirely in the African tongue employed by the group in its rituals, blesses the drums while sprinkling them with the sacred liquid (Herskovits 1944: 484).

While this might still be true nowadays among the Caboclos, it is not the case among the Gêge-Nagô groups. The sacred liquid results from the maceration of sacred plants which are believed to have great power (*axé*) and are the secret of each cult center. The presence of this liquid is indeed signified by the special plant songs which appear in the sequence to be described. Plant songs (*cantigas de fôlhas* in Portuguese) would have no place in that sequence if it were not for the very nature of this liquid.

The liturgical setting of the drum "baptism" ceremony may be further considered. Each center is primarily dedicated to the cult of the *orixá* to whom the cult leader was initiated. The drums become, therefore, one of the main vehicles of communication with that god (another being divination). The baptismal ritual will be placed under the sign of that god. The preparation of the drums entails painting their bodies with the characteristic colors of the god. In the specific performance to be described, Xangó, the god of thunder, fire, and lightning, is represented by the colors red and white. Although not a requirement, the drums are sometimes dressed for the occasion. This dressing consists of encircling them with a cloth called *odjá*, following the same practice as for the initiates in a state of possession.

In most cult groups, drums are played in a battery of three, in conjunction with an iron gong or bell (*agogô*) or a shaken rattle. In the Gêge-Nagô cult groups, the trio always comes in three different sizes. In these cults they are played with sticks (*aguidavis*), while in the Congo-Angola and Caboclo cults the hands are used exclusively. A religious hierarchy exists between the *rum* (the largest drum) and the *rumpi* and *lê*. The *rum* is played by the master drummer and is considered the most important because it determines the various changes in the choreography. Its religious function of inducing spirit possession is paramount. While dancing, the initiates pay more attention to it than to the other ones, because they are expected to respond to its calls. By improvising, the *rum* establishes a contrast with the smaller drums which usually repeat a single steady ostinato pattern, as does the *agogô*. The following example sketches the structure of the *rum* in specific rhythmic patterns: [Example 1]. Functionally and musically the *rum* appears to be, therefore, the instrument par excellence. This hierarchy, however, is not manifested in the baptismal rites. Each drum is treated equally.

The ritual takes place shortly after a new drum has been constructed. In most instances, the three drums of the set are built at the same time. There is no basic difference between this first ceremony and the subsequent annual feeding of the drums (with the exception of the painting and occasional naming of the instruments). The *babalorixá*, or less frequently the master drummer (*alabê*), officiates. He or she begins by consulting the gods through divination to make sure that the particular day chosen for the ceremony is appropriate for the god under whose sign the ceremony takes place (*obi*, i.e., kola nuts, or cowry shells are used for divination purposes). *Orikis* or prayers of offering are said concurrently with the divination game. If the divination signs (there are 256 in West Africa according to Bascom and Verger) should prove consistently negative, the ceremony would be postponed, although in actual practice such an occurrence is very rare. The drums are placed in a slanting position, which is only permissible on this occasion. Normally they are always in an upright position for actual performance (as opposed to comparable ceremonies witnessed in Dahomey-Bénin). Several dishes for the food offerings are placed in front of the drum heads. This food includes blood, the sacred liquid mentioned earlier, salt,

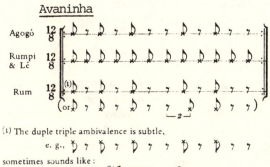

Avaninha

Agogó 12/8

Rumpi & Lê 12/8

Rum 12/8

(1)

(or, —2—)

(1) The duple triple ambivalence is subtle,

e. g.,

sometimes sounds like: —8:6— —2—

Toque de Iansã

The 4/4 gong pattern often approaches the triple feel, as for example:

—3— —3— —3— —3—

Agogó 4/4

Rumpi & Lê 12/8

Rum 12/8

The *rum* also gets into a duple feel, like the gong:

4/4

Bravum

Agogó 2/4

—3—

Rumpi & Lê 6/8

Rum 6/8

Opanijé

Agogó 4/4

Rumpi & Lê 4/4

Rum 4/4

Example 1   Some Schematic Basic Patterns in *Candomblé* Drumming palm oil (*epô*), and honey. Of these, the foods believed to have real *axé* are the blood and the herbs or plants. The ritual use of blood is clearly an African trait in this context. As the most manifest symbol of life, blood, especially running blood, is necessary in the most liturgically significant Afro-Bahian rituals. Such a necessity appears quite consistent with the animistic nature of the Yoruba African religion. A feathered animal (a chicken, preferably a cock) will be sacrificed for each drum. At the moment the head of the animal begins to be severed, an appropriate song ("sacrificial" song as a native category) is sung: "*Ogum chorô, chorô . . . Eje chorô, ilu paô,*" i.e., "Ogum conducts ceremony . . . the blood is flowing, ilu." The reference to the god Ogum is justified by the fact that Ogum, the god of war and metal tools, should be invoked in conjunction with the use of the sacrificial knife. (See Example 2).

Example 2   Sacrificial Song

Two more songs ("*E eje ofere bará lajê,*" and "*Oniê kilo paô*"), presenting the same pentatonic or hexatonic melodic structure, are performed as a further offering of the blood to the *ilus*. All the songs are accompanied by the *agogô* alone (occasionally the *adjá* or *xerê*, a shaken double-coned bell, is also used to call on the spirit of the deity), the "baptism" being one of the few musical occasions of *candomblé* in which singing is not accompanied by drums. The cycle of plant songs follows, introduced by the greeting word *Assá* (repeated three times) to Ossanha, the god of all vegetation. (See Example 3). In theory (i.e., according to the most orthodox tradition), the order in which the plants (or leaves) should be invoked is well set, involving sixteen different plants grown in both the West African and the Brazilian Northeastern coasts. Most of the Yoruba names of plants continue to be used in Bahia: *irokô, odundun, eurepepê, agtibá olá,* etc. These plants are known by all cult leaders, who also act as medicine men in most cases. Since herbs and plants are considered to be one of the critical secrets of a given cult center, all plant songs are not generally sung if a member of another (rival) center is present, in order to avoid revealing these secrets. The song-texts are, in general, traditional Yoruba or Fon texts although the numerous linguistic and phonetic alterations prevent a meaningful literal translation of such texts, even by a Yoruba-speaking person. The tones of the language especially have been lost.

With the performance of these songs a true baptism, i.e. in the sense of

Example 3   Plant Song (text omitted)

immersion, takes place. The drums are sprinkled with the sacred liquid, the sacralization of which occurs at the time of the gathering and maceration of the plants and involves offerings to Ossanha and singing. Plant songs may include songs for *Ipessam* (there is no common equivalent in English; these are plants of the mimosa, begonia and borage families), *Agba-ô* (a type of morning glory), *Eurepepê* (a water primrose) and *Peregum* (a dracaena type). The song *"Pelebe ni tobeô"* or *"Peleme mi kobeô"* (flat is my knife) appears in the middle of the plant cycle, presumably as a reference to the tool used to collect the plants.[3] (See Example 4).

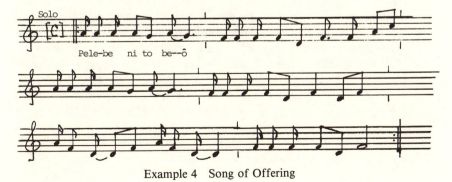

Example 4   Song of Offering

The last plant song of this cycle *"Ifa-ô, Ifa-omon"* corresponds to the *Mariwo*, the African oilpalm. The Yoruba songtext signifies good wishes of wealth and good fortune (*ifa-omon* means to attract money). Four songs of greetings to the drums follow, in which *ilu* is already associated with *Oba*, the "King," that is, the King Xangô. The placement of the chicken's or cock's head in one of the dishes in front of the drums is signified by the song *"Ori abodi o gueguê maniô,"* (the severed head is the fulfillment). (*Ori* = head; *abodi* = cut, severed; *ogueguê* = fulfillment; *maniô* = this is; cf. Verger 1957: 84). (See Example 5).

Example 5   Head Offering Song

The greeting words of the text of this song mix Yoruba (e.g. *ajê-um* = food; *omo* = money; *Achò* = clothing) and Portuguese (e.g. *paz, prosperidade, sossêgo,* peace, prosperity, tranquility). Food offering songs follow in the order of salt (*iyô*), honey (*oyin*), and palm oil (*epô*). These three ingredients are mixed in a bowl and poured on the drums' heads. Covering the drum bodies with the feathers of the sacrificial animals, the *babalorixá* sings *"Iorô, koko bo-ô"* referring to the feathers (*iyé*). The last offering—perhaps the most significant from a strictly religious viewpoint— is that of the head of the animal. Indeed, the head symbolizes the new life conferred upon the instruments (*"Ilu, bori ia-um"*). This is why this offering is followed by two songs of general joy (*"Opê irê"* = "I call happiness, cheerfulness") and thanksgiving (*Oni-wagogô,* the bell-playing greeting the drums).

The last songs (ten to fifteen) generally belong to the specific repertory associated with the *orixá* for whom the drums were "baptized." In the specific case of Xangô, it is by greeting Xangô that the worshippers reveal the fulfillment of the rite of passage: Xangô takes possession of his drums. The latter are referred to in the songtexts as *"omorobá"* or "children of Xangô." The greeting shout *"Kawô, kabie sile"* (translated by William Bascom [1972: 3-4] as "Welcome, we prostrate ourselves before you"), specific to Xangô, is uttered several times, indicating the imminent presence of the god, who may or may not manifest himself at that time. A few songs may be singled out. For example, *"E mirê mirê xorobê eje koba, benaô"* forms an integral part of the *obrigação* to Xangô. The only difference here is the addition of the word *ilu*. Greeting songs to Obá, the King, and *Obá otá,* the King of stone (i.e. thunderstone) are also part of the cycle. The song "*Oku, la ilá*" is, from a liturgical viewpoint, the climax of the ceremony (and almost the ending), because in the Xangô repertory, this song is of special *fundamento*. (See Example 6).

O –ku   la   i   lá

Example 6   Song of "Fundamento"

The presence of this song at the end of the sequence is significant since it is supposed to help establish a direct communication with the *orixá*. The ceremony ends with a consultation game (again with *orikis*) to make sure that the deity has accepted his new children and devotees. The positive result of the game is expressed through applause and shouting and general rejoicing of the limited congregation (see Béhague 1977). The drums remain in the sacred space (*barracão*) where the ceremony took place for several hours with a lit candle in front of each drum. After that period, drum heads and bodies are cleaned. The hides are left in the sun to dry. They are properly tuned, and then ready to fulfill their crucial role.

Thus, the "baptism" ceremony is a clear illustration of the close relationship existing between liturgical behavior and musical repertories. More specifically, music operates as an integral component of that behavior since music alone, in this instance, corroborates the very meaning of the ceremony which is the sacralization of the instruments.

3. A Public Musical Occasion: The "Xirê" Ceremony

The numerous public rituals of *candomblé* include several phases of initiation (*Saida de iaôs*, or the first public appearance of the new initiates; *orunkó*, the new name-giving ceremony; and *panan* or *quitanda das iaôs*, a rite of transition of the initiates from the sacred to the secular world), purification rituals such as the *Água de Oxalá*, communion rites such as the *Pilão de Oxalá* and *Olubajé* for the *orixá* Omolu or Obaluaiê (the deity of smallpox and other contagious diseases), aspects of funeral ceremonies such as the *Axêxê*, and confirmation rites such as those for the *ogans* and *alabês*. While many of these public rituals take place at specific dates during the year, the *xirê* may occur at any date, depending on the occasion for which it is held, for the *xirê* really concludes a whole period of festive events. This is why it is the most generalized public ritual, open to all, including outsiders such as tourists. In the local language, *xirê* is simply referred to as *candomblé* or *festa*, which confirms the frequency of its performance, since the generic term is used to refer to that ceremony as a sort of epitome of the Afro-Bahian religious complex (see Béhague 1975).

The *xirê* takes place at night in the main dancing room (*barracão*), the largest area of a cult center. The *barracão* is decorated for the occasion with paper garlands in the colors of the main *orixá* of the house or those of the particular deity of the person(s) being honored at that occasion. The drums are often dressed with an *odjá* of the same colors. Seats and benches surround the central dancing space. The hierarchy of *candomblé* personnel is made evident through the types and placement of seats within the *barracão*. A large armchair occupying a central position belongs to the cult head, on both sides of whom sit other dignitaries such as the *iakekerê*, the various *ogans* of the house and distinguished visitors and friends. Members of the community and outsiders sit on benches generally on both sides of the main entrance of the *barracão*. Men and women sit separately. The drummers and *agogô* player occupy another focal point often enhanced by a platform covered with special decorations.

The *xirê* begins with the entrance of the *filhas de santo* into the *barracão* to a march-like rhythm known as *avaninha* in the Gêge groups (cf. Béhague 1977), followed by the *despacho de Exu* (the sending away of the trickster-deity, Exu, or Legba to the Fon people, the guardian of the crossroads and a symbol of generative power), if a *padê de Exu* (i.e., a special sacrificial offering) was not performed during that same afternoon. When the *padê* is observed, there is no need for a *despacho de Exu*. In this case, the ceremony begins with a direct invocation of Ogum. For the *despacho*, three to seven songs are sung to Exu (cf. Herskovits & Herskovits, n.d.) while offering him water, sugar-cane alcohol (*cachaça*) or manioc flour. (See Example 7).

Example 7   Song to Exu

These offerings are thrown outside through the doorway of the main entrance where Exu is believed to reside. This *despacho* is essential because it assures the proper, uninterrupted course of the ceremony.

The ritual clearly follows a two-part sequence of varying length, with subdivisions within each part. The first part could be designated from a functional viewpoint as the "call to the gods" (first the greeting then the call) and the second as the "presence of the gods." The main liturgical function of the first part is to bring about spirit possession, which signifies the response of the gods. This is done exclusively through ritual dancing and music; i.e., no artificial means can be utilized. Again three to seven songs should be performed for each *orixá* in the following sequence: Ogum, Oxossi (the hunting god), Ossanha, Oxumaré (the rainbow, symbol of life continuity), Omolu, Nanã (an old female deity, considered the mother of all *orixás*), Iemanjá (goddess of the sea), Iansã (also known as Oyá, goddess of tempest and wind), Obá (the goddess of the Nigerian river of the same name, one of Xangô's wives), Euá (goddess of the Nigerian river and lagoon Iewa), Xangô, and Oxalá (the god of creation, son of the Supreme Being, Olorun). In practice, however, there are many deviations from this sequence, but the types and functions of songs in this cycle are not altered. The number of songs for each deity also varies in practice depending on the special occasion for which the ceremony is being performed and on the response of the initiates to the songs of their own specific gods. It falls upon the solo singer (most frequently the cult head or the master drummer, at times an *ogan*) to select those songs associated with each deity that he or she knows will incite a better response from the initiates. The latter dance to and sing the whole cycle of songs regardless of their own god association until spirit possession occurs. Thus, one can say that the most general functional category of the songs is to induce spirit possession. But specific songs function subjectively for each initiate according to the type of psychological association and conditioning developed during his/her period of initiation.

The structure of the possession phenomenon finds its basic explanation in sociocultural conditioning, as shown by the studies of Herskovits, Bastide and Verger. Bastide considered spirit possession the result of social pressure on the individual, part of a cultural pattern following a certain number of collective representation. "A mystic manifestation," he wrote, "which begins and ends at a given time, always according to certain rules, can only be explained through the antecedence of the social over the mystic [nature of such a manifestation]" (Bastide 1958: 121). On later occasions, however, Bastide stressed the mythical aspect of Afro-Bahian culture, when he stated "the religious trance is regulated according to mythical models, it actually is a repetition of the myths" (Bastide 1958: 122). Indeed, one could interpret the ceremony as a reenactment of specific myths. Such a reenactment is meaningfully expressed through music and dance. The ceremony primarily entails a collective choreography whose structure for the most part is dictated by the dramatic representation of certain mythological stories involving the *orixás*. The fact that the gods are, in practical terms, initiates in trance and yet interact with each other, according to religious beliefs, tells us a great deal about the nature of spirit possession; namely, trance does not prevent the initiates from watching each other's behavior and thus being stimulated by outside factors. To give a specific example, let me refer to the well-known legend of Xangô and his three wives, Iansã, Oxum and

Obá. Of these, Oxum was the favorite and Obá the most neglected (other versions mention Iansã as the preferred wife). One day, Obá asked Oxum to reveal her secret for being able to seduce so easily the fearful Xangô. Oxum answered that she had devised a magic trick: she had cut off her ear and had cooked it in the *caruru* (special dish) of Xangô. Thus, Xangô had developed a constant sexual desire for her. The gullible Obá in desperation for her husband's love did just that, but when Xangô tasted his food and found out what had happened, he repudiated her forever. In the *xirê*, one of the most typical choreographic traits of Obá's dancing consists of hiding her left ear, or of a mock fight against Oxum, should the latter deity be present at the same time. It is clear, then, that the religious dances are not the result of simple individual trances of the initiates separate from one another. On the contrary, they seem to complement each other by responding to each other, in a complex of stimuli and responses, according to the mythical tradition. This almost theatrical nature of spirit possession may make one wonder whether there might not be some simulacrum of the real possession. The answer is, in most cases, negative, for the trance phenomenon is actually tested frequently during the initiation.

By the time the worshippers reach the Xangô songs in the first part of the ceremony, numerous possessions may have occurred. However, if after the many songs and the sacred dances (lasting from two to three hours as a rule) some initiates seem to have difficulty in reaching the state of possession, some cult centers may resort to a specific rhythm known as *adarrum* whose function is to call all the gods at once. Few people can avoid responding to the dynamic level and the fast tempo of this rhythm. Cross-cultural studies of possession drumming made by psychologists and neurologists have revealed that the "rhythmic stimulation of the organ of hearing can be accomplished only by using a sound stimulus containing components of supraliminal intensity over the whole gamut of auditory frequencies . . . as from an untuned percussion instrument or an explosion" (Walter & Walter 1949: 57). Moreover, whatever the prevailing rhythmic patterns of possession drumming may be, it has been shown that rhythmic stimulation (as opposed to continuous stimulation) elicits a greater driving response, and actual neurophysiological alterations in the brain waves. There is little doubt, however, that rhythmic stimulation and response to specific patterns are culturally determined. In Bahia the conditioning to *adarrum* (originally only found in Gêge cult centers) is such that some of the most orthodox or purist cult leaders forbid its performance in their center on the grounds that it is an unnatural way of calling the gods, and the resulting trances may be too violent. This may also be the reason why *adarrum* is not too frequently performed. In a recorded performance in actual ritual context (see Béhague 1977, Side I, band 5), one can notice how the *adarrum* was brought about suddenly. The timing of the solo leader was perfect; from his singing to Ogum, he cued the initiates so that they would know that this was the final call for spirit possession. It is quite clear that the whole religious behavior was dictated and determined through musical means alone.

As the call to the gods materializes, each initiate backs out (a god cannot turn his back on the drums) into the "room of the *orixás*" inside the cult center, where each one will be dressed as a god and will be given the sacred ritual tools (daggers, fans, scepters, etc.). Depending on the occasion, female deities (*iabás*) also carry bouquets of flowers. After an interval of up to one hour, depending on the number of gods to appear, and during which feelings of high anticipation build up, the cult leader, the drummers, and the whole community of spectators begin one of the special entrance songs, known as "*Agolonā*," (lit., please open the way), accompanied by a *batá* rhythm (reserved for some of the most solemn and important liturgical moments). (See Example 8). This performance signals the beginning of the

Example 8   Entrance Song

second major part of the ceremony. In single file, the gods enter the *barracāo*, dancing to the *batá* rhythm in a march-like, solemn and majestic fashion. Again social hierarchy within the group is observed in the order of appearance of the gods. This order is dictated by seniority of initiation and neglects the relative importance of the *orixás* represented by the initiates, a significant case of human over supernatural prevalence. While the spectators stand, firecrackers are detonated outside, announcing the coming of the gods to the whole community. The song *"Agolonã"* is repeated as long as it takes for each god to circle the *barracão*, to salute the drums and to pay homage to the cult leader or any other official of the cult center.

This is an intensely emotional, dramatic moment for the worshippers of the particular cult house. Man is at last face to face with the supernatural power of the *orixás*, a power governing his destiny to a great extent and inspiring respect, admiration and awe. Yet, in spite of the possessed initiates' uncommonly hardened, mask-like facial expressions representing their new personalities, they appear as gods in the very physical configuration of their fellow men, and as such become tangible, concrete entities with whom man can easily identify. Whatever communication might be established between gods and men during the remainder of the ceremony assumes a mostly non-verbal form of interchange, through music and dancing.

As opposed to the first part, in which collective dancing prevails, the second part stresses the individual choreography of the gods. When there are several initiates to a god, they often dance together, but as their dancing abilities are quite evidently displayed, attention is generally focused on the most skillful dancers. Once more three to seven songs may be sung for each deity, but more than seven may be sung for a specific *orixá*, depending on the occasion. The gods themselves may sing or speak (answering questions or conveying messages), and sometimes they intone specific canticles to which they wish to dance. Conversely, they may refuse to dance to other songs if and when such songs selected by the solo leader do not correspond to the proper *fundamento* of that god; in such cases, the solo leader switches to another appropriate song. It is significant to note that the vocal quality of an individual is totally altered when he/she sings as an *orixá*, logically following the idea that the initiates personify gods.

Specific rhythms correspond to specific gods. For example, a rhythm known as *bravum* may be associated with Ogum, Oxumaré, or Nanã; *aguerê* is reserved for Oxossi and Iansã; *opanijé* for Omolu; *alujá*, *tonibobé* and *bajubá* for Xangô; and *igbim* for Oxalá. Whenever any such rhythm is played, the god with whom it is associated reacts immediately by shouting his or her individual ritual cries known as *ilá* or *kê* (from the Yoruba: to shout). Most of the ritual behavior of the gods is controlled through such rhythms and appropriate songs by the *babalorixá* or the master drummer who decide when one god should stop dancing and another should begin.

The musical structure of the second part of the ceremony cannot be as well defined as that of the first part since the sequence of songs and drum rhythms is dependent upon the religious observance of a specific day or occasion. Yet, as a general rule, once each of the gods or groups of gods have danced for a reasonable amount of time, they may all participate in special rounds, such as the Xangô Round. After these, the gods are led out of the *barracão* one at a time, or they may all retreat from the *barracão* to the same *avaninha* or *bravum* rhythms which opened the specific ritual.

At any time during the second part of this ceremony, social interaction develops at various levels. The splendid costumes of the gods and the various "tools" they display (sacred objects symbolizing their specific attributes) become the subject of much praise and discussion among the observers or spectators. The display of their choreographic skills and occasional disclosure of individually creative dancing figures may provoke visible signs of esthetic approval among the members of the cult house and visitors alike. Another form of social interchange occurs when the gods go around and embrace the dignitaries of the cult house or anyone they choose to single out for this special honor. Often worshippers take advantage of this close contact with the gods to speak to them briefly, either uttering a few words of greeting or consulting them about any problems in their life. In this exchange, the gods may respond or may simply mimic a few comforting gestures, such as placing their hands for a few seconds on the worshipper's head.

Music appears as the vehicle par excellence of social fellowship. Frequently, an important visitor signifies his/her friendship toward the cult center and the specific occasion of the ceremony by leading the singing (the local expression is *puxar a cantiga*, i.e., to draw out the song). The more *fundamento* the songs selected for such occasions may exhibit, the more positive and friendly a response will be elicited. The same reverence is expressed when an *ogan*, for example, begins leading the singing for a particular dance of a god. In such cases, the choral response becomes more animated (both in numbers of people responding and in the dynamic level of performance), a sure sign of approval and gratitude. Likewise, drummers of another cult house present at the ceremony may be invited by the *alabês* of the house to pay homage to the gods/initiates of this specific occasion by performing a few pieces.

4. Performance at Funeral Rites

Ancestor worship and the cult of the dead among *candomblé* groups have been explained with great insight by Juana Elbein dos Santos (1976) who provided elaborate descriptions and interpretations of the various ritual institutions and mechanisms related to Nagô's conception of death. Her rather subjective analyses of ritual symbolism in the liturgy of death appear nevertheless as the necessary adjunct to any description of music performance at funeral occasions.

A. The Cult of the "Eguns"

The Nagô oppose the concept of the real, concrete universe, *aiyé*, which includes in it the life of all living beings with that of the supernatural world, *orun*, whose conceptualization is essentially abstract yet closely related with *aiyé*. "*Ọ̀rún* is a world parallel to the real world which coexists with all the contents of the latter. Each individual, each tree, each animal, each city, etc. possesses a spiritual and abstract double in the *ọ̀rún* . . ." (Elbein dos Santos 1976: 54). All supernatural entities are believed to reside in the *orun*, to which human beings go after death. The *eguns* are spirits or souls of the ancestral dead who come back to *aiyé* during certain ritual ceremonies. As opposed to the *ọ̀rixás* who are associated with and represent the forces of nature and cosmos, the *eguns* have a direct relationship with human history and thus are associated with the social structure and order of a given group. Since *orixás* are not conceived as *eguns*, the cult of the former is clearly differentiated from that of the latter. While in Nigeria and Dahomey (Bénin) there exist numerous secret societies for the cult of the *eguns*, in Brazil only two such societies remain, the Ilê Agboulá (in Bela Vista) and the related Ilê Oyá (Rouxinho) in the Itaparica Island, next to Salvador, Bahia. At present, the cult of the ancestral spirits takes place only in the *terreiros* or cult centers which contain a special secret room (*igbalé* in Yoruba, translated into *ibalé* and *balé* in Brazil) or a special house known as *Ilê-ibó-aku*, where the dead are worshipped through food offerings and special rituals that only the men of the center can attend. The same cosmological dualism prevailing in Yoruban mythology appears in the native classification of the *eguns*. On the one hand, the male ancestors (*babá-eguns*) belong to the right of the world (*otun-aiyé*), on the other, the female ancestors (*iamis*) occupy the left (*osi-aiyé*). Moreover, while the female ancestors do not seem "to have individualized representations in the *aiyé*, as their symbols carry a collective meaning, the male ancestors have, besides their collective symbols, well defined individualized representations" (Elbein dos Santos 1976: 105). This explains the corporeal representations of the *eguns* as men, individualized through special costumes and special names and cultivated by members of their family and their descendants. (Ibid.) *Iku* (Death) is itself conceived as a man and male symbol.

While the cult of the *eguns* has remained institutionalized in Bahia through the society known as *Egun* (*Egungun* in West Africa), that of the *iamis* has its own grouping in the societies *Geledé* and *Elekô*, still existing in Nigeria and Dahomey, but no longer active in Brazil (cf. Verger 1965; Elbein dos Santos 1976). This does not mean that the female ancestral power is not recognized. On the contrary, numerous myths involving the *iamis*, and particularly *Iami Oxorongá* or *Ajé Mãe* (the collective representative of the *iamis*) are interwoven with numerous beliefs and ritual practices (Elbein dos Santos 1976: 107-118). In Brazil, the *iamis'* generative power is still symbolized by a calabash (womb) containing a bird, the symbol of the element procreated, although specific *assentos* (the consecrated places for worship and sacrifices) of *Iami Oxorongá* in Salvador exhibit different symbols.

The major rituals of the *eguns* in which music and dance performances occur include several ceremonial occasions in which the spirits of the dead need to be invoked. Moreover, the Egun society observes annual festivals with much singing and dancing. The ritual performance itself entails first the summoning of the *eguns*, by the *ojê* (or *babá ojê*) or initiated priests of the *Egun* society, the "intermediaries between the living and the dead" (dos Santos & dos Santos 1969: 101), who go through a first stage of initiation as *omo ixā* before becoming *ojê*. This summoning begins with the call of the *eguns* by hitting the ground three times with a special ritual staff, known as *ixā*, and enunciating secret verbal formulas. After the last invocation the *eguns* must appear. The first to be invoked and worshipped is *Onilé*, a god conceived as "the collective representative of the ancestors," to whom people sing: *"Onilé iba ré, Onilé mo jubá"* ("Onilé, you are venerated, Onilé, I present you my humble respects, or I bow in front of you") (dos Santos & dos Santos 1969: 90). The *eguns* appear dressed in phantasmagoric fashion, in vividly colored strips of cloth, richly embroidered and ornamented with shells, mirrors, and spangles (cf. illustrations in Verger 1957). "It is believed that under the strips of cloth which cover the bodily forms is the *Egun* of a dead person, a known ancestor, or, in the event that the bodily form is not recognizable, some aspect related to death. In the latter case the *Egúngún* represent collective ancestors who symbolize moral concepts and are the guardians of inherited customs and traditions. These collective ancestors are the most respected and feared of all the *Egúngún*, keepers as they are of the ethics and moral discipline of the group" (dos Santos & dos Santos 1969: 86). This fear emerges from the mystery of death (*awô*) as symbolized by the *eguns*, a mystery acknowledged intangible to men, as the following song text confirms: *"Gégé orô axó lari, lari, lari. Gégé orô axó lémon, ako mó Babá"* ("According to the ritual, cloth is what we see, that which we see, pieces of cloth is what we see, we do not know, Father").

Besides using the *ixā*, the *ojê* also invoke the ancestors with a large ritual scepter known as *opá* whose symbol of authority is linked directly to *Olorun*, the supreme being of Yoruba religion, as stated in the text of the song *"Olorun, Olorun Olo Opá"* ("Olorun, the master of the Opá") performed in Bahia in the *Egun* society (Elbein dos Santos 1976: 125). The *ojê* control and guide the performance of the *eguns* with the *ixā*, making sure that the spirits of the ancestors remain physically separated from the mortals present at the ceremony. The performance of the *eguns* consists essentially of receiving the offerings prepared for them by the descendants of a given *egun*, and giving men their blessings, transmitting specific messages and rejoicing, in general terms, with their descendants. The *eguns* sing and dance on such occasions. Their performance takes place in a special sacred space, part of the *barracão*, where the throne and chairs of the *eguns* stand and non-initiates are allowed to penetrate only when accompanied by an *ojê* or the leader of the *terreiro*. As with the *orixás*, the *eguns* possess greeting formulas, specific shouts (known as *Pé*, as for the *orixás*) and songs which identify them. In its various manifestations, sound appears, therefore, as the most fundamental sign of identification and communication. This is why the rites of preparation and invocation of the *eguns* include the "opening of speech" (Portuguese *abrir a fala*) of the *eguns*, done by only those *ojê* with special position and knowledge. The essential difference between the music associated with the cult of the *orixás* and that of the *eguns*, besides their respective song cycles, is the unusually fast tempo of the music for the *eguns*. An *alujá* of Xangô, for example, performed for an *egun* of Xangô, is rendered almost twice as fast as for the same dance of the *orixá*. The reason for the "fast music of the *Eguns*" is not verbalized, but an educated guess would indicate that the pace is an expression of the essential difference between *orun* and *aiyé*.

B. The Axêxê Ceremonies

The funeral ritual cycle of *axêxê* (*azeri* for the Gêge, *sirrum* for the Congo-Angola) is performed soon after the burial of an initiate, more specifically any *adoxu* of the cult center. When a *babalorixá* or *ialorixá* dies, the *axêxê* (from the Yoruba meaning origin, or beginning) cycle involves more complex rites, since as "father" and "mother" of the *axé* of the center, the cult leader "has his/her hand" (to use a native expression) on all the initiates of the center. Upon his/her death, it is necessary, therefore, to "pull the hand" (Portuguese *tirar a mão*) of the cult leader so as to assure the continuity of the *axé* of the *terreiro*. In effect, the fundamental principle of the *axêxê* rites resides in the transfer of the *axé*. In Elbein dos Santos's words ". . . once his life cycle is fulfilled, each human being disintegrates to return in part to the ancestral bodies and to reinforce the *àṣẹ* of the latter. . . . In the case of the *adóṣù*, depending on their hierarchy, part of their components represented by their 'assentos' may remain in the *àiyé* and be venerated. But let us remember that the 'assentos' represent the priestess's individual elements of the *òrun*; her elements of the *àiyé* will be unfailingly reabsorbed by the ancestral bodies . . ." (Elbein dos Santos 1976: 229-230). The *axêxê* cycle assures the smooth transition from one world to the other. Once the ceremony is completed, the *adoxu* herself (or himself) becomes an *axêxê*. Through this transformation, all *axêxês* are, therefore, "the first ancestors of creation, the beginning and the origin of the universe, of a lineage, of a family, of a 'terreiro'" (Ibid. 231-232). The immediate, practical function of the *axêxê* ceremonies is to send Iku (Death) away and to call the *egun* of the dead person.

In principle, the full *axêxê* cycle, which lasts seven days, is observed for any initiate with three or more years of initiation. For those initiates with less than three years, frequently a simple *carrego* (lit. a load—see below) is prepared and taken away. Thus, the complexity and duration of the rites vary according to the importance of the post held in the *candomblé* hierarchy by the dead person. In general, however, the same ceremonies are performed during the first five days, including the *padê* (see description in Elbein dos Santos 1976: 187ff) celebrated in the *barracão* at sunset, with the corresponding song cycle. Around an empty container, generally made of a half-calabash (known as *cuia*), standing in the middle of the room, the members of the center and relatives of the dead, all dressed in white, wait for one of the priests officiating to light the candle next to the container. The lit candle is believed to indicate the presence of the dead's spirit. With their heads and bodies covered with a large white cloth (*ojá*), each member of the center (beginning with the cult leader, then in order of seniority, with each of the priestesses and with pairs of initiates) dances around the *cuia*, greeting all those present, and deposits coins in it after making the symbolic gesture of rotating the coins over one's head to signify the entrustment of one's person to the spirit of the dead. The cult leader begins the performance of the first song of the cycle, paying special homage to all *axêxês:* "*Axêxê, Axêxê o, Axêxê mo jubá*" ("Axêxê, I bow in front of you, I present my respects"), and "*Axêxê, o ku Agbá o*" ("Axêxê, I greet the Old Ones"). The second song of the cycle refers to Odê Arolê, i.e., the *orixá* Oxossi, the hunting god, who, according to Elbein dos Santos, is the "mythical ancestor-founder of the Ketu 'terreiros' and, consequently, Aṣèṣe of the sons of the 'terreiro'" (1976: 232). This is indeed confirmed by the songtext "*Odê Arolê lo bi wa*" ("Odê Arolê brought us to the world"). Canticles of farewell to the dead are sung by each member while depositing the coins. After the individual dancing and singing around the *cuia*, paying respects to the dead, a collective performance involving the whole membership takes place in the form of a large round with dances and songs, invoking the protection of the *egun and orixá*. Specific songs refer at that point to the fact that the dead person will go to the *orun*. Special food for the occasion as well as an *obi* (kola nut) are placed next to the *cuia* by several *adoxus*. Several priests come in to put out the candle and carry the *cuia* and the food outside next to all the belongings of the dead person. Finally, with their heads uncovered, the members of the center perform a second danced round, specifically greeting and paying their respects to the *orixás*. The invocation of all the major *orixás* in such funeral rites is perfectly natural. Herskovits's indication that "songs addressed to certain deities who 'run away' from the contact with Death may not be performed" (Herskovits and Waterman 1949: 99) has, to my knowledge, no empirical validity, since all *orixás* need to be saluted without discrimination. Likewise, the information related to musical instruments and rhythmic organization of the *axêxê* musical occasion provided by Herskovits is sketchy. While the use of the *agogô* and of calabash drums played with sticks is indeed traditional in both Ketu and Gêge cults, it is erroneous to state that "the main instrument is a pottery jar played by striking the opening of the jar with a fire-fan . . ." (Ibid.). The pottery jar (Portuguese *pote*) is, according to local tradition, specific to the Gêge cult and the corresponding *azeri* rites. Consequently, the assertion that "drums consecrated to the gods are never present" (Ibid.) in the *axêxê* is incorrect.

In those cult centers professing a Ketu-Gêge affiliation, it is possible, of course for jars to be used instead of regular drums. Furthermore, while *axêxê* songs have distinct rhythmic patterns, there is no evidence to support the predication that it is "the rhythmic accompaniment of the melodies performed to the gods during ordinary ceremonies that transforms these canticles [or melodies] into those used for the death rites." (Ibid.). In effect, only two distinct rhythms are performed on the pottery jar: the *bravum* and the *sató*, the latter a Gêge rhythm not exclusive to funeral rites. All other rhythmic accompaniments played on calabash drums and regular *atabaques* follow the common pattern known as *corrido*.

The last two days of the *axêxê* cycle involve special rites which include, among others, animal sacrifices with the performance of the appropriate "sacrificial" songs, and the last call of the dead, with the *assentos*, *cuia*, food offerings, animals, and three new containers made of clay, all brought together in the *Ilê-ibo Aku*. A circle is drawn on the ground with sand, in the middle of which the *obi* is cracked and used for divination to discover the oracle that will dictate the resting place of the *assentos* and objects of the dead person. Sometimes the spirit of the dead is consulted in order to determine if any of his/her belongings should remain in the *terreiro*. The priest of highest rank present strikes the ground three times with a new *ixā* to summon the dead so that he/she will take away his/her *carrego* (load) and will therefore sever forever his/her ties with the *terreiro*. After the third call the dead responds and, at once, everything that belonged to the dead is broken with the *ixā* (including the *cuia* full of coins, the calabash drums, and when used, the pottery jars). The animals are then sacrificed and their bodies placed on top of everything destroyed. One deposits some sand on top of the remains, and proceeds to prepare the *carrego*, also known as *eru*. The exit of the *carrego* (*eru Iku*, i.e., the load of Death) is hailed with special sung words: *"Beru le maló, A-fi-bô"* ("The *eru* is leaving, let us cover ourselves"). The dreaded *carrego* is taken by special priests to the place indicated by the oracle so that Exu Aleru, the "patron of the *eru*," will make final disposition of it. Upon the return of the priests, who reveal the happy fulfillment of their assignment, the members of the group dance a final round in the *barracão* and sing to all *orixás*, concluding with two songs of farewell to the dead. This phase of the ceremony is sometimes designated as the *arremate*, i.e., the end or conclusion. At sunset of the seventh day, a final *padê* is sung, after which a *sacudimento* (lit. shaking, a prophylactic rite) is executed, consisting of washing and sweeping the cult house with branches of sacred plants. For an *ialorixá*, *babalorixá*, and other members of high rank and prestige, the *axêxê* is repeated at regular periods, generally thirty days after death, then six months, one, three, seven and fourteen years, with a rare maximum of twenty-one years for exceptional cases.

As we have seen, there is hardly a ritual gesture in *candomblé* performance that is sanctioned and brought into effective reality without music. The funeral rites which assure the communication with the *orun*, the "passage of the individual existence of the *àiyé* to the generic existence in the *òrún*" (Elbein dos Santos 1976: 235), and, consequently, the very existential continuity of the group, are brought into focus, as performance and events, through music and dance.

CONCLUSIONS

Perhaps because of the tightly structured nature of *candomblé* rituals and the high level of specificity in ritual behavior dictated by the religious dogmas themselves, musical and dance performance appears inseparable from the prescribed ritual behavior. Yet, musical performance behavior differs somewhat from other aspects of ritual behavior in that the sets of rules determining that behavior recognize implicitly a certain degree of individual competence, and allow, consequently, some flexibility in the compliance with them. For example, while it is expected that the *ialorixá* or *babalorixá* should lead the singing, in actuality numerous cult leaders delegated that responsibility to others whom they considered better singers than themselves, without a single alteration in the expected ritual effect of the music. Other non-musical responsibilities are seldom delegated. Likewise, a certain degree of variance in the actual melodic rendition of ritual songs is quite common among various cult centers of Salvador and does not affect the ritual behavior of initiates in those centers. What remains fairly strict, however, is the proper observance of the sequence of songs in a given ceremony. The *ejó* of *candomblé* (i.e., gossip) frequently centers on criticism of a given *terreiro* for lack of compliance or knowledge of the proper songs to be performed at the appropriate liturgical moment. Another subject of frequent derisive criticism between *candomblé* centers concerns the performance of songtexts. Very few people in Bahia speak or understand Yoruba or Fon, but *candomblé* worshippers know the specific functional meaning of the songs, although they may not know the literal meaning of each word. Thus, frequent phonetic alterations occur and one can observe a general Brazilianization of Yoruba or Fon words. The tones of the African words have been lost and while numerous African words have become part of the daily vocabulary of most Bahians, no creole language as such ever developed in Brazil. The most orthodox cult leaders and a few persons affiliated with *candomblé* who have had the opportunity to sojourn in Nigeria or Dahomey in recent years point to the deficiencies and general impoverishment of the local ritual language. It is clear, however, that any effort toward the re-Africanization of the local religions, particularly through language, is bound to fail because its artificiality goes against well-established cultural dynamics, resulting from the whole complex of local cultural and historical contexts.

Of particular interest and significance in *candomblé* patterns of music performance is the integrated concept of performers and audience. In effect, on numerous public occasions, members who initially appear passive in their observation of the ritual activities may, in the course of the ceremonies, become very active participants-performers, depending on the religious stimulation of such occasions. The traditional dichotomy between performers and audience in such cases breaks down. Likewise, the interaction between performers and audience (defined by means of conventional behavior in performance contexts) frequently becomes so intense that those members of the "audience" end up behaving, through performance, as full-fledged participants. Furthermore, in some funeral rites the very division of performers and audience ceases to exist, as worshippers act and interact in both capacities at regular intervals.

Most importantly, it is primarily through musical and dance performance that religious fulfillment takes place. While the traditional religious dogmas of *candomblé* maintain their African animistic nature, the supernatural function of sacred tools (such as drums and plants) is mostly established through the power of musical performance. Ritual songs, in effect, when performed at specifically appropriate times, make possible the expected results of the ritual, and operate as the essential sacralizing elements of the religious complex. Musical performance therefore is the absolute prerequisite for the very existence and operation of *candomblé* religion.

NOTES

1. Various etymologies have been proposed. The term *candomblé*, which first appears in the literature only in the latter part of the nineteenth century, is most likely derived from the contraction *candombe* (a dance of African origin in Brazil and the Río de la Plata area) and *ilê*, from the Yoruba, meaning "house." Thus, *candomblé* would mean literally the "house of the dance."

2. In the spelling of African words, I follow the Portuguese phonetic rendition of such words, without the diacritical marks indicating the various tones of a word, since those tones no longer operate in Brazil. Diacritical marks are maintained, however, in quotations from the literature in which they are observed.

3. Herskovits says that this is a proverb meaning that a Yoruba remains one whatever happens to him (cf. Herskovits and Herskovits, n.d.:4).

REFERENCES CITED

Bascom, William
   1969   *Ifa-Divination: Communication between Gods and Men in West Africa.* Bloomington, Indiana: Indiana University Press.
   1972   *Shango in the New World.* Austin, Texas: African and Afro-American Research Institute.
Bastide, Roger
   1958   *Le Candomblé da Bahia, Rite Nagô.* The Hague: Mouton & Cie.
Béhague, Gerard
   1975   Notes on Regional and National Trends in Afro-Brazilian Cult Music. In Merlin H. Forster, ed., *Tradition and Renewal.* Urbana, Chicago, London: University of Illinois Press. 68-80.

1977 *Afro-Brazilian Religious Songs. Cantigas de Candomblé/Candomblé Songs.* Lyrichord Discs. Stereo LLST 7315.

Carneiro, Edison
1954 *Candomblées da Bahia.* 2nd ed. Rio de Janeiro: Editorial Andes, Ltda.

Falcon, R. P. Paul
1970 Religion du Vodun. *Etudes Dahoméennes,* Nos. 18-19 (July-October).

Geertz, Clifford
1958 Ethos, World View and the Analysis of Sacred Symbols. *The Antioch Review* 58: 421-437.

1966 Religion as a Cultural System. In M. Banton, ed., *Anthropological Approaches to the Study of Religion.* London: Tavistock Publications. 204-215.

Herskovits, Melville J.
1944 Drums and Drummers in Afrobrazilian Cult Life. In *Musical Quarterly* 30 (4): 477-492.

Herskovits, Melville J. & Frances Herskovits
n.d. *Afro-Bahian Religious Songs.* Album XIII. Archive of American Folk Song. Washington, D.C. The Library of Congress.

Herskovits, Melville J. & Richard Waterman
1949 Música de culto afrobahiana. In *Revista de Estudios Musicales,* Año 1, no. 2, 65-127.

Lima, Vivaldo da Costa
1977 *A família-de-santo nos Candomblés Jeje Nagôs da Bahia: Um estudo de relações intra-grupais.* Salvador, Bahia: n.p.

Merriam, Alan P.
1951 *Songs of the Afro-Bahian Cults. An Ethnomusicological Analysis.* Doctoral dissertation. Northwestern University.

Radcliffe-Brown, Alfred R.
1922 *The Andaman Islanders; A Study in Social Anthropology.* Cambridge: The University Press.

Santos, Juana Elbein dos
1976 *Os Nàgô e a morte. Pàde, Àsèsè e o Culto Égun na Bahia.* Petrópolis: Editora Vozes, Ltda.

Santos, Juana Elbein dos and Deoscoredes M. dos Santos
1969 Ancestor Worship in Bahia: The Égun-Cult. *Journal de la Société des Américanistes,* 58: 79-108.

Verger, Pierre
1957 *Notes sur le Culte des Oriṣa et Vodun.* Dakar: Institut Français d'Afrique Noire.

1965 Grandeur et Décadence du Culte de Iyámi Òsòròngá. *Journal de la Société des Africanistes.* Vol. 35.

1968 *Flux et reflux de la traite des nègres entre le Golfe de Bénin et Bahia de Todos os Santos du dix-septième au dix-neuvième siècle.* The Hague: Mouton & Cie.

Viana Filho, Luiz
1976 *O Negro na Bahia.* Brasília: Livraria Martins Editora.

Walter & Walter
1949 The Central Effects of Rhythmic Sensory Stimulation. In *Electro-encephallographic and Clinical Neurophysiology,* 1: 57-86.

GLOSSARY OF MAIN TERMS USED IN BAHIAN "CANDOMBLÉ"

Abébé—Fan of the *orixás* Iemanjá, Oxum and Oxalá.

Abian—Designation of the pre-initiation stage of a young girl or woman.

Adarrum—A special drum rhythm whose function is to induce possession.

Adê—Crown, especially Oxum's crown in Angola *candomblés*.

Adjá—Bell-like instrument "to call" the *orixás* (white metal for Oxalá, copper for Xangô). Also see *Xerê*.

Agogô—Musical instrument (cow-bell type), including one or two bells (different sizes), struck with a metal stick.

Àgua de oxalá—(lit. "Water of Oxalá") Purification ceremony of *candomblés*.

Água dos axés—Liquid containing some blood of all sacrificed animals, kept in the *pejí*.

Agüê—(also *Agbé*) Musical instrument, consisting of a calabash covered with beads. The typical rattle of Caboclo *candomblés*.

Alabê—Player of *atabaque*. Also used to refer to the master drummer.

Alujá—Special drum rhythm for Xangô.

Ariaxé—Ritual baths (with special herbs and plants) during initiation.

Assentar o Santo—To prepare the body of the *abian* for *orixá* penetration.

Assento—Altar of the *orixás* (related to *pejí*).

Assentamentos—All the paraphernalia associated with the *orixás* and placed on the altar.

Atin—The ensemble of herbs and leaves special of each *orixá*.

Axé—Spiritual force. Magnetic force of a *candomblé* house.

Axêxê—Funeral ceremonies.

Atabaques—Drums.

Axogun—The person who sacrifices the animals.

Babá—Father.

Babalaô—Diviner, Ifá priest.

Babalorixá—Same as *Pai-de-santo*. Cult house leader.

Baixar—"To come down," lit. to possess the initiate's body (by the *orixá*).

Banho de fôlhas—Ritual bath, with infusion of certain plants, during initiation or for illness cures.

Barco das iaôs:Ensemble of *iaôs* who come out of initiation, each year.

Barracão—Locale in which public (some private) ceremonies take place.

Barravento—1. The mental and physical disturbance that precedes possession. 2. One of the three drum rhythms in Angola *candomblé*.

Borí—Ceremony with animal sacrifices for the "owner" of one's head (to feed the head). Purification ceremony.

Búzios—Cowries (cowry shells).

Caboclo—1. *Orixá* of the Caboclo *candomblés*. 2. Designation of *candomblé* in which prevails a strong local influence (Amerindian among others) as opposed to the more traditional, African-related Ketu, Gêge, Ijexá or Angola cults.

Cair no santo—To be possessed by the *orixá*.

Camarinha—Special room of the cult center where the *iaôs* remain during the period of initiation. (also *Runkó*).

Candomblé—1. Afro-Bahian religious cults. 2. Locale of cult center. 3. Public ceremony (*Orô/Xiré*).

Caruru—Food including okra, shrimp, palm oil and rice.

Cachaça—Sugar cane alcohol.

Cavalo do Santo—(Horse of the saint) The person possessed by the *orixá* (according to the general belief, the *orixá* cannot be on foot).

Couro—(Lit. leather) Popular designation of drums.

Deká—Ritual involving the installation of a new *babalorixá* or *ialorixá*.

Despacho—Gen. animal sacrifice to the *orixás*. More specifically, offering of food to Exú. (Often used as a synonym of *Padê*).

Despachar—1. To sacrifice to the *orixás*. 2. To send away, hence, to remove the *orixá* from the body of the possessed initiate.

Dobalé—Special form of salutation for those who have feminine *orixás*.

Ebó—Animal and other food offerings to the *orixás* (used especially for Exú).

Ebomim—Initiated person for more than seven years.

Efun—Ritual act of depilating the *abian*'s body (more specifically, her head) during initiation. Also white drawings painted on the head and body of the initiates.

Egun—The dead. Dead's souls, ancestors. (The Yoruba word is *egúngún* = skeleton).

Êini—Soul.

Êiru—Ox tail, one of the attributes of Oxossi.

Ekede—Those in charge of the *iaôs* (helpers).

Eluô—Diviner.

Engoma—General designation for drum in Congo-Angola *candomblés*.

Erê—1. Generic name of an inferior spirit accompanying gods and men. 2. A type of childlike trance.

Fazer santo—To be initiated.

Filá—Straw hood worn by Omolu (deity of smallpox and other contagious diseases).

Filha-de-santo—(Lit. daughter of the Saint). Initiate.

Gan—Often used to designate the *agogô* with one bell only.

Iaô—(Yoruba *yawô* = bride) Initiate with less than seven years of initiation.

Ialorixá—Cult head (woman). Same of *Mãe-de-santo*.

Igbim—Drum rhythm for Oxalá.

Iká—Special form of salutation for those who have male *orixás*.

Ilê—House.

Itá—Fetish stone of the *orixás*.

Iyabá—Any female *orixá*.

Iyá bassê—Cook of the *orixás*.

Iyá kekerê—Same as *Mãe pequena*, immediate substitute of the *Mãe de Santo*.

Iyalaxé—The one who has charge of the *axé*.

Iyá Tebexê—Soloist, the woman who sings the solo part of the canticles in public ceremonies.

Jurema—1. A sacred tree where the Caboclo Juremeiro lives. 2. Alcoholic beverage made with the Jurema's fruit and roots used in Caboclo *candomblé*.

Kelé—(In Portuguese the tie of the *orixá*). Collar worn by the *iaôs* as a sign of their subjection to the *babalorixá* or *ialorixá*.

Lê—The smallest drum.

Liquaqua—Hand clapping to accompany a canticle.

Lorogun—Ceremony to close the cult houses (send back the *orixás*) during Lent.

Mãe-de-santo—*Ialorixá*, female cult head.

Mãe-pequena—*Iyá kekerê*. Substitute of *mãe-de-santo*.

Mandinga—Magic, witchcraft.

Matança—Animal sacrifices.

Mesa—Table—Altar.

Mironga—Secret.

Obá—King (*Obás de Xangô*). The 12 ministers of Xangô. Also, the Yoruba deity of the river Obá, Xangô's third wife.

Obe—Knife.

Obí—Kola nut.

Ogan—Civil protector of the *candomblés*, chosen by the *orixás*.

Oguidavis—Drum (wooden) sticks.

Ogé or *Babaogé*—Priest in charge of the cult of the dead.

Ojá—Piece of white cloth used by the *filhas-de-santo* on their thorax, as an extra ornament. Also, piece of cloth used as drum ornament.

Omalá—Special *caruru* of Xangô.

Opelé ifá—*Ifá* rosary (collar) for divinatory practice.

Orixá—Deity.

Oriki—Prayer, praise.

Orô—Ritual. Also, sequence of songs accompanying public ceremonies (*Xirê*).

Ossé—Food offering to the *orixás* by the *filhas-de-santo*.

Oxé—Xangô's double ax.

Padê—gen. used as synonym of *Despacho*. But *Padê* implies the ritual sacrifice of a four-leg animal to Exú, in theory accompanied by 36 songs.

Pai-de-santo—Same as *Babalorixá*. Cult head.

Panam—(See also *Quitanda*) Ceremony in which initiates act as every day working individuals, symbolizing their reintegration into the secular world, at the very end of the initiation period.

Paxorô—Ceremonial cane of Oxalá.

Pejí—Altar of the *orixás*.

Pomba gira—Female Exú, of the Caboclos.

Pontos cantados—Canticles in Umbanda cult to call the *orixás*.

Pontos riscados—Drawings on the floor symbolizing the spirits in Umbanda cult, in order to attract those spirits.

Quitanda das iaôs—See *Panam*.

Roça—The actual place of the cult house.

Rum—The largest *atabaque*.

Rumpí—Medium size *atabaque*.

Sirrúm—Funeral ceremony in Angola *candomblé*, same as *Axêxê*.

Sundide—The bath of blood. Part of initiatory rites.

Terreiro—Same as *Roça*.

Xaorô—Bracelet or ornamental chain worn at the ankles by the *iaôs* with small bells, sign of subjection.

Xaxará—Straw scepter type, ornamented with cowry shells, an attribute of Omolu.

Xeré—Bell to call the *orixás* (see *Adjá*).

Xiré—1. Offering to Exú in the form of a two-leg animal or simply food. 2. Particular sequence of canticles sung at public ceremonies (see *Orô*).

Index

Contributors _____

Gerard Béhague (Ph.D., Tulane University), Professor of musicology/ethnomusicology at The University of Texas at Austin, has carried out field research in several South American countries, particularly Brazil, and among Fon and Yoruba communities in Nigeria and Bénin.

Linda C. Burman-Hall (Ph.D., Princeton University), Professor of music at the University of California, Santa Cruz, is an ethnomusicologist and harpsichordist. She specializes in traditional American music and has also carried out field work in Europe and Indonesia.

Roderic Knight (Ph.D., University of California at Los Angeles), Professor of ethnomusicology at Oberlin College Conservatory, has done extensive field research in West Africa and India.

Philip D. Schuyler (Ph.D., University of Washington), teaches ethnomusicology at Columbia University. He has carried out field work in North Africa and has published extensively on traditional Moroccan music.

Bonnie C. Wade (Ph.D., University of California at Los Angeles), Professor of ethnomusicology at the University of California, Berkeley, specializes in the study of classical Indian and other Asian musics. She has published numerous articles and books on Indian music.

About the Editor

GERARD BÉHAGUE is Professor of Ethnomusicology and Chairman of the Music Department at the University of Texas, Austin. His earlier books include *Music in Latin America: An Introduction* and *The Beginnings of Musical Nationalism in Brazil*. He has also contributed to *Ethnomusicology*, *The World of Music*, *The New Grove's Dictionary of Music and Musicians*, and the *Yearbook* of the Inter-American Institute for Musical Research. He is Past-President of the Society for Ethnomusicology, Inc., and the founder and editor of *Latin American Music Review*.